John Nash
&
The Village Picturesque

John Nash & The Village Picturesque

with special reference to the Reptons and Nash at the Blaise Castle Estate, Bristol

NIGEL TEMPLE

ALAN SUTTON
1979

Alan Sutton Publishing Limited
17a Brunswick Road
Gloucester GL1 1HG

First published 1979

ISBN 0 904387 24 0

British Library Cataloguing in Publication Data
Temple, Nigel Hal Longdale
John Nash and the village picturesque.
1. Architecture, Georgian — England — Bristol
2. Bristol, Eng. — Buildings
3. Blaise Hamlet, Bristol, Eng. — Buildings
I. Title
720'.9423'93 NA 971.B/
ISNB 0-904387-24-0

Typesetting and orgination by Alan Sutton Publishing Limited
Set in Stempel Garamond 11/13

Printed in Great Britain by
Redwood Burn Limited, Trowbridge

Bound by Western Book Company Limited, Maesteg

Contents

The Illustrations

Acknowledgements are made to those persons and institutions, as identified below, who have kindly given permission for material in their ownership or custody to be reproduced in this book.

Plates *(after page 178)*

Illustrations in the Text

Page

End Papers

Wrapper

Acknowledgements

Over a period of years assistance has been given by many people, institutions and organisations. Although the following account resulted directly from a personal response to Blaise Hamlet, I owe my thanks especially to Sir John Summerson for the lead given by his own writings on Nash, for his advice, and for the kindness he has shown. Miss Mary Williams (in whose keeping are the Harford Papers) and Dr. Howard Colvin have both been good enough to read and make valuable comments on my typescript and I have also benefited from their help in other ways.

I would like to thank those whom I have approached privately, some allowing access to their houses, gardens, estate papers, or other written and graphic material in their keeping, and often offering appreciated hospitality as well. Sir Timothy Harford Bt., who with Mr. Piers Harford placed the Harford Papers on deposit at the Bristol Record Office, has given valuable advice. Similarly, Mr. Charles Cornwall-Legh gave the Cornwall-Legh Muniments to the John Rylands University Library of Manchester. I am grateful to them both for permission to quote from or reproduce material in their respective ownerships and for other help they have given. Brother James Oakley and Mr. Bryan Turner contributed by supplying photographs and information. Major Francis Jones, Mr. Victor Lodwick and Dr. David Watkin I would like to thank for their advice. Others who have helped in various ways include Dr. Stephen Blake, Sister Bonaventure, Mr. Patrick Brown, Mr. John Bowler, Mr. Eustace Button, Mrs. A. Chichester, Mrs. Evelyn Christmas, Mr. Robert Cooper, Major D.J.C. Davenport, Mr. Denys Delhanty, Mr. Richard Dufty, Mr. and Mrs. R.A. Gladwyn, Mr. Arthur Harford, Mr. Lionel Harford, Mr. David Havard, Mr. Simon Houfe, Mme. Thérèse Houin, Mr. Lewis Hurley, Commander and Mrs. B.S. Jones, Mr. and Mrs. J. Ivor Jones, Major D.P.H. Lennox, Mr. T.P. Lewes, Mr. Hugh Lucius and Baroness Irene Lucius, Mr. Sutherland Lyall, Miss Annette Macarthur-Onslow, Mrs. L. Motley, Dr. Clifford Musgrave, Mr. Robert Paterson, Sir Nikolaus Pevsner, Mr. Malcolm Pinhorn, Miss Elsie Pritchard, Mr. Percy Pritchard, Mrs. W.D. Reynolds, Mr. Ian Rogerson, Mr. Peter

Silsby, Miss Dorothy Stroud, Mr. W.H. Wykeham-Musgrave and the tenants of Blaise Hamlet.

For their personal assistance, in some cases intermittent over several years, I would like to thank the following representatives of public offices, institutions, organisations and business concerns. First Mr. John Harris and Mr. John Morley for their co-operation in making available many drawings from the Collections in their respective charges; also Mr. Norman Higham, Mr. Geoffrey Langley, Dr. F.W. Ratcliffe, Mr. Nicholas Thomas and Mr. Arnold Wilson; Mr. L. Edwards, Mrs. Mary Halford, Miss Jane Isaac, Miss Meryl Jancey, Miss Glenise Matheson, Miss Jean Mauldon, Miss Eileen Simpson and Mr. Brian Smith. Mr. Merlin Waterson, of the National Trust, found the paintings at Attingham and made them available. They led to my findings on Atcham of 1972. Mr. W. Baker, Mr. John Barrow, Miss Joyce Beals, Miss Susan Beckley, Miss Clare Crick, Mr. Ivor Collis, Mr. Nicholas Cooper, Mr. Harry Dickens, Mr. Alun Edwards, Mr. H. Turner Evans, Mr. Francis Greenacre, Mr. J. Griffin, Miss Daphne Hubbard, Mrs. Jill Lever, Miss Gwyneth Lewis, Miss Pamela Lewis, Mr. G. Maby, Miss Philippa MacLiesh, Miss Jean McKinney, Mr. A. Meecham, Mr. Brian Redwood, Mr. J. Risebrook, Mr. Henry Sandon, Miss E.H. Sargeant, Mr. Peter Smith, Mrs. B. Strong, Mr. Brian Turner, Mr. B. Whitehouse and Mr. D.E. Williams.

The following public offices, institutions, business concerns and organisations have been co-operative in providing material, services and sometimes their hospitality also:

Borough of Altrincham Central Library, Jonah Arnold and Smith, Ashmolean Museum, Avon County Library, City of Bath Administrative and Legal Services, City of Bath Record Office, Bodleian Library (Department of Western Mss.), Brecon Museum, Brighton Art Gallery and Museums and Royal Pavilion, *Bristol Evening Post,* City Art Gallery and City Museum, Bristol, Bristol Record Office, University of Bristol Library, British Aluminium Company, The British Library, The British Museum, Cardiganshire Joint Library, *Carmarthen Times,* Carmarthenshire County Library, Carmarthenshire Record Office, Cheltenham Public Library, Cheshire Record Office, Courtauld Institute of Art, Forestry Commission, Glamorgan Record Office, Gloucester City Library, Gloucestershire College of Art and Design Library, Gloucestershire College of Education Library, Gloucestershire County Library, Gloucestershire Record Office, Gwent County Library, Gwent County Record Office, Hafod — the Caravan Club, Hereford Library, The County Council of Hereford and Worcester Record Office, The Hutchinson Publishing Group, Isle of Wight County Library, Isle of Wight County Record Office, Kent County Library, Lichfield Joint

Record Office, John Rylands University Library of Manchester, Paul Mellon Collection, Monmouth Record Office, National Gallery, London, National Library of Wales, National Monuments Record, National Museum of Wales, National Register of Archives, The National Trust, Norfolk and Norwich Record Office, Pembrokeshire Record Office, Penguin Books Limited, Public Record Office, Royal Academy of Arts, London, Royal Commission on Historical Manuscripts, Royal Commission on Historical Monuments (England), Royal Commission on Historical Monuments (Wales and Monmouthshire), Royal Institute of British Architects (Drawings Collection and Library), Royal Society of Arts, Royal West of England Academy, Salop County Library, Salop Record Office, Shrewsbury Borough Library, Sir John Soane's Museum, Society of Antiquaries of London, Somerset Record Office, Thames and Hudson Limited, Tithe Redemption Office, Victoria and Albert Museum, West Glamorgan County Library, Worcester Royal Porcelain Company.

Individual owners and numerous institutions and organisations have kindly granted permission for me to quote from or reproduce material in their keeping. The sources of items used have been identified elsewhere, as appropriate.

Finally, I would particularly like to thank Gordon Priest for his advice, and my typist, Jenepher Green. My wife, Judith, gave her help in many valuable ways.

Introduction

For the one hundred and sixty-odd years of its existence, Blaise Hamlet, Bristol, has been a focus of interest and a place of pilgrimage for those who quicken to the peculiarities of romantic rustic cottages and to visual and historical attributes of the village picturesque.

While some elusive qualities they embody suggest that the cottage forms owe a debt to some national and regional vernacular building traditions, the Hamlet as an entity is distinctly artificial; a consciously contrived object created, if not overnight, in a short space of time and in compliance with an all-embracing vision. Its irregularities and its harmonising devices have been arrived at and articulated more by inspired calculation than through those often fortuitous social, technological, economic and human needs that are associated with innovation and transition over centuries of gradual change.

Once completed, Blaise Hamlet became a topographical celebrity. Commercial printmakers soon published lithographic portraits of the pretty creeper-clad cottages. Several produced variations on nine miniature 'postage stamp' views on one sheet. Panoramas, in sets of two or four, depicted the broader scene and artists such as Hugh O'Neill, J.D. Harding, Francis Danby and John Linnell were all moved to record this matchless rustic spectacle. Early photographers also paid their tribute and untold numbers of amateur draughtsmen carefully delineated 'Omega' or 'Windmill' cottage on peach-tinted, embossed, or perforated pages of sumptuously-bound Sunday albums. Diarists and guide-book writers praised the display, and prints were carefully trimmed, to be neatly pasted into Victorian scrap books. Models of the cottages were constructed, coloured ceramic plaques were manufactured. A duke, a prince and a queen dowager paid their compliments. It was not long after completion that a handsome folio volume, describing Blaise Hamlet and containing a large lithographic drawing and plan of each cottage, was in print.

Such acclaim for so small a group of new almshouses must be rare, if not unique. But despite its having been lionised, Blaise Hamlet might have slipped almost un-noticed into oblivion after the Second World War, had not Mr. Donald Hughes of Bristol been instrumental in securing its future. Now, under National Trust care, the Hamlet is probably visited more than ever before.

John Nash, architect to King George IV, is famed for his metropolitan improvements, splendid country houses, dazzling terraces, Buckingham Palace and the Royal Pavilion at Brighton. Yet his parallel concern with cottages, lodges and garden buildings is relatively little known and the possibility of Nash having planned or even built precursors appears not to have been considered. It must be conceded that the chance of one so famous and criticised in his own lifetime having created an additional rural village, and for it to have passed quite unrecorded, is indeed remote.

There the matter might have rested, had not two sources of manuscript material become newly available for research at the time Blaise Hamlet was being reconsidered by the present writer: not that the material itself divulged anything directly concerning other village designs possibly attributable to Nash. However, one thing does tend to lead to another. Our first new source, the Harford Papers, was deposited with the Bristol Record Office in 1969 and 1970 (see Appendix VII). The Papers tell us a great deal about John Scandrett Harford's operations on the Blaise Castle Estate from later in the eighteenth century, and of specific interest to our subject is the correspondence that passed between him and Nash's office when Blaise Hamlet was being built. The other newly available source was George Repton's Notebook at Brighton Pavilion and Art Gallery. It contains, among numerous others, small working drawings for all Harford's cottages at Blaise Hamlet and is referred to here as the *Pavilion Notebook*, to distinguish it from George Repton's similar record at the Royal Institute of British Architects. That is referred to here as the *RIBA Notebook* (see Appendix VII).

Many questions had already arisen by the time these papers and drawings had been located. Did Nash really design Blaise Hamlet without previously attempting similar groupings? In fact, what undeniable evidence was there that he planned it at all; or the cottages either, for that matter? What inspired those massive chimney shafts? Why were the almshouses hidden away instead of lined up at Harford's gates, or displayed along the village street? How far was Harford responsible for the appearance of his scheme? Who built the cottages and to what extent was their construction supervised by the architect employed? The major sources of manuscript material referred to in the course of attempting to answer questions such as these are noted under Appendix VII. Other manuscript sources, sometimes a single letter or drawing, or perhaps a small collection, such as are referred to in the text, are detailed in the Notes or (as seems most appropriate and convenient) elsewhere.

Three books, all of which refer to and illustrate Blaise Hamlet within the context of Nash's career and work as a whole, are essential reading. Sir John Summerson's pioneering biography, *John Nash — Architect to King George IV*, was first published in 1935 and stood alone until followed by Terence Davis's *The Architecture of John Nash* (1960), and *John Nash — the Prince Regent's Architect* (1966). They outline or detail Nash's life, illustrate his buildings extensively and give lists of his known and attributed works. Dr. Howard Colvin's *A Biographical Dictionary of British Architects, 1600-1840* (1978), gives invaluable information on other architects encountered, as well as on Nash and the Reptons, while Dorothy Stroud's *Capability Brown* (1975) and *Humphry Repton* (1962), are indispensable detailed biographies.

The search for precedents for Blaise Hamlet will take us far from Henbury village, in which it was built, to Shropshire, Cheshire, Carmarthen, Rheola, Hafod, Aberystwyth, Herefordshire and the Isle of Wight. The finding of several painted panels at Attingham Park and the leads they offered will be seen as encouraging evidence and the estate papers of the Cornwall-Legh family, of High Legh, near Knutsford, brought their reward.

No attempt has been made to cover in detail the development and ramifications of the theory of the Picturesque in this book as the copious literature it generated is complex and continuing. The inter-relationships of painting, architecture, landscape, poetry and aesthetic philosophy of the movement are intricate. They have already been discussed at very great length elsewhere. In view of this, a selection from earlier writings relating to the Picturesque (essays, letters, poems and journals, mostly) is drawn upon here to illuminate some of the personalities involved. Nevertheless, it is hoped that the nature of the aesthetic climate in which they lived and worked has also been suggested for the benefit of readers new to the subject: those familiar with it I ask to bear with me in such passages as relate to events already well known to them. *The Picturesque: Studies in a Point of View* (1927), by Christopher Hussey, offers an able general survey of the theories and practices evolving during our period and Walter Hipple, in *The Beautiful, The Sublime, and The Picturesque in Eighteenth Century British Aesthetic Theory* (1957), takes a scholarly and analytical view, considering the work of many essayists and painters of the time. Elizabeth Wheeler Manwaring's *Italian Landscape in Eighteenth Century England* (1925), discusses with insight and in detail particularly the influences of continental painters on the English scene. No attempt is made in this present work to enter into the overall development of the estate village, but readers will find Gillian Darley's *Villages of Vision* (1975) a well illustrated guide to the subject.

The political and economic background, obviously, cannot be ignored, as problems of international moment reached crisis point in North America during Harford's time and potentially perilous relations developed with France. Transatlantic trade was vital to Bristol — intimately and inextricably involved as it was with tobacco, sugar, timber, cocoa, grain, shipping, warehousing, industry and finance. Local political activity was intense and the repercussions at times calamitous. Bryan Little, in *The City and County of Bristol* (1954), has dealt helpfully with these hazardous years.

Of John Scandrett Harford, senior, a great deal more could now be told; but for the purpose of this account only his activities at Blaise will be considered in any detail. Alice Harford apparently used the papers recently deposited when preparing her well-produced *Annals of the Harford Family* (1909), in which she traced relationships, fortunes and events over several centuries. She records at some length Harford's work at the Blaise Estate and the building of his new house, but Blaise Hamlet passes with no more than a few lines devoted to it. Something of its significance in terms of architectural history and Nash's career will become apparent below. So what can be said of Blaise Hamlet in a brief introductory note that will not be repeated? Perhaps we might be reflective at a moment when both popular and professional opinion are critical of those vast impersonal housing estates, towering point blocks and unselective town-centre re-developments that we have come to know, if not to love. Perhaps we can see beyond political influences, architectural style and physical dimension. Old-fashioned and minute as it is, Blaise Hamlet might remind us of some qualities that can help make planned housing estates a pleasure to live in and a joy to visit. Consideration of privacy within a community, identity and security, variety, harmony and daily human needs are involved: articulate relationships between buildings, nature, activity and space can also be as relevant today as in 1810.

N.H.L.T. Cheltenham,
January 1979.

1 *One Beauteous, Nicely Blended Whole*

Harford's paternal seat contiguous lies,
Where ev'ry varied charm romantic vies;
Where Blaize and Henbury, by turns delight —
One charms the soul, each gratifies the sight.
That, its protecting form majestic rears,
This cheers the widow's heart and dries her tears;
Here well-tim'd bounty, on a princely plan,
Proclaims at once the Christian and the Man.

Thus wrote J. Antrobus in *Clifton; or, Thoughts and Scenes* (1834), which was dedicated to the ladies of Clifton and the lovers of Nature.

The nine cottages comprising Blaise Hamlet border, but do not necessarily open on to, the irregularly shaped and naturally undulating green, an asymmetrically placed monumental village pump acting as its focal point. Most cottages appear to turn their faces modestly aside from each other and the beholder. It is told that they were so placed to discourage idle gossip by tenants at their doors: but perhaps this arrangement was intended to keep the frontages very neat — architecturally as well as socially — by discouraging cottagers from intruding into the delectable composition.

Like the ground on which they so confidently stand, the cottages are irregular in form. In levels, spacing, orientation, plans, surfaces and profiles they also vary (Plate 1).

Yet it cannot be denied that order is present. All the cottages have dormer windows and casements. Some chimneys are alike. Coursed stone rubble walls are common to all the dwellings: they are carefully constructed and angled. A common scale prevails. Variety excites, yet is contained, a wider vision embracing the parts.

The green has its long axis and its short one, the former being accentuated by responding dove-cote gable ends fronting Vine and Double Cottages, while Diamond Cottage is cunningly set askew, holding Jasmine Cottage

(Plate 2) from view. As Richard Payne Knight, a philosopher of the Picturesque to whom we shall return later, had written:—

> But cautiously will taste its stores reveal;
> Its greatest art is aptly to conceal;
> To lead, with secret guile, the prying sight
> To where component parts may best unite,
> And form one beauteous, nicely blended whole,
> To charm the eye and captivate the soul.[1]

Blaise Hamlet, superficially an irregular grouping of cottages in the vernacular idiom is, in fact, a professional essay in estate village design. The cottages recall pre-renaissance traditions in their comfortable forms. Yet these, though built of stone, owe more perhaps to Surrey and Sussex timber and brick than to local traditional styles. Only two arches are gothic in shape and barely a trace of renaissance detail can be found. Tudoresque chimneys — if memorable — hardly convince, so theatrically have they been contrived.

If elusive in their origins, the cottages are instantly familiar and native in their warmth; if discernibly eclectic in style, they are sophisticated in form. Although apparently so casually grouped, the overall composition suggests that an experienced hand has been very much in control, as has an eye, instinctively acting from familiarity with the precision and discipline of classical rules, yet not blinded by them to the possibilities of stylistic innovation.

Blaise Hamlet is a product of that phase in which the Picturesque, as an architectural style, could be identified and defined: when Burlington's scholarly and stabilising influence had long since declined and a painterly vision was ascendant. The Picturesque point of view embraced a visual understanding inherent in the canons of classical design. While acting as a dilutent of that very style on which it drew, the Picturesque was simultaneously setting the stage for more-romantic and more-pedantic revivals to come with the advent of the Victorian age.

When William Fuller Pocock (1779-1849) was commenting on his proposed plans for a hunting establishment in *Architectural Designs for Rustic Cottages* in 1807, his ideas were relevant to us in that they were published only three years before work on Blaise Hamlet began. As a concept, his group of miscellaneous buildings, which included a huntsman's house, dwellings for the whipper-in and a dog kennel 'with proper Feeding and Sleeping Rooms', would have shared much with Blaise Hamlet. Pocock attempted '. . . to shew how in the necessary Buildings on a large estate, picturesque beauty may be joined to utility for the same expence as would be incurred without attending thereto . . . I have arranged the whole so as to give the idea of a Village, which, in many situations, will become an object both pleasing and picturesque'. He also burst into verse about it all, improbable a subject as Kennels might be.

The Blaise cottages, like the buildings Pocock proposed, were primarily practical. They were hardly spacious by today's standards, but Harford gave his tenants a quality of accommodation apparently quite exceptional for the working class of that time. Generally, it seems rural cottagers accepted overcrowding in squalid hovels as their lot. Demonstrably well-built, the Hamlet cottages hardly complied though with Pocock's economic forecast, as even Harford (who assessed his assets at around £300,000) was aware of mounting costs.

With numerous other pattern book authors of his times, Pocock did not hide the fact that he was out for trade. He had a larger-scale drawing of his hunting establishment 'village' for those who would like to see it and 'Mr. Pocock requests those Noblemen and Gentlemen who favour him with their commands, to address their communications to his Office'. He also brought in many devices to catch a client's interest: not only winning drawings, but also mention of economy, safety, comfort, imagination, practicality, testing, caution, novelty, variety, effect and the picturesque. However, Pocock was not totally heedless of human needs any more than he was of those of horse and hound. With reference to the advantages of a bold and numerous peasantry, he added that rustic cottages were of the highest importance, as comfortable habitations favoured a numerous peasantry: and a small garden could divert them from intemperance which might lead to industrially relaxed habits and corrupt morals, too. They would also prove to be more worthy members of society and better fitted to the defence of their country in times of war; and these were unsettled times.

Over one-hundred architectural pattern books advocating picturesque principles appeared in Britain during eighty years, some running to several editions. The flood — between 1790 and 1810 — was preceded by a long and noble line of classical publications by masters of their art. Palladio, Burlington, Ware, Campbell, Gibbs, Paine, Kent, Langley and Chambers all produced such scholarly works, informed in their texts and accurate in their delineations: lines engraved, as suited their authors' purposes, with precision and skill. Although Soane, who produced *Sketches in Architecture* (1793), and Papworth, renowned for his *Rural Residences* (1818), are notable exceptions, some of the later pattern book authors are little known as architects today. It is rather by their writings and designs than by their identifiable buildings that they are best remembered.

As books usually come to people more readily than people to selected buildings, it is probable that some authors had, through their pattern books, a considerable influence over many years. For example, John Weale's *Designs and Examples of Cottages, Villas, and Country Houses* included specimens by

C.A. Busby (1788-1834), typical of about 1810: these, in a volume of unusually mixed content, not published until years after the Great Exhibition had closed.[2] Such pattern books commonly possessed great charm and perhaps opened with a rather racy history of architecture, to continue with a number of carefully drawn plates. Elevations or perspectives were frequently displayed against darker and romantically arranged groupings of trees, or some other suitable — frequently 'natural' — landscape setting. But innocuous as these backgrounds were, their inclusion was important as they implied that the buildings they accompanied were calculated to be seen as complementary to romantic or picturesque landscape effects.

With the development of new graphic techniques such as aquatint, lithography and steel engraving, tonal richness and linear accuracy of a previously unattainable quality were commercially possible: subtleties denied to the Palladian academics of generations before, who illustrated their works almost always by copper plates engraved as formally as the texts were written. Although, by the use of technical devices such as gradations and cross-hatching surface modelling and shaded voids could be suggested, the idea of showing buildings in normal settings for pattern book purposes appears generally not to have been applied. By late in the eighteenth century the fashion was changing, and by the 1830's lithography was a popular commercial medium, P.F. Robinson (1776-1858), for example, illustrating his *Rural Architecture* with some fully-detailed landscape settings drawn by J.D. Harding and printed by none less than Hullmandel in its fourth edition of 1836. Writing in the first edition (1823), Peter Robinson noted that 'In the most beautiful parts of this Country, the scenery is disfigured by the impotent attempts of the Workman, unaided by the pencil of the Artist . . . Cottage Architecture has so material an effect among the features of a country, and occupies so conspicuous a place in the picture, that it is well to consider what forms are most pleasing, and least intrusive.' Some earlier writers sensed this. He was one who also stated the need in words and illustrated his principles with the assistance of a noted lithographic draughtsman.

By 1860 James Sanderson's book of *Rural Architecture* was in its second edition.[3] 'This little work . . . is simply addressed to a class who are daily increasing in number and importance, whose general intelligence only requires a slight amount of technical knowledge to make it practically useful': Robinson's 'Workmen', for example? The second edition of this paperback, pocket-sized pattern book contained 112 pages of text, and over thirty wood-engraved plates — many of them double-folding. It illustrates a tremendous shift in purpose, patronage and public from the Georgian publications. Sanderson's plans and specifications were intended to help the artisan to help himself, and the volume sold for as little as a shilling — no more than a modest illustrated children's book would have cost at about that time.

Photographic illustrations might be thought potentially ideal for visualising cottages to be built in picturesque landscape. None of early date have been located. Photographically illustrated books had been introduced by the 1840s and were becoming popular a decade later. Some early ones included architectural subjects. William and Mary Howitt's *Ruined Abbeys and Castles* (1862) is well known; F.G. Stevens' *Normandy, its Gothic Architecture and History* (1865), less so. Perhaps the greatest disincentive to its adoption lay in the marginal advantage of reproducing built designs by photography, despite the temptation of showing real landscape settings. Every sepia print had to be trimmed and pasted down on to the page: and whereas a Harding could use his considerable graphic skills and some licence to idealise and heighten a point in design, a photograph could not so readily be adjusted to the same effect.

The majority of picturesque pattern books must here go unmentioned although some pre-Blaise Hamlet ones should not be passed by completely. Nathaniel Kent's *Hints to Gentlemen* of 1775 was probably the first with plans for labourers' cottages, and six years later John Wood (1728-81) the younger, of Bath, produced a *Series of Plans, for Cottages or Habitations of the Labourer, either in Husbandry or the Mechanical Arts:* that is, in the year of his death. Village plans appeared in John Plaw's *Ferme Ornée; or Rural Improvements* of 1795, and James Malton was first to advocate perpetuation of 'that peculiar mode of building, which was originally the effect of Chance' in his *Essay on British Cottage Architecture*, of 1798.

Pattern books will be returned to from time to time, as relevant to specific issues. But two minor architectural themes important in the context of Blaise Hamlet and picturesque villages generally, and exemplified by some of the pattern books, must first be noted.[4]

Although John Plaw (1745-1820) appears to have been first to use the term specifically in a pattern book title, the *ferme ornée* had in fact existed in England as much as a decade before that author's birth. William Kent (*c.* 1685-1748) was also influential. His 'natural taste' allowed for views of the countryside to be contained within his classical garden horizons. Yet, it is generally to Philip Southcote (*c.* 1697-1758), that credit is given, from as early as the mid-1730s, for first embracing a farmstead within contrived rustic walks and landscape views. This was at Woburn, near Chertsey, in Surrey. By the '40s, his achievements were already celebrated and his example is believed to have influenced Brown. Of Southcote's 150 acres, thirty five were 'adorned to the highest degree', farmland — arable and grazing — being bounded by a scenic walk, powdered with wild flowers.[5]

Henry Bolingbroke (1678-1751), developed another such feature at

Dawley, Middlesex. Of that perfection it was written that he

> Himself neglects what must all others charm
> And what he built a Palace calls a FARM.[6]

In France, the fashion also caught on. It produced some rather splendid farmsteads and dairies, including l'Hameau at Chantilly (1774-75), another at Bellevue (1799), the best-known — Marie Antoinette's Hameau at the Petit Trianon — and the queen's dairy at Rambouillet (1785-88). The painter, Hubert Robert (1733-1808), with the architect, Richard Mique (1728-94), brought Antoinette's cottages, stables and dairy into being, beside an artificial lake, but l'Hameau (1782-85), really was a working farm.[7]

For perhaps a thousand years conscious attempts have been made in Britain to create compact building complexes to house communities in architecturally considered environments. Especially in ecclesiastical and collegiate establishments the tradition is long and strong and one remarkable early surviving example is in Bishop Ralf's living quarters for his vice-prebendaries at Vicars' Close in Wells. Built in the 1340s, two 450-foot-long terraces form a broad tapering street, closed at one end by a chapel and at the other by a hall. Almshouses, sometimes ranged around a central court, carried such traditions closer in time and recently there have been attempts in the urban context to plan again such village-scale communities within cities and in redeveloped areas of long established towns.

It is possible that through the attempts of progressive owners of agricultural estates and their efforts to consolidate assets in the interests of farming efficiency around 1700, a link in the planned-community chain of architectural development was forged. By clearing old villages, re-composing and building anew housing for labourers and retainers in terraces or compact clusters of dwellings, enterprising landlords might have encouraged more-efficient husbandry and simultaneously improved standards of dwellings and amenities. Moreover, the ambitious could take matters further, and by employing an architect to site and design his private village or hamlet, could both embellish his estate and elevate his social prestige. By having a cottage group at his gates, visual and landscape miracles could be performed, even if the accommodation offered was little better than the miserable places that cottagers knew before. With a planned village outside the mansion gates an architectural extension to the landscaped grounds within could be achieved.

New villages could therefore be architectural exercises for the rich, or they might genuinely improve conditions of the poor; even contribute to the local or national economy. Layouts could be formal or romantic and the dwellings traditional, or in fashionable style. The last was to prevail, and it is likely that the proliferation of pattern books, with their relatively sophisticated cottage designs, contributed to the decline of vernacular building style and regional character in some localities.

A few examples of the inorganic village should be mentioned as precedents for Blaise Hamlet. Perhaps the first-built was Chippenham, Cambridgeshire, redeveloped by Edward Russell in the early eighteenth century. By the 1730s Robert Walpole had followed suit at New Houghton, not many miles distant, clearing the old and building anew at his impressive gates a group of cottages formally aligned on either side of a straight village street.[8]

Professional architects soon appeared on the scene. They might create a new unity in the whole, as well as design cottages in sophisticated styles. In 1760, John Carr produced a sizeable and rather formal village outside the gates of Harewood House, in Yorkshire, and about five years later the Adam brothers planned a miniature 'circus' redevelopment at Lowther, by the Lakes. But perhaps, in terms of a new village with buildings of varied form and purpose set within a calculated landscape, Milton Abbas (1773) is of greatest interest among these earlier groups, for here an architect and landscape improver, both of first rank, contributed their skills. However, William Chambers and Lancelot Brown hardly had their client's tenants in the front of their minds when drawing up plans for Lord Milton's village. Cottages might be for as many as four families — two up and two down. The whole scheme, eventually with almshouses, church, bakery and school, was again formally aligned, but along a gently winding street, into which the landscape entered with considerable visual effect (Plate 3). And, one wonders, did the horizontally-aligned rurally rehoused produce any more successful a social mix than the vertically-stacked rehoused of recent times?

Madame D'Arblay, better known as Fanny Burney (1752-1840), even from what must have been an arbitrary examination, sensed that the Milton project was not all that it might have been, when visiting the place in 1791. She recorded in her *Diary* that after an early dinner on Sunday August 7, she and her party arrived, through very bad roads, at Milton Abbas. The village, regularly built, was 'of white plaster, cut stone fashion and thatched, though every house was square and meant to resemble a gentleman's abode: a very miserable mistake in his good Lordship, of an intended fine effect; for the sight of the common people and of the poor, labouring or strolling in and about these dwellings, made them appear rather to be reduced from better days than flourishing in a primitive or natural state.' As will be seen, she was not a lone critic of such sweeping schemes for rural rehousing.[9]

About a hundred years after the building of Milton Abbas, a philanthropic approach to re-housing the poorer classes had become something of a national cause. Organised reformers were appalled that so prosperous a country could tolerate the living conditions frequently suffered by those — in industry and agriculture — who actually forged the wealth: conditions for many apparently worse than those in which one of Pocock's more enterprising clients might have kept his hounds. It was people like Harford who, quite early in the course of events, struck a balance between practical re-housing, aesthetic quality and social conscience, though at Blaise, of necessity, on so minute a scale.

Now we must return to Harford and those who helped him reform his estate. Blaise Hamlet, so nearly lost by default and recently restored by the National Trust, might be judged the most accomplished realisation of picturesque estate village design. That it will be shown to reflect also a less-familiar face of an architect who changed the plan of London might intrigue those who know Nash well for his imaginative metropolitan achievements, but little for his rustic work. Because of its demure nature and frequently remote situation, it would usually less-readily have caught the eye of topographers and the public than, say, his palaces, country houses, terraces and streets.

Notes to Chapter One

1. Richard Payne KNIGHT, *The Landscape, a Didactic Poem. In Three Books*, 1795 (2nd edn.), p. 14. First published in 1794. The second edition has additional text and all quotations are taken from this edition.
2. John WEALE (ed.), *Designs and Examples of Cottages, Villas, and Country Houses, being the Studies of several eminent Architects and Builders*, 1857. BUSBY produced *Designs for Villas and Country Houses* in 1808.
3. *Rural Architecture: being a Series of Designs for Rural and other Dwellings*, 1860 (2nd edn.), revised by George MORGAN. The 1st edn. (*Handbook of Rural Architecture*), was largely by SANDERSON. Morgan added an essay on labourers' cottages and additional designs were provided by the Cottage Improvement Society.
4. Sandra BLUTMAN, 'Books of Designs for Country Houses, 1780-1815', *Architectural History*, xi, 1968: and Michael McMORDIE, 'Picturesque Pattern Books and pre-Victorian Designers', *Architectural History*, xviii, 1975, discuss various pattern books originating from the period being considered.

5. Christopher HUSSEY, *English Gardens and Landscapes 1700-1750*, 1967, p.48. See also R.W. KING, 'The "Ferme Ornée"; Philip Southcote and Wooburn Farm', *Garden History*, summer 1974, pp. 27-60. J.C. LOUDON, *An Encyclopaedia of Gardening*, 1835 (new edn.), p.320; he visited Woburn in 1830 and found the principal walks still existing, but the shrubberies overgrown, or gone, whereas George JOHNSON, in *A History of English Gardening*, 1829, while stating that Southcote 'invented' the *ferme ornée*, found that at Woburn it 'no longer exists'. Woburn is engagingly described in Thomas WHATELY, *Observations on Modern Gardening*, 1770. William MASON, *The English Garden*, Bk. i (1778), p. 33:

   On thee too, SOUTHCOTE, shall the Muse bestow
   No vulgar praise: for thou to humblest things
   Could'st give ennobling beauties; deck'd by thee,
   The simple FARM eclips'd the Garden's pride,

6. Edward MALINS, *English Landscaping and Literature*, 1966, p. 36. Morris BROWNELL, *Alexander Pope and the Arts of Georgian England*, 1978, was received after printing of this present book was well advanced. See especially Ch. 9: Appscourt Manor, Dawley Park, Riskins, Woburn Farm, Leasowes. See also John Martin ROBINSON, 'Model Farm Buildings of the Age of Improvement', *Architectural History*, xix, 1976, pp. 17-[31], which includes a gazetteer, *c.* 1730 -*c.* 1820.

7. Henry-Russell HITCHCOCK, *Architecture: Nineteenth and Twentieth Centuries*, 1968 (3rd edn.), p. 110. See also Wend Graf KALNEIN & Michael LEVEY, *Art and Architecture of the Eighteenth Century in France*, 1972, p.335; Vincent CRONIN, *Louis & Antoinette*, 1974, p.194; and Dora WIEBENSON, *The Picturesque Garden in France*, 1978.

8. Gillian DARLEY, *Villages of Vision*, 1975, pp. 3-5.

9. Charlotte BARRETT (ed.), *Diary and Letters of Madame D'Arblay*, (1904-) 1905, v, pp. 13-14.

2 *A Convergence of Talents*

On July 20th 1789, within a week of the fall of the Bastille, Bristol banker, merchant and Quaker, John Scandrett Harford, agreed to buy the Blaise Castle Estate at Henbury from a Bath lawyer, Dr. Denham Skeet, for £13,000.[1]

In the same year Thomas Paty and his son John, Bristol architects, both died, leaving John's partner and brother, William Paty, to continue alone the practice inherited from their father. Also in 1789, 37-year-old John Nash saw the stones of his first public building — Carmarthen Gaol — rise. Humphry Repton, botanist, failed merchant, security coach proprietor and recently a diplomat's secretary, was also 37 and at what was to be the turning point of his hitherto unsettled career. He had made a decision, and recorded in a letter written to the Reverend Norton Nicholls his intention to follow the late 'Capability' Brown and take steps that could lead him to the head of his profession. 'My habit of Landscape Sketching I have considerably improved by Practice & this may be of great use in Shewing effects where descriptions are not sufficient', he wrote.[2] As events proved, it was. He bought surveying equipment in 1789 and completed one of his celebrated *Red Books*.

William Paty (1758-1800), John Nash (1752-1835) and Humphry Repton (1752-1818), with two sons, followed paths which were to intersect at Blaise: Paty by way of a long-established provincial family business of surveyors, monumental sculptors and masons; Nash as an ambitious and socially aspiring architect; and Repton — by all appearances a gentler person than Nash, but like him, starting again — by means of commissions probably secured initially through the good offices of his influential friends, to whom he sent introductory addresses to be passed to their associates.

For Harford, Paty was to produce a fine new classical mansion. Nash added a conservatory to it and secondary buildings about the estate as well, perhaps advising Paty on the house itself. Repton, seizing opportunities offered by the wooded site, sought out within nature's own impressive composition as dramatic a sequence of landscaping events as any Picturesque enthusiast could hope to encounter nearby. His suggested improvements, largely adopted by Harford and substantially extant, make a fitting introduction to the celebrated complex of buildings which were constructed during the thirty years of Harford's reign at Blaise.

Repton, having calculated to use his recently-polished skill as a water-colourist to profitable ends, soon put intentions into practice. Usually bound in red leather and presented to clients, the *Red Books* detailed in his own hand his recommendations to landowners for the improvement of their grounds. By means of water-colour drawings, Repton depicted carefully selected scenes as he found them. Then, by overlaying areas of some of these paintings with flaps painted in the same style, he was able to illustrate — in an instant — how his recommendations might improve or recompose the scene.[3] By 1816 he had submitted over four hundred reports, many in the form of *Red Books.*[4]

With six years' energetic and successful application of his newly-established profession behind him, Repton visited Blaise in August and October 1795 and duly presented the *Red Book for Blaise*[5] early in the following year — that during which Nash, emerging from exile in Wales after bankruptcy at the opening of his career, set up his new London office. He took on Repton's eldest son, John Adey Repton (1775-1860), as assistant, to join Augustus Charles Pugin (1762-1832) who, since escaping from France in 1793 after the execution of Louis XVI, had landed in Wales and responded to Nash's advertisement for a draughtsman — if possible a foreigner: an appointment by chance or by design?

Pugin was no doubt a great asset to Nash's practice, so skilled was he at his work. Nash found gothick irksome; as Lord Clark records in *The Gothic Revival* (1964), 'one window costs more trouble in designing than two houses ought to do.' Pugin grew to fame for his architectural drawings and contributed to many publications, including a learned pattern book of his own, *Specimens of Gothic Architecture* (1821-23), which, incidentally, delineated details and followed the earlier tradition of precisely engraved plates. The work was dedicated to John Nash, Esq. Architect to the Office of Works, Private Architect to the King, etc. etc. etc.: 'Sir, Soon after my arrival in this country, I was very fortunately introduced to you, and prosecuted my architectural studies in your office, with much gratification and advantage to myself. It is, therefore, with no small degree of pleasure that I inscribe to you the present volume of Specimens, which none, better than yourself, know how to appropriate and to appreciate. Indeed, from your friendly and judicious counsel I have already profited much;' and with further plans probably already in mind, he concluded his courteous dedication: '. . . and I trust that the present Work, as well as any other I may hereafter be induced to undertake, may merit the approbation of so distinguished a judge.'

Charles Pugin married Catherine Welby. Their dynamic, but short-lived son Augustus Welby Northmore Pugin (1812-1852), ridiculed the crenellated style so much favoured by Nash for a number of impressive country houses in England and Ireland, not to mention his own mansion on the Isle of Wight. 'What absurdities, what anomalies, what utter contradictions do not the builders of modern castles perpetrate!' railed Pugin: 'On one side of the house machicolated parapets, embrasures, bastions, and all the show of strong defence, and round the corner of the building a conservatory leading to the principal rooms, through which a whole company of horsemen might penetrate at one smash into the very heart of the mansion!'[6] A year after Nash's death, he had already tilted at the architect himself, rather than the mode, when discussing what he saw as current fashionable absurdities and incongruities: '. . . we have only to look into those nests of monstrosities, the Regent's Park and Regent Street, where all kinds of styles are jumbled together to make up a mass.'[7] Just what, one speculates, would Pugin the younger have made of Blaise Hamlet.

Humphry Repton's direct contribution to Blaise appears to have ended on completion of the drive and such works as were connected immediately with it, although a tenuous link with the Hamlet was retained as Humphry's fourth son, George Stanley Repton (1786-1858), became an assistant to Nash. It was he who survived the break-up of a professional relationship between his father and Nash at about the time of their working at Blaise Castle estate, later to become involved with the nearby Hamlet during his master's absence when attending to commissions elsewhere. Humphry and John Adey Repton continued in separate practice for years to come.

It would now be helpful to have some appreciation of the then developing philosophy of the Picturesque[8] and to know of some aspects of Nash's experience as an architect before Blaise Hamlet was built; to follow earlier progress at the Blaise Castle estate generally, and to estimate what was there before Harford started on his improvements, will clarify for us his point of departure. Did Harford acquire landscape ingredients other than fields, a rather rambling house, a wild and wooded gorge and a soaring vantage point, or had the civilising hand of man already tamed the scene that was to be the focus of so much activity during Harford's years of dominion? To what extent had Thomas Farr already developed the grounds at the time of his bankruptcy in 1780 and subsequent sale to Skeet, apart from adding a substantial embattled circular tower — Blaise Castle?

In order to sense the aesthetic climate in which Harford, with Nash and the Reptons, worked it will be necessary to consider some painters (as the term 'Picturesque' might suggest). As Nash and Repton had made contact with Richard Payne Knight and Uvedale Price — leading promoters of the

Picturesque — the professionals' involvement with these land-owners must also be noted. To the painters we now turn.

Notes to Chapter Two

1. Bristol R.O. 28048, P43/3, copy agreement, 20 July, 1789, between Harford & Skeet for the purchase of Blaise Castle estate, the Inn, Blacksmith's Shop, etc., for £13,000, £100 being a deposit, the remainder to be paid by 29 Sept. next. See Appendix VII re the Harford Papers.
2. University of Bristol Library. DM 180/1; letter from H. Repton to Rev. Norton Nicholls, 26 Aug. 1788.
3. *The Red Books of Humphry Repton* (Antony House, Attingham Park & Sheringham Hall), were reproduced in *facsimile*, with an explanation by Edward Malins, by the Basilisk Press, 1976.
4. Dorothy STROUD, *Humphry Repton*, 1962.
5. Humphry REPTON, *The Red Book for Blaise Castle Estate;* 'on the spot August and October, 1795. Plan'd at Hare street by Romford Feb. 7, 1796.' City Museum and Art Gallery, Bristol.
6. A. Welby PUGIN, *The True Principles of Pointed or Christian Architecture*, 1841, pp.58-59. See Benjamin FERREY, *Recollections of A.W.N. Pugin and his father, Augustus Pugin* (introduced by Clive WAINWRIGHT), 1978, re these two men and their publications.
7. A. Welby PUGIN, *Contrasts*, 1836, p. 31.
8. Christopher HUSSEY, *The Picturesque: Studies in a Point of View*, 1927.

Pitts Cottage, Tunbridge Wells, from a plan and elevations dated 1799

3 *The Picturesque: Landscape, Painting and Words*

The Reverend William Gilpin (1724-1804) wrote several important books about his tours in Britain in search of the Picturesque, and Fanny Burney was sufficiently interested in landscape aesthetics to read his words at breakfast. In the second volume of *The Mountains and Lakes* (1786) he states that:—

> The horse, in itself, is certainly a nobler animal, than the cow. His form is more elegant; and his spirit gives fire and grace to his actions. But in a *picturesque light* the cow has undoubtedly the advantage; and is every way better suited to receive the graces of the pencil.
>
> In the first place, the lines of the horse are round and smooth; and admit little variety: whereas the bones of the cow are high, and vary the line, here and there, by a squareness, which is very picturesque. There is a greater proportion also of concavity in them; the lines of the horse being chiefly convex.[1]

Numerous painters and writers have heightened our awareness of visual qualities in landscape. Artists such as Nicolas Poussin (1593/4-1665), Claude Lorrain (1600-82) and Gaspard Dughet (otherwise Gaspard Poussin, 1615-75), went further. As Palladio influenced the style and form of the English house, these painters, through the appeal of their Italianate landscapes to eighteenth century men of taste, contributed to the appearance of great expanses of parkland as the English countryside was refashioned or embellished in an enthusiastic wave of scenic improvements.

All three French-born painters worked in Rome and their pictures were keenly sought after by English collectors. While it would be rash to attempt a summary of the qualities common to all three in their total body of work, some pastoral scenes, typically, are bathed in light and glimpse distant horizons. More varied nearer landforms embrace in their broad tonal passages animals and figures — grouped or in isolation — pursuing peaceful activities in an atmosphere of serenity and warmth. Lost and found; rough and smooth; foreground and distance; some peasant hovel, stony pediment or crumbling tower — consummately poised — breaks, yet parodies, undulations of a near horizon, or arrests the eye with catching light. Fair-weather cumulus echoes the heads of leafy trees as higher layers laze in mid-day sun or dissolve in glowing evening haze. In the foreground, deep shadow: recumbent cattle rest, ruminate and take solace.

Country gentlemen, philosophers, gardeners and writers, as well as painters, drew inspiration from these evocative scenes and some like the Reverend William Mason (1725-97), expressed their feelings about the new landscape ideal by deeds and in words. Mason practised the gardener's art and also propagated a developing philosophy through his verse. The possibility of transforming the English countryside into painterly equivalents of landscapes created under Italian influence was envisaged:

> Meanwhile, of old and classic aid
> Tho' fruitless be the search, your eyes entranc'd
> Shall catch those glowing scenes, that taught a CLAUDE
> To grace his canvass with Hesperian hues,
> And scenes like these, on Memory's tablet drawn,
> Bring back to Britain; there give local form
> To each Idea; and, if Nature lend
> Materials fit of torrent, rock, and shade,
> Produce new TIVOLIS.[2]

Landscapes of the kind by Poussin, so favoured by the arbiters in Britain, were only one aspect of his life's work, but as R.H. Wilenski puts it, 'His picturesque landscapes are works of architecture realised with marvellous completeness; they are microcosmic symbols, records of the true classical attitude to art.'[3] Claude, Wilenski continues, converted Poussin's landscapes into objects of luxury, but as his mind was relatively trivial and his intention mainly decorative, he produced furniture pictures — though of the highest class.

While Poussin's landscapes were more firmly structured, Gaspard's could be more free: Claude's softer and mistier, with saturating glowing light. But all landscape paintings, normally, have their viewing point fixed. Serial vision, as experienced when moving physically through space, could not readily be recorded in two-dimensional pictorial form. The surface of water, reflecting an ever-changing cloudscape and modifying light, the impingement of close walls, the engulfing capacity of shadowy woods and flickering rhythms of a colonnade experienced while walking, cannot be reproduced by traditional landscape painting techniques. Interactions of foreground and distance, the mobility and elusiveness of a spire, the smell of blossom or a dank pond and the increasing chill of evening air can, at best, only be implied. The painter can go so far, the sympathetic observer extending experience, feeling, imagination, association and time, as he may, in response to the painter's selection and skills.

There are then limitations on traditional landscape painting which do not confine the eyesight in real, three-dimensional space. But with an idealised vision, as these painters and their patrons sought to capture, the idyllic image and spirit might be crystallised, eventually to permeate northern homesteads. And apart from decorating the draughtiest of mansions on bleak and foggy winter evenings, paintings might stimulate dreams, even inspire noble thoughts of transformations that might be undertaken about the grounds, of long Arcadian summer days to come. From what features — already existing naturally — might not a Wiltshire vale be transfigured to recapture the atmosphere of a Gaspard paysage? How apt a symbol of perfection might not the temple from Poussin's *Gathering of the Ashes of Phocion* appear if transplanted as a distant focal point in a sylvan park? (Plate 4). And how many devotees were to over-reach their financial means in attempting to realise such landscape fancies? Mason, in continuing his poem, warns of dangers even worse:

> Great Nature scorns controul: she will not bear
> One beauty foreign to the spot or soil
> She gives thee to adorn: 'tis thine alone
> To mend, not change her features. Does her hand
> Stretch forth a level lawn? ah, hope not thou
> To lift the mountain there. Do mountains frown
> Around? ah, wish not there the level lawn.
> Yet she permits thy art, discreetly us'd,
> To smooth or scoop the rugged and the plain.
> But dare with caution; else expect, bold man!
> The injur'd Genius of the place to rise
> In self-defence, and, like some giant fiend
> That frowns in Gothic story, swift destroy,
> By night, the puny labours of thy day.

Salvator Rosa (1615-73), a native of Italy, was admired for some qualities not likely to be found in Poussin or Claude, but still in sympathy with picturesque principles. His moods are more passionate, his landscapes more turbulent. Tempests rage against beetling cliffs and high winds sweep untamed cloud-laden skies. Of Rosa, Constable could write that he was a great favourite with novel-writers, particularly the ladies;[4] but of Gaspard, that his pictures contained the highest feeling of landscape painting yet seen.[5]

Horace Walpole (1717-97) also looked up to Gaspard and Claude. He expressed his appreciation of the picturesque point of view, and urged, 'Enough has been done to establish such a school of landscape, as cannot be found on the rest of the globe.' He appealed for a native master to emerge: 'If we have the seeds of a Claud or a Gasper amongst us, he must come forth. If wood, water, groves, vallies, glades, can inspire or poet or painter, this is the country, this is the age to produce them.'[6]

Richard Wilson (1714-82) might have assumed such a role. Wood, water and glades did inspire him, but the position was unlikely to come to one who lost his temper, offended the King and tampered with works submitted to the Royal Academy. As it was, his genius lived: but he died unhonoured. No painter answered Walpole's call. Foreigners — and there were others more Northern, also influential and sought — secured their place in the hearts of aesthetes and pockets of the rich. Rembrandt, Ruisdael and Rubens, too, held sway, and through their special qualities of vision, poetry and skill, Continental painters were to leave their trace on the British scene.

In 1756 Edmund Burke's treatise, *A Philosophical Enquiry into the Origin of our Ideas of the Sublime and Beautiful,* appeared. Towards the close of this essay, Burke compares his 'Sublime' and his 'Beautiful': '. . . and in this comparison there appears a remarkable contrast. For sublime objects are vast in their dimensions, beautiful ones comparatively small; beauty should be smooth, and polished; the great, rugged and negligent; beauty should shun the right line, yet deviate from it insensibly; the great in many cases loves the right line, and when it deviates, if often makes a strong deviation; beauty should not be obscure; the great ought to be dark and gloomy; beauty should be light and delicate; the great ought to be solid, and even massive. They are indeed ideas of a very different nature, one being founded on pain, the other on pleasure; and however they may vary afterwards from the direct nature of their causes, yet these causes keep up an eternal distinction between them, a distinction never to be forgotten by any whose business it is to affect the passions.'[7]

Statements such as these could hardly have passed unchallenged and Burke's treatise was followed by an extended debate. The term 'Picturesque', as an additional category of visual-emotional stimulation to Burke's two classes, was promoted by Uvedale Price (1747-1829) who developed his own inherited estate at Foxley, near Hereford, on picturesque lines. For him, picturesque qualities included roughness, intricacy and sudden variations associated with irregularity of form, light, colour, physical decay and perhaps even sound. The relationship of landscape practice and appreciation to paintings was vital.

Quite apart from the inspired amateurs and men of letters, professional 'landscape gardeners' (as they were later to be known), were increasingly making themselves felt in effecting change — away from formal Dutch gardens and symmetrical or geometrical compositions, towards nature, then landscape painting, in creating their schemes. William Eames (d. 1803) and

Richard Woods are two recorded as being in sympathy with Lancelot 'Capability' Brown (1716-83). Once he had become established, both the scale and pace of professional operations were transformed. He dominated the field and by his death had undertaken two hundred schemes of improvement. Brown did not succeed in landscaping the whole of England, but made a very impressive start. Price had little time for Brown and his works. He wrote in opposition to his principles and was no doubt delighted to record that Owen Cambridge (himself a gentleman gardener, poet and friend of Fanny Burney's) had assigned to Brown '. . . a higher sphere for his operations than any of those I have mentioned.' On Brown's 'vapouring' about the extent of his changes to the face of the country, Cambridge said, " 'Mr. Brown, I very earnestly wish that I may die before you;' 'why so?' said Brown with great surprise; 'because,' said he, 'I should like to see heaven before you had improved it.' "[8]

Brown was seen by opponents to have blighted the kingdom with stereotyped parklands. He was over-concerned, they would argue, with apparent extent, laying all bare to disclose it, shaving the lawns and polishing the water's edge, isolating mansions from nature's forms by setting them in contrast. He was insensitive to native qualities of a given scene. Particularly after his death, there was much criticism of his principles and achievements.

Richard Payne Knight (1750-1824) was also in disagreement with Brown. A neighbour of Price and fellow Etonian, Knight was a scholar and noted collector of Claudes. He is also remembered for his writings on aesthetics, the collections he left to the British Museum and for Downton Castle, in Shropshire, which by his mid-twenties he had already built and in doing so quietly effected a remarkable architectural innovation — in styles, plan, siting and form — at a time when Nash had still several years to serve in the office of Sir Robert Taylor.

Downton Castle (Knight inherited the estate), was in bold, embattled, mediaeval style (Plate 5). Poised above the wooded Teme valley, it looks across to agricultural country on the hillside opposite. For its time it was remarkable as a newbuilt country house for its asymmetry of plan. Sir Nikolaus Pevsner has written that 'It is evidently the accepted view that the Gothic Revival with its crenellations and ogee-headed windows is wholly a matter of rediscovering a national baronial past.

Nor may Payne Knight's Downton Castle . . . at first sight appear to contradict this view. Its round and polygonal towers and its battlements do not seem to be of a kind fundamentally different from those of Strawberry Hill. Yet Knight's source was indeed of quite another kind', continues Pevsner; 'The compactness of Downton Castle is perhaps the only visual hint at the buildings to which he went for inspiration. They were not buildings ever built; they were buildings drawn and painted.'[9] *The Enchanted Castle,*[10] by

Claude, was such a place.

Downton Castle was 'the prototype of the "castellated" style which flourished for nearly half a century from 1790', writes Sir John Summerson.[11] Yet, inside, Knight's romantically sited and fashioned mansion was classical, like most other country house interiors of its day.

Knight was to write of this paradox retrospectively in *An Analytical Inquiry into the Principles of Taste* (1805): 'It is now more than thirty years since the author of this inquiry ventured to build a house, ornamented with what are called Gothic towers and battlements without, and with Grecian ceilings, columns, and entablatures within; and though his example has not been much followed, he has every reason to congratulate himself upon the success of the experiment'. He advances the opinion of his '. . . having at once, the advantage of a picturesque object, and of an elegant and convenient dwelling; though less perfect in both respects than if he had executed it at a maturer age. It has, however, the advantage of being capable of receiving alterations and additions in almost any direction, without any injury to its genuine and original character.'[12]

Romantic and irregular qualities of the kind demonstrated by Downton and attacked by Pugin were echoed many times by Nash in later years, but it appears that only in the light of recent evidence has the name of John Nash been directly associated with the building of Downton Castle itself. It has been suggested that young Knight might have consulted Nash when contemplating building his house; that is, at a date when Nash (Knight's junior by two years) was in his early twenties.[13] If so, it was a propitious encounter, for in the words of Sir John Summerson, 'If the history of "picturesque" architecture — including the "castellated" style and Gothic and Italian equivalents — starts with Downton, its further progress is associated with a remarkable partnership — the partnership between the landscape-gardener, Humphry Repton, and the architect, John Nash.'[14]

At Downton, picturesque landscape was indigenous — there to be sought, revealed, embellished. Knight was fortunate in so readily being able to put his thoughts into practice: *The Landscape, a Didactic Poem. In Three Books* (1794),[15] put them into print. The work was addressed to Uvedale Price, who followed quickly with his own *Essay*, the full title of which accurately suggests the gist of his argument. *An Essay on the Picturesque, as Compared with the Sublime and the Beautiful; and, on the Use of Studying Pictures, for the Purpose of Improving Real Landscape*[16] appeared in the same year, and between them, Knight and Price were to develop their respective philosophies in a series of letters, replies and editions of their printed works.

Humphry Repton was at one point sufficiently friendly with Knight to have wanted, and been able, to record in watercolour the incident in 'Epping

Forest — with Mr. Knight cutting our joint names' on a tree.[17] This touching moment in their relationship is not suggestive of the troublesome one that developed by way of more enduring writings elsewhere. Having, early, stated his intention to succeed Brown and that his works, with those of Kent and Richmond, were the places of his worship, it would have been difficult for Repton not to have defended his idol almost as himself. Later, in *Theory and Practice* (1803), Repton nailed his colours to the mast, praising Brown as an architect in his own right, but as one whose work was eclipsed by his outstanding success as a landscape gardener — which art Repton was determined to establish as a true profession and to become its leader. He had to defend it and himself against what probably appeared to be the half-informed criticisms of landed amateurs and theoreticians, who perhaps had attitudes of superiority over the emerging 'coxcomical' practitioner — a mere commercial gardener as it were: one little better than a tradesman. And worse, he was a self-confessed addict of Brown into the bargain.

Drawing as he was on Brown's example, Repton did not, in fact, copy his effects. He favoured atmosphere, irregularity, the lost-and-found, and cultivated his sensitivity to 'the genius of the place' — which, once discerned intimated to him a point of departure for betterment of the site. Repton's approach was the more intuitive. The organic nature of a landscape concerned him, as did visual quality.

Knight's *Landscape*, a second edition of which appeared in 1795, included footnotes (largely critical or argumentative) possibly outweighing in words his verse. Brown and Repton personally, and landscape gardeners as a newly-emerging breed, were the butt of unkind attacks. But the poem itself hardly eulogised them either:

> Hence, hence! thou haggard fiend, however call'd,
> Thin, meagre genius of the bare and bald;
> Thy spade and mattock here at length lay down
> And follow to the tomb thy favourite Brown:
> Thy favourite Brown, whose innovating hand
> First dealt thy curses o'er this fertile land;
> First taught the walk in formal spires to move,
> And from their haunts the secret Dryads drove;
> With clumps bespotted o'er the mountain's side,
> And bade the stream 'twixt banks close shaven glide;
> Banish'd the thickets of high-bowering wood,
> Which hung, reflected, o'er the glassy flood . . .'[18]

In the 'Advertisement' to the second edition, Knight replied curtly to *A Sketch from the Landscape: a Didactic Poem* (1794) (Plate 6), which among other things implied that Knight had pillaged Mason's *English Garden* 'to decorate *The Landscape.*' This anonymous and 'contemptible publication' was possibly written by another neighbour, John Matthews, who had recently built Belmont (only seven miles from Foxley), and who was later a client of Nash. In August of the year in which *A Sketch* was published, Matthews breakfasted with Joseph Farington (1747-1821), and passed the comment that he thought very moderately of Knight's poem — didactic only in title. Price, he thought more of in that his *Essays* were written with information and spirit.[19]

Repton's disagreement with the connoisseurs was to develop into open conflict. In a letter dated November 6, 1794, Repton wrote complaining that he had no time to see the sheets of his first book as they were printed. An editor was employed: 'The work will, however, soon make its appearance'. It did. Repton continued with thinly veiled bitterness, '. . . I have been obliged to defend myself from the false & I may say malicious attack of Mr: Knight with whom I have lived in some habits of intimacy & had no reason to suspect this contumelious treatment of my profession — especially as I am actually endeavouring to raise it in the Scale of Polite Arts.'[20]

Repton wrote again after publication of *Sketches and Hints on Landscape Gardening,*[21] '. . . my fame is not to be hurt by the jealous nibbling of a rival Critic, who is puffing himself into notice under the title of Rural Artist — Marshall I suppose has reviewd my work, as he did Knights & Prices, & this will account for all the malice & pecking of this Critique.

The Compliments I daily receive from literary Correspondents & the more solid proof of its merit by the increase of my professional engagements, leaves me no reason to shrink from the detection of grammatical errors — in a work that teaches to improve Scenery & not language'. Repton also wrote of his 'peculiar pleasure' in sending his correspondent a copy of the finished work and he was, that day, answering half-a-dozen noble personages and three times that number of other people who fancied it in Repton's power to furnish them with copies.[22] Clearly, he was taking strides in his chosen direction.

In *Essays on the Picturesque* Price stated that 'the qualities which make objects picturesque, are not only as distinct as those which make them beautiful or sublime, but are equally extended to all our sensations by whatever organs they are received; and that music (though it appears like a solecism) may be as truly picturesque, according to the general principles of picturesqueness, as it may be beautiful or sublime.' He was persuaded that the two opposite qualities of roughness and of sudden variation, joined to that of irregularity, were the most efficient causes of the picturesque.[23]

The theories of Price, as of Knight, were not wholly agreeable to Repton, who argued against imitating painting in landscape design. For example, it was quite impractical to view landscape from a single point of view from a multi-windowed house. In defending Brown's approach against Knight's attack he conceded that the *Landscape* was not without ingenious observations, but added that 'the only source of disgust excited in this gentleman's mind, on viewing the scenes improved by Mr. Brown, proceeds from their not being fit objects for the representation of the pencil. The painter turns with indignation from the trim-mown grass, and swept gravel-walk; but the gardener, who knows his duty, will remove such unsightly weeds as offend the view from a drawing-room window, although perfectly in harmony with the savage pride and dignity of the forest . . .'[24]

Time can atone and attitudes change in the light of subsequent experience. John Claudius Loudon (1783-1843), in *Country Residences* (1806), nagged Repton in the second of his two volumes.[25] Yet it was he, Loudon, who three years before his own death, edited and republished sympathetically Repton's major works. Of Price's aesthetic, Loudon wrote that although Repton disputed its application to landscape gardening, he largely demonstrated it in his later works.[26] Blaise was being planned very shortly after Price's *Essay* was first in print and Repton's written advice to Harford, and the place itself, are available evidence by which to judge. They may serve as an illustration of Repton's move from Brown's example towards Price's view.

The controversy was serious, complex and protracted. Price and his contemporaries were, after all, developing an aesthetic philosophy related to current practice and, as it proved, to important future revelations in the broader field of the Arts. Ruskin, in 'Memory' — the sixth of his *Seven Lamps of Architecture* (1849) — considered that probably no word in the language, exclusive of theological expressions, had been the subject of so frequent or so prolonged dispute as 'Picturesque'.[27]

Here, this brief introduction to the aesthetic climate in which Blaise evolved might be left, but just two more points must be made. The first concerns the notion — the germ — of the Picturesque: the second, popularisation and degeneration of the cult. We must refer first to Vanbrugh, to his work at Blenheim, eighty-five years before Price went to print.

Had the Duchess of Marlborough not questioned her architect about his restoring nearby Woodstock Manor, Vanbrugh probably would not have written his *Memorandum* (1709). He had hoped (without the Duchess's permission) to refurbish the place for his personal use. In his reply to her, Vanbrugh wrote not only of the associative value of retaining old buildings (unusual enough in itself), but explained that judicious use of planting and buildings could improve an otherwise uninteresting view. In Dr. Watkin's view, Vanbrugh summed up in a hasty excuse the essence of what was later to take decades to discuss.[28]

Vanbrugh, writing about buildings and plantations, gives his opinion:

'And the most agreeable disposition is to mix them: in which this old Manour gives so happy an occasion for; that were the enclosure filled with Trees (principally fine Yews & Hollys) promiscuously set to grow up in a wild thicket, so that all the buildings left might appear in two risings amongst 'em, it would make one of the most agreeable objects that the best of Landskip painters can invent.'[29] Dr. Watkin adds that late-century theoreticians 'produced hardly a single idea that the Memorandum does not contain in embryo'.

Writers such as Gilpin, combining their analytical descriptions and topographical recordings with the newly developing commercially viable graphic techniques, encouraged enthusiasts to search out the sublime, beautiful and picturesque in natural landscape and improved estates for themselves. Troubled times in France and published itineraries are likely to have contributed to the popularity of everyman's 'Grand Tour' of the homeland, the Wye Valley, the Lakes and wilder parts of Wales being considered particularly conducive to aesthetic satisfaction.

Bearing in mind Lord Clark's caution that 'Exquisite and awful sensations cannot be shared with the vulgar, and the appearance of *Dr Syntax* showed that picturesque beauty was no longer a subject for the polite',[30] we might fittingly close with some lines extracted from that anonymous work.

William Combe (1741-1823), would-be lawyer, trooper, waiter, spendthrift, Old Etonian, prisoner for debt and satirist, author of *The Tour of Doctor Syntax, in Search of the Picturesque,* poked fun at the writings of both Gilpin and Price in summarising the fashionable view in his doggerel, later to be illustrated by Rowlandson (Plate 7).

> The first, the middle, and the last,
> In *Picturesque,* is *bold contrast;*
> And painting has no nobler use
> Than this grand object to produce.
> Such is my thought, and I'll pursue it;
> There's an example — you shall view it:
> Look at that tree — then take a glance —
> At its fine, bold protuberance;
> Behold those branches — how their shade
> Is by the mass of light display'd;
> Look at that light, and see how fine
> The backward shadows make it shine:
> The sombre clouds that spot the sky
> Make the blue vaulting twice as high;
> And where the sunbeams warmly glow,
> They make the hollow twice as low.
> The Flemish painters all surpass

In making pictures smooth as glass:
In Cuyp's best works there's pretty painting:
But the bold *picturesque* is wanting.[31]

Notes to Chapter Three

1. William GILPIN, *Observations, Relative Chiefly to Picturesque Beauty, made in the year 1772, on several parts of England; particularly the Mountains, and Lakes of Cumberland, and Westmoreland,* 1786, ii, p. 252.
2. William MASON, *The English Garden,* Bk. i, 1778 (first in 1772), pp. 4-5. Gilpin dedicated *Observations on the River Wye* (1782), to William Mason. In it he attempted to convey his understanding of picturesque qualities by the analysis of scenery in painterly terms.
3. R.H. WILENSKI, *English Painting,* 1933, p. 89. With acknowledgements to the author and Faber & Faber Ltd.
4. C.R. LESLIE, *Memoirs of the life of John Constable, Esq. R.A.,* 1843, p. 141, lecture II, 1836.
5. R.B. BECKETT (ed.), *John Constable's Correspondence,* 1968, vi, p. 66.
6. Horace WALPOLE, *Essay on Modern Gardening,* 1785, p. 85: first published in Horace WALPOLE, *Anecdotes of Painting in England,* 1762-71, iv. The former work was reprinted in [William MARSHALL] *Planting and Rural Ornament,* 1796, i, pp. 197-244.
7. Edmund BURKE (1729-97), *A Philosophical Enquiry into the Origin of Our Ideas of the Sublime and Beautiful,* 1756. The quotation is from the edition of 1759, pp. 237-238.
8. Uvedale PRICE, *Essays on the Picturesque,* 1810, ii, xix, n.
9. Nikolaus PEVSNER, 'Richard Payne Knight', *The Art Bulletin* xxxi, 1949. Reprinted in PEVSNER, *Studies in Art, Architecture and Design,* i, 1968, p. 112.
10. *c.* 1664. Courtauld Institute of Art, London, currently on loan to the National Gallery, London.
11. John SUMMERSON, *Architecture in Britain 1530-1830,* 1953, p. 292.
12. Richard Payne KNIGHT, *An Analytical Inquiry into the Principles of Taste,* 1805. Quotations are from the 4th edn., 1808, p. 223.
13. Alistair ROWAN, 'Downton Castle, Herefordshire', Howard COLVIN and John HARRIS (eds.), *The Country Seat,* 1970, pp. 170-173.

14. SUMMERSON, *op. cit.*, p. 292.
15. R.P. KNIGHT, *The Landscape, a Didactic Poem. In Three Books*, 1794; 2nd edn., 1795, amended, quoted in this book.
16. Uvedale PRICE, *An Essay on the Picturesque, as Compared with the Sublime and the Beautiful; and, on the Use of Studying Pictures, for the Purpose of Improving Real Landscape*, 1794. A second volume appeared in 1798 and a collected 3-volume edition in 1810. This includes a summary of the whole argument. Quotations are from this edition. '*Essays . . .*' was used in the title from 1798.
17. Kay SANECKI, *Humphry Repton*, 1974, p. 13, reproduces the water-colour, undated.
18. KNIGHT, *op. cit.*, p. 25.
19. James GREIG (ed.), *The Farington Diary*, 1922-1928, i, pp. 68-69, 31 Aug. 1794.
20. University of Bristol Library. DM 180/3. See Appendix I.
21. Humphry REPTON, *Sketches and Hints on Landscape Gardening*, 1794. There are footnotes and an important Appendix in which Repton explains reasons for the delay in publication and takes both Price and Knight to task.
    Sketches and Hints was republished in 1840 together with Repton's *Observations on the Theory and Practice of Landscape Gardening*, 1803; *An Inquiry into the Changes of Taste in Landscape Gardening*, 1806; *Designs for the Pavilion at Brighton*, 1808; and *Fragments on the Theory and Practice of Landscape Gardening*, 1816, by J.C. Loudon, who edited the collected works under the title *The Landscape Gardening and Landscape Architecture of the late Humphry Repton, Esq., being his entire works on these subjects*. Loudon's edition is quoted throughout this present work.
22. University of Bristol Library. DM 180/4 13 Feb. 1796. See Appendix I.
23. PRICE, *op. cit.*, i, pp. 43-44: 50-51.
24. REPTON. *op. cit.*, Loudon's edn., p. 101 (*Sketches and Hints*).
25. John LOUDON, *A Treatise on Forming, Improving and Managing Country Residences*, 1806.
26. J.C. LOUDON, *An Encyclopaedia of Gardening*, 1835 (new edn.), pp. 322-326; he also relates many facts and opinions concerning the works of Brown, Price, Repton, *et al.*
27. John RUSKIN, *The Seven Lamps of Architecture*, 1897 (7th edn.), pp. 341-342.
28. David WATKIN, *Thomas Hope and the Neo-Classical Idea*, 1968, p. 126.
29. *Ibid.*, pp. 125-127.
30. Kenneth CLARK, *The Gothic Revival*, 1964, p. 55. With acknowledgements to the author & John Murray (Publishers) Ltd.
31. [William COMBE], *The Tour of Doctor Syntax, In search of the Picturesque*, 1815 (5th edn.), p. 117.

4 *John Nash — Formative Years*

Even if the summits and depths of the Cambrian Range are unlikely to have raised in young Nash's breast the exquisite emotional pain experienced by some later grand tourists on first seeing the vertiginous Alps, it is not likely that he was totally unmoved by them.

Visits to Dolau Cothi, Ffynone and Hafod would have taken him through wild tracts of great scenic spledour. Cross-country travelling was slow at best and remote mountain routes arduous. There would have been plenty of time, when the going was easier, to reflect on the moods of close valleys, the architectural character and detail of rustic farmsteads, precarious ruins and modulations of light, while visualising one notional mansion, or another being built.

Nash might well have recalled the lines of John Dyer (1699-1758), born in the Carmarthen area and writing of scenery around the river Towey, in his mid-twenties:

> Old castles on the cliffs arise,
> Proudly tow'ring in the skies!
> Rushing from the woods, the spires
> Seem from hence ascending fires![1]
>
> and
>
> Ever charming, ever new,
> When will the landskip tire the view!
> The fountain's fall, the river's flow,
> The woody vallies, warm and low;
> The windy summit, wild and high,
> Roughly rushing on the sky!
> The pleasant seat, the ruin'd tow'r,
> The naked rock, the shady bow'r;
> The town and village, dome and farm,
> Each give each a double charm,
> As pearls upon an Æthiop's arm. [2]

It is difficult, perhaps even impossible, to enter deeply into the mental and imaginative processes of other people. The ways in which a landscape sequence, for example, may be semi-consciously scanned then possibly years later be consciously reconstructed in painterly, architectural, musical or literary forms might not be appreciated by one who thinks more abstractly than pictorially. Some think visually, receiving, selecting, assimilating and restructuring fragmented images — perhaps image on image, compressing or reversing dimensions of time and space, superimposing fact on fancy, changing scale and context. Some have the ability to communicate the more memorable or significant of them in a coherent and articulate two or three-dimensional form.

If Nash was such a thinker, he could have experienced intense visions during, and probably after, those years in Wales: visions significant in a developing architectural perception. One can only speculate on impact, assimilation and manifestations. But had early bankruptcy not forced Nash's retreat to Carmarthen and had he remained in London, it is conceivable that his sensibilities might have revealed themselves differently later in his career.

Conjecture and the possibility of fertile visual encounters quite apart, there is evidence that he made human contacts in Wales which could well have had a direct bearing on his feeling for the picturesque and on his development as an architect.

At Carmarthen, Nolton House (once called Green Gardens), is generally believed to have been Nash's own residence, built by and for himself. Perhaps financial constraint accounts for its ordinariness, inside and out. His work at St. Peter's church had to be rebuilt and some other early buildings have vanished, although the County Gaol survived until 1938. Jeremy's Hotel, a pleasant vertical house with a deeply curved bow running the full height of its painted front, is associated locally with Nash's name, but as Nolton House might be the sole building of his left in the town, there is little to commemorate him here. This building, one end demolished and the other converted to a school lavatory, is an unassuming memorial to the designer of Buckingham Palace. He was though presented with a gold box 'in consideration of valuable services rendered to the Corporation and the inhabitants at large'[3] about forty years later, after completion of the Picton Monument, in 1828. Whether or not he retained such high esteem locally is questionable. The £3,000 doric column and appurtenances were shortly afterwards considered both inelegant and unsafe.[4] Their demolition in 1846 was ironically symbolic of Nash's earlier fall from public favour on the demise of his notorious patron, George IV, who had been censured by Parliament for his impossibly extravagant ways. Nash, because of lavish royal favour, was inevitably the victim of some jealousy and spite. He had taken over the work at the Royal Pavilion from Repton, then Buckingham Palace from Soane. But before the report of a committee appointed to investigate royal expenditure was drawn up England had lost its spendthrift king and Nash his excessively improvident patron. Corruption was not proved against Nash, but the damage had been done. He was a convenient and vulnerable public whipping-boy and in 1831 Nash retreated again, nearly eighty years old, to East Cowes Castle, and without the knighthood that might have been his.

Nash did not escape personal criticism either. We are left the captious comment of a diarist. In an entry for January 12, 1817 we read:–

'I convers'd with Mr. Lee about Nash the architect in London, who is a great coxcomb. He is about 60 years of age. He is very fond of women, although he is married, & attempted even Mrs. Parker, his wife's sister. He lives in Dover Street in London, has a charming place in the Isle of Wight, and drives four horses.'[5]

When Farington visited Nash at his 'charming place' in 1821 and recorded Nash's own account of early days in Wales, the architect could hardly have forgotten completely a personal financial disaster and his fresh start. Having left Taylor's office 'he passed his time in country exercises and amusements till he was 29 years old, when his attention was roused by a report of the good success of his late fellow pupil Mr [S.P.] Cockerell.' Nash claimed that as a result, instead of turning to Law, he now resolved to make an effort in the field for which he had studied.[6] Sir John Summerson has shown that Nash's tale deviated from facts: the *London Gazette* confirms his bankruptcy of 1783.

If Nash's early building activities in Carmarthen appear to have been modest, his years there were not wasted. He was ambitious, confident and pushing. As his experience and circle of contacts grew, so did his rewards. They included a socially more elevated and a geographically more widely distributed clientele, these in turn leading to professional success encouraging enough for Nash to return to London. His first fee, Farington tells us, was for designing a bath for John Vaughan, at Golden Grove, a little to the north of Carmarthen; and so pleased was his client that a *Rouleau* of guineas was put into Nash's travelling baggage. 'Within a year he had employment which produced him £500.' Nash was writing from 30 Duke Street by March 1795. Presumably this was a period of transition, as correspondence about alterations at Dolau Cothi for John Johnes was from Carmarthen in June 1792 and January 1796. In a further letter from 30 Duke Street, dated February 1796, Nash refers to a copy bill for Johnes' chimney-piece as still being at Carmarthen.[7] On re-marriage, Nash moved to 28 Dover Street, while simultaneously converting number 29 into splendid new quarters, which he eventually occupied in about 1800, although writing of such intentions four years earlier. He must have been a very busy man on his own account alone, as work on East Cowes Castle was in progress before the turn of the century, and he let it be known to Farington later that his chaise hire cost £1,500 in one year to cover the 11,000 miles necessary to secure and discharge commissions in the three kingdoms.

A collection of letters in Carmarthen,[8] testifies to Nash's having been politically aware during his years there: an awareness that he might well have calculated could bring contacts, if not patrons, to turn his retreat into advance. Although he preferred to forget what must in many ways have been difficult times, they were probably of great importance to his career as it was later to evolve.

Before Nash left Wales he had built half-a-dozen or so country houses for the gentry. Llanayron (*c.* 1794: near Aberayron) stands largely as built, although Temple Druid (*c.* 1795: near Pembroke) has suffered grievously. Much-altered Llysnewydd (*c.* 1795: near Cardigan), was recently demolished and Ffynone (1792-96), stands resplendent, though remodelled.[9]

Important as the early country houses are in Nash's rise to fame, two other commissions in Wales were of particular significance to his association with the picturesque. One, possibly his first major building, was the triangular and embattled Castle House (*c.* 1794),[10] which stood on the front at Aberystwyth (Plate 8). Another undertaking was a few miles inland from Castle House, where he produced an octagonal library for Thomas Johnes, in 1794. With surrounding hillside plantations mostly felled, Hafod — recently blasted into a massive pile of rocky rubble and now beset by caravans and motor cars — is a forlorn spectacle. Yet poignant reminders of Johnes' fertile rule remain: the site of Mariamne's flower garden can be traced, and Francis Chantrey's splendid fire-scorched monument to this precocious child may be seen in the church nearby.[11]

Johnes, who left Croft Castle in Herefordshire in order to face the challenge presented by the Welsh estate, was cousin of none other than Richard Payne Knight of Downton Castle: and it was Uvedale Price who had employed Nash to build Castle House as a holiday retreat.[12]

Only recently has proof of Nash's responsibility for Johnes' library been found. Samuel Cockerell's son, Charles, made a tour of Wales when he was nineteen with the Daniells — noted topographical artists. Cockerell recorded these observations in his journal, 1806:

'House is not very good, chiefly by Nash; the library is a good room but affected as Nash's things generally are — 8 marble columns of slim Doric supporting a gallery. A[n] antique mosaic very fine.' One side of the octagon led into a Conservatory: 'a good idea.'[13] (Plate 9).

Nash and the building of Hafod are firmly linked only by young Cockerell's faint praise of buildings long since destroyed. Repton's association with the place is remembered by something less flattering still:

> Far hence! let REPTON, BROWN, and EAMES,
> Zig-zag their walks, and torture streams;
> But let them not my dells profane,
> Or violate my Naiad train;
> Nor let their arrogance invade
> My meanest Dryad's secret shade,
> And with fantastic knots disgrace
> The native honours of the place;
> Making the vet'ran oak give way,
> Some spruce exotic to display.
> Their petty labours be defy'd
> Who *taste* and *nature* would divide.

These lines, Loudon records, were left written on a seat at Hafod.[14]

There appears to be no evidence to establish the date or circumstances under which Nash and Repton first met. Miss Stroud suggests that this might have been at Hafod, or in Herefordshire when Repton was visiting Stoke Edith or Sufton and Nash was working on the County Gaol at Hereford.[15] Edward Hyams, while considering it probable that they first met in Wales, states that the partnership had been entered into by May 1796.[16] Their first joint venture materialised at Corsham Court, Wiltshire, in the following year — which also saw them working at Southgate Grove in Middlesex and at Dulwich. And it will be seen that by May the partners were already planning a project of importance to this enquiry.

There is less certainty about the date when the partnership ended. Edward Hyams states that their last year of working together was 1799,[17] while Terence Davis considers it to have been 1803,[18] though co-operation was still possible, he adds, at Longner Hall, in Shropshire, as late as 1806, if with some unease. Nash had apparently done less than full justice to John Repton for his part in some work and Humphry was aggrieved that his own good will and connections had been exploited. Nash received the larger commission on work secured through the partnership and it will be seen that very early in their relationship Nash, particulary, might be judged not always strictly loyal to his colleague, professionally speaking, when corresponding with one joint client. In view of their respective personalities, any or all of these possibilities might have contributed to the breakdown of their business arrangement.

Judging by the dates above, the partnership might have lasted for as little as two to three years, and Repton could have introduced Nash to Harford very shortly after completion of the *Red Book for Blaise* early in 1796, should they not, in fact, already have been acquainted.

Notes to Chapter Four

1. John DYER, *Grongar Hill,* 1726. Lines quoted are from John DYER, L.L.B. *Poems,* 1761, p. 11. This is a posthumous collected edition comprising *Grongar Hill, The Ruins of Rome* and *The Fleece.*
2. *Ibid.*, p. 14. Dyer was a painter. In *Observations on the River Wye*, 1782, pp. 59-61, Gilpin compares unfavourably with Milton's, Dyer's ability to convey picturesque qualities in his verse.
3. J. and V. LODWICK, *The Story of Carmarthen,* 1972, p. 153.
4. *Ibid.*, p. 155.
5. Bodleian Library. Finch MS. d. 19, fol. 19v.
6. James GREIG (ed.), *The Farington Diary,* viii, p. 301.
7. National Library of Wales. Dolau Cothi Papers, 1705-1826. John Johnes was cousin of Thomas Johnes of Hafod. Nash refronted his farmhouse and did other work there *c.* 1792-95. Apart from a minor building, Dolau Cothi was recently demolished. Those Dolau Cothi Papers concerning Nash are drawn on by Francis JONES, 'The Hand of Nash in West Wales', *Transactions of the Cambrian Antiquarian and Field Society,* 1939, pp. 93-96. For some recent references to Thomas Johnes of Hafod and John Johnes of Dolau Cothi see R.G. THORNE, 'Herbert Lloyd of Carmarthen', *Transactions of the Honourable Society of Cymmrodorion,* 1977, pp. 103-130.
8. Carmarthen County R.O. Cwmgwili Collection.
9. For a more detailed account of these and other early buildings by Nash, as well as for accounts of his professional career and aspects of his private life, see:
   i John SUMMERSON, *John Nash — Architect to King George IV,* 1935 (2nd edn., 1949).
   ii Howard COLVIN, *A Biographical Dictionary of British Architects 1600-1840,* 1978.
   iii Terence DAVIS, *The Architecture of John Nash*, 1960, and
   iv Terence DAVIS, *John Nash — The Prince Regent's Architect*, 1966 (2nd edn., 1973).
10. DAVIS, *ibid.*, Pl. 4.

11. Elisabeth INGLIS-JONES, *Peacocks in Paradise,* 1971. This biography of Thomas Johnes describes accomplishments and disasters at Hafod.
12. Elisabeth INGLIS-JONES, 'An Eccentric's Castle House', *Country Life,* 4 July 1952, p. 33, discusses the building and shows a Worcester tea caddy resembling it. No record of such a design can be traced in the Royal Worcester archives.
13. David WATKIN, *The Life and Work of C.R. Cockerell,* 1974, p. 5, quoting from Cockerell's unpublished journal of 1806.
14. John LOUDON, *A Treatise on Forming, Improving and Managing Country Residences,* 1806, p. 439.
15. Dorothy STROUD, *Humphry Repton,* 1962, p. 94.
16. Edward HYAMS, *Capability Brown and Humphry Repton,* 1971, p. 166 *et seq.*
17. *Ibid.,* p. 171.
18. DAVIS, *op. cit.,* p. 34, 39.

Nolton House, Carmarthen, in 1971

5 Neatness, Nature and Vapoury Repose

'The capricious taste of that sweeping improver, Mr. Repton, has made this naturally beautiful place still more whimsically fantastical than it originally was', wrote the Reverend John Evans in *The Picture of Bristol,* in about the year 1818, when describing Blaise.

Despite the magnificent views that made Thomas Farr's tower so tempting to seek out and scale, Repton would not have recommended Harford to set his mansion on that same rare hill-top site — so well suited for panoramic viewing, but wholly inappropriate to a family residence. A landscape gardener could not hope to compete with the prospect of nature's horizons seen from such boundless situations, although an exposed hill site might be quite satisfactory for a villa used as an occasional retreat.[1] However, Repton need have had no fears as the decision on siting had already been taken. He also recorded observations on orientation. Harford's new house should face the sun and also take advantage of the scenery. It appears that site work could not have been far advanced by the time he arrived, as Repton wrote, '. . . it is therefore very fortunate that in this instance the best views are towards the south, and the two living fronts will be so placed as to command them to advantage, especially if the house be raised a few feet above the present level, which will make it appear to stand on a small knoll with the ground gently sloping from it in every direction.'[2] Tower and mansion were complementary, not competitive, in their siting. Their relationship visually also added a spatial quality to the open parkland, which might not have been realised had Harford not placed his house near Henbury village, half a mile from the hill-top tower.

Before considering further Repton's part in the development of Blaise, it is necessary to identify three major landscape components contributing to the physical composition of the site. First, there was the heavily wooded gorge, threaded by gently winding Hazel Brook: second, the hill rising above the north-west cliff of the gorge and topped by the embattled circular tower: third was the flat green parkland lying between that hill and Harford's mansion (Plate 10). Aligned with the tower and running across that park, were the remains of Sir Samuel Astry's double avenue of elms, which had linked the hill with his earlier Great House, once to the north-east of Harford's estate.[3]

Repton's *Red Book* plan shows the avenue already in disarray. Even had it been otherwise he might well have wished it gone, as geometrically insistent features on a scale such as this could be out of sympathy with principles of irregularity in landscape, as was later to be observed in *Mansfield Park* (1814), by Jane Austen (1775-1817).

Mr. Rushworth, enthused by the improvements at a friend's estate, was considering rather grandiose schemes himself: '. . . Repton, or anybody of that sort, would certainly have the avenue at Sotherton down; the avenue that leads from the west front to the top of the hill you know' . . . 'Cut down an avenue! What a pity! Does not it make you think of Cowper? "Ye fallen avenues, once more I mourn your fate unmerited." '

He smiled as he answered, 'I am afraid the avenue stands a bad chance, Fanny.'

His site defined and commission entered into, Repton's procedure was first to sense and then to draw out the essence of a landscape by experiencing it at first-hand and allowing the site to suggest what might be done to satisfy his own aesthetic insights and his client's practical needs: a process of divining and realising, rather than imposing a preconceived formula. Around Blaise Castle, built to the design of Robert Mylne[4] who was working at Vanbrugh's neighbouring Kingsweston at that time, relatively little needed to be done as the expansive views — towards South Wales, Chepstow, distant mountains, and Johnes' Hafod far beyond — offered everchanging and large-scale panoramas. As well as revealing latent landscape qualities to advantage, Repton was at pains sometimes to suppress or correct scenic defects by the use of suitable cosmetic devices. A good example of his technique was illustrated in *Fragments on the Theory and Practice of Landscape Gardening* (1816). Some improvements to his own cottage garden at Hare Street were made to screen undesirable visual intrusions into this haven to which he retreated for upwards of thirty years from 'the pomp of palaces, the elegances of fashion, or the allurements of dissipation.'[5]

The obvious access point to Harford's new mansion would have been, as today, straight from the village; quick, direct and simple. But the hundred-yard drive, while convenient enough as a short cut for domestic servicing, would hardly have exercised Repton's greatest talents to the full, or have exploited the scenic potential of Harford's richly endowed estate (Plate 11).

Repton's means of approach was not the obvious one. 'A stranger to the shapes of the ground in this romantic Place would be at a loss to account for the crooked and distorted lines represented on the map, which can only be explained by stating, that a deep ravine crosses the wood and seemed at first to render hopeless all attempt to make any approach except that thro' the village of Henbury. I trust however that the line of road will be found perfectly easy and accessible on the ground, however violent it may appear on paper'.[6] He wrote again later on the problems of Blaise: 'However, by cutting away the face of the rock in some places, and building lofty walls in others, to support the road, and by taking advantage of the natural projections and recesses to make the necessary curvatures, carriages now pass this tremendous chasm with perfect ease and safety.'[7] Previously unrealised landscape experiences were revealed to the view-taking traveller in an unhurried quarter-hour serpentine and precipitous carriage drive from the romantic entrance lodge to the carefully poised classical house. Avoidance of the village was essential to Repton's envisaged scheme, presuming that visitors would normally approach from the Bristol side of Henbury, where a number of villas and country houses seemed to dispute with each other because of their grandeur or size.[8]

By heading-off the village completely Repton obliged travellers to see those delights they might otherwise have missed and gave them the impression that Blaise Castle House and the church were set deeply in secluded country-side. They were actually close to England's second city and only a few yards from the village so by-passed. Having teased out his woodland drive Repton marked its entrance with a substantial, though not grandiose lodge — an architectural device with which he attempted to reconcile the then prominent gothick castle giving name to the place with the new formal mansion — invisible from the highway, then to be glimpsed, withheld, and gradually unveiled during the circuitous approach. With subsequent tree growth, much of the intended effect has been lost.

Repton, in deciding in what style the Lodge should be built, was faced with the classical-romantic dilemma. He settled for compromise in his explanation, and on embattled Tudor for his style (Plate 12). Thus, Repton wrote, the main entrance lodge was in character with the castle to which it was a prelude, introducing a wood with which it was in harmony. He anticipated the stranger's agreeable surprise on quitting the wood to find that he was not in fact visiting a mouldering castle at all, but a mansion of elegance, cheerfulness, and hospitality, where the comfort of neatness would blend with the rude features of nature, 'without committing great violence on the Genius of the Place.'[9]

Once past the Lodge, and before descending the steepsided ravine, visitors encountered a cottage set deeply in the woods and alongside the drive. Such an object was needed to enliven the scenery. A temple or pavilion in this situation would have reflected light and formed a contrast with the dark woods. But Repton needed an inhabited building. A sculptural symbol was not enough. Later, he wrote, '. . . this cottage, therefore, derives its chief beauty from that which cannot easily be expressed by painting — the ideas of motion, animation, and inhabitancy, contrasted with those of stillness and solitude.' The form had to be humble, yet not mean. It should appear to be what it was — the cottage of the labourer who had care of the woods. Its simplicity should be the effect of art and not of neglect or accident. It should seem to belong to the proprietor of the mansion and castle, without affecting the character of either.[10]

Clearly, Repton was aware not only of picturesque, beautiful and sublime qualities in landscape, but also of practical, transient and social niceties, some of which he was capable of wrapping up in high-flown turns of phrase: 'It may perhaps be urged that I have made a road where nature never intended the foot of man to tread, much less that he should be conveyed in the vehicles of modern luxury, but where man resides, Nature must be conquered by Art, and it is only the ostentation of her triumph, and not her victory, that ought never to offend the correct Eye of Taste,' he wrote to Harford in his *Red Book*.

The importance of such passages of Repton's prose lies partly in that they reveal his attitudes and approach to solutions of several specific aspects of landscape design. He went further into his ideas of motion and atmosphere by explaining that on a summer's evening it would frequently happen that smoke from the cottage would spread a thin veil along the glen, and produce 'that kind of vapoury repose over the opposite wood which painters often attempt to describe, and which in appearance so separates the two sides of the valley that the imagination will conceive it to be much wider and more extensive than it really is.'[11]

Repton apportioned the splendours and sights of Blaise to two categories. There were those to be seen on approaching the mansion by way of Harford's new carriage drive, and those for the more curious of leisured sight-seers setting out from the house. 'I must therefore assume to myself the merit of shewing this situation in a manner before unthought of, and while I reserve some scenes for those who can walk to them, and who can climb steps and creep thro' caverns, I must endeavour to display others from the windows of a carriage with all the interest of surprize and novelty.'[12]

Closing his *Red Book for Blaise* with lines sometimes as obsequious as earlier ones might have been informative or florid, Repton congratulated Harford on having attained command of such romantic scenes and rejoiced that they had fallen into his hands. He was highly gratified and flattered by having been called on 'to direct how best to preserve or heighten the native beauties of such a delightful subject.'

In putting Repton's proposals into practice, Harford was committed to felling rather than to planting trees. As Repton himself put it on writing of the view from mansion to cottage, 'This is the first instance in which I have been consulted where all improvement must depend on the axe, and tho' fully aware of the common objection to cutting down trees, yet, it is only by a bold use of that instrument that the wonders of Blaise Castle can be properly displayed.'[13]

Harford was already well aware of the concern that felling at Blaise stirred in hearts of local conservationists. He had, perhaps, mentioned to Repton his difficulty of four years earlier when Charles Fenwick Noel complained that 'The Depredations daily committing on your Property in Blaze Wood are beyond description bad not even Sunday is suffered to pass without your property being Destroyed.' Noel actually took away the woodman's offending axe and dared Harford to take legal action. 'Should you think proper to Prosecute we Shall most readily attend.'[14]

Few would deny that Repton went far towards achieving his stated goals, and no doubt his influence was such that the popularity of Blaise as a place of pilgrimage for seekers of the picturesque increased. However its charms had not passed entirely unrecognised by the public before Repton's visits and Harford had made determined attempts to discourage them, though running into difficulties from the start. He wrote to Farr (by then at Whitechapel) in September 1789,[15] stating his plight and seeking Farr's advice. Harford, the townsman, was probably unwise to announce so early his intention to keep the place very much to himself, the problem of public access being aggravated by neighbours (as in Farr's day) holding keys. Harford intended to give access on their ringing a bell, but his plans met with resistance: '. . . I think myself very ungenteely treated by the Gent[ry?] of Henbury, to be thus threatened before I have even possession of the Place'. Farr replied in rather philosophical terms, advising an unhurried approach, though recalling that no other problem had caused him so much concern and illustrating his craftiness with a case history. It had been 'the constant Walk for the late Vicar Mr Gardiner and Mr Sampson for many Years, but as I manured the Field very plentifully, they were obliged at last from necessity to quit a Path which was in general too Wet from no one walking in it but themselves.'[16]

It must have been a rewarding moment for John Harford when Repton's drive through the woods was ready for use. He left an account of that proud occasion in the summer of 1799: 'Friday, July 26, Drove Mr. Battersby[17] in his Phaeton, entering the new Road in the Woods opposite Mr. Brooke's, to the New House and back again, returning through the Village; the first time a four-wheel Carriage was ever driven through the new road, and afterwards drove my Wife in the Phaeton through the woods and back again.'[18]

The question arises: whose was the vision — Farr's, Harford's, or Repton's? It was not Skeet's, but Farr made a substantial start in developing, on a smaller acreage than Harford's estate was to become, his own kind of paradise. His 'Castle' survives; but he left more than that. He is said to have created woodland walks and to have explored those visual qualities of landscape indigenous to Blaise. While Repton despised earlier attempts to set up a system of water control, it could well be that he incorporated some of Farr's walks — cuttings through the woods — and vistas within his own recommendations for the place. However, on the evidence of Harford's additional purchases of land, his immediate attempts to close paths and his having sited the mansion, all before Repton is known to have arrived on the scene, it does seem possible that he knew not only who he wanted to help him, but (to a considerable degree) what he wanted, too. And if Blaise, from the time of Harford's purchase until the building of Blaise Hamlet, is seen as a significant architectural and landscaping achievement developing from what the unfortunate Thomas Farr begun, we are faced with a further question: what inspired Farr?

Quite apart from vision and energy, there was a third, and essential force that contributed to the realisation of plans for Blaise. This was money. Farr had been a prominent Bristol citizen and merchant, but whereas Harford's pocket was relatively bottomless, Farr's sugar fortune (like his dreams for Blaise) dissolved. The War of American Independence cut him short in his plans for Blaise and he was forced to sell to Dr. Denham Skeet who 'resided here for several years, but without effecting any alterations of importance'.[19]

Improvements of the kind undertaken by Harford needed substantial long-term as well as more immediate financial support, not to mention the optimism and tenacity associated with a successful large-scale landscaping enterprise. He certainly had the means.

Embracing, as they do, the critical years of development at Blaise, Harford's journals and ledgers offer a guide to the style of living by one in his position: not an aristocrat, but a provincial banker and business man, he could spend in a year on horses and carriages very many times an agricultural worker's annual wages. While James Franks earned £16 10s. 0d. hauling 360 tons of stones for the new dwelling house at Henbury in 1796, the same sum could be paid for a lottery ticket, or £100 be spent on greenhouse and hothouse exotics several times over a decade. But it is perhaps misleading to make such a simple comparison of apparent values, and Harford made many charitable donations over the years.[20]

The accounts are not sufficiently detailed to provide all the information that could be wished for. However, there are helpful and sometimes tantalising clues to landscaping and building works at Blaise, such as regular payments for improvements at Ashgrove, which are phased out by about 1801. There are almost monthly and seemingly never-ending expenses at Blaise Woods. There are the estate and farm disbursements and the costs of building and furnishing the new mansion at Henbury. The house at which Harford was born, in Brunswick Square, and the setting up of another substantial dwelling (in which he was to die) at 25 Great George Street in 1802, all added considerably to his outgoings. There were new stables to be built at Henbury, a lodge at Coombe Hill, and numerous other ventures that contributed to Harford's luxurious surroundings — in which Blaise Hamlet was the crowning enrichment — to be financed.

The sources of Harford's capital and income were widely based. His business involvements were substantial. A partner in the Harford Bank, director of the Bristol Dock Company and of Harford's Bristol Brass and Copper Co., he also had an interest in mining rights at Wednesbury and many other concerns.[21] 1782 saw him Warden and 1798 Master of the Merchant Venturers.

His personal accounts were carefully kept until illness (which began with a chill in the summer of 1812) was reflected a year later in his books, which became progressively less detailed, less tidily written and apparently hastily entered. Whereas earlier there might have been many entries every month, there is only a brief annual summary for 1814.

John Scandrett Harford died, aged 60, on 23rd January, 1815 and his son, John Scandrett Harford junior, inherited the estate. He had renounced Quakerism in 1809 and became a convinced Anglican, a traveller, scholar and author of books largely about classical and aesthetic matters. He developed a strong social conscience, kept diaries and journals, and wrote over twenty pages in memory of his father who, although a member of the Society of Friends, 'did not feel himself called upon strictly to adopt all their customs or practises, but in cases where his conscience called for conformity, he never drew back in the face of the world from a manly avowal of his principles.'

The son's appreciation confirms, from first-hand knowledge, the father's apparent character: 'Great order and regularity marked the conduct of his affairs. He was punctual in his payments, and his accounts were kept with particular exactness. Every department of his expenditure was therefore clearly open to his inspection. By this means he avoided all the uncertainty and embarrassment to which men of irregular habits in this respect are exposed': and he was always deeply anxious that his sons should conduct their affairs as he did himself.

'In an especial manner I would dwell upon the integrity and uprightness which eminently marked his daily conduct, both in the bosom of his family, and in his commerce with the world. These qualities produced a most punctual discharge of his promises & engagements; a marked detestation of every practice bordering on equivocation or meanness: and above all a most scrupulous and undeviating regard to Truth.'[22]

Such, in the eyes of his son, was the man who commissioned Repton, Paty and Nash to create for him a haven within 'the quiet and sequestered scenery in which this place so remarkably abounds.'[23] Within weeks of his father's death John Harford junior had completed his Address on the pernicious influence of Bristol Gaol. Published in that same year, it was a pointer to his developing philanthropic attitudes.

Notes to Chapter Five

1. Humphry REPTON, *The Red Book for Blaise.* City Museum and Art Gallery, Bristol.
2. REPTON, *ibid.*
3. Robert ATKYNS, *The Ancient and Present State of Glocestershire,* 1768 (2nd ed.), Pls. 248, 249, Kip's (*c.* 1712) engravings of Henbury. A large canvas in Blaise Castle Museum gives further detail, as does the recently discovered painting by Thomas Robins.
4. John STEEGMANN [*sic*], 'Humphry Repton at Blaize Castle', *Architectural Review,* May 1938, p. 249. See Chapter 6; 'Blaise Castle', below.
5. J.C. LOUDON (ed.), *The Landscape Gardening and Landscape Architecture of the late Humphry Repton, Esq.*, 1840, pp. 603-604.
6. REPTON, *op.cit.*
7. LOUDON, *op.cit.*, p. 251, n.
8. REPTON, *op. cit.*
9. REPTON, *op. cit.*; see also J.C. LOUDON (ed.), *The Landscape Gardening . . . of Humphry Repton,* 1840, pp. 250-251, which show 'before and after' views of this entrance.
10. LOUDON, *op. cit.*, pp. 256-257.
11. REPTON, *op. cit.*; see also J.C. LOUDON (ed.), *The Landscape Gardening . . . of Humphry Repton,* 1840, pp. 256-257, which show 'before and after' views of the cottage as seen from the mansion.
12. REPTON, *op. cit.*

13. *Ibid.*
14. Bristol R.O. 28048, P43/18, 28 Feb. 1791. Noel, of Cote House, Durdham Down.
15. *Ibid.*, P 41/1, 7 Sept. 1789, copy letter.
16. *Ibid.*, P 41/2, 10 Sept. 1789, copy letter.
17. Probably his relation William Battersby (1737-1812), who left his fortune (on the death of his widow, in 1815) to John Harford junior's brother Abraham (1786-1851) on condition that he adopted the name Battersby, which he did.
18. Alice Harford (ed.), *Annals of the Harford Family*, 1909, p. 56.
19. J. and H.S. STORER (del./sc.) & J.N. BREWER, *Delineations of Gloucestershire*, 1824, p. 105.
20. Bristol R.O. 28048, F1-F19, ledgers, journals and cash books, 1748-1815.
21. Charles CAVE, *A History of Banking in Bristol*, 1899, pp. 90-99.
22. Bristol R.O. 28048, M24/1-5. Harford listed five Rosas, two Gaspars and a Poussin in his collection of pictures which he valued at over £10,000.
23. REPTON, *op. cit.*

A cow house for Lord Robert Spencer, after a drawing by George Repton

6 *Building at Blaise*

The Hamlet apart, there are several buildings at Blaise deserving our attention. Humphry Repton's name has been linked with three of them, his sons' have been associated with at least as many projects, and Nash's (if tenuously so in a couple of instances) with no fewer than five. Blaise Castle, built to a design delivered in 1766 by Robert Mylne (1733-1811), was a major influence on the recommendations made by Humphry Repton which, as we have seen, included the siting and architectural style of the Main Lodge: but, as in the case of the mansion, it has been suggested that Nash had a hand in its design.

Farr is said also to have built one of those atmosphere-producing garden embellishments known as a root house. No detailed description or depiction of it appears to have been previously recorded. Timber Lodge, alongside Repton's drive, has been tentatively indentified with the root house, but has also been attributed to Humphry Repton. The handsome conservatory has long been connected with Nash's name and various dates have been ascribed to it, while the dairy, so much in the spirit of Blaise Hamlet, has been attributed to Nash, with the assistance of both of Humphry's architect sons.

Bearing in mind that the *Red Book* proposals were in general adopted by Harford, it is clear that Blaise owes a great deal of its character to the imagination, influence and skills of the Reptons and Nash. It is also apparent that there is some confusion about who did what and when.

In this chapter an attempt is made to consolidate some previously recorded data and expand on it with new, in order to isolate some remaining questions and clarify the course of events. If these ends are met, a better understanding of the respective contributions made to Harford's Blaise by those he employed, of Harford's character and tastes, and thereby of the immediate background from which Blaise Hamlet came into being, might be gained. Attention may then be turned to the Hamlet itself and to some excursions made in search of Nash's cottage and village architecture elsewhere.

Blaise Castle

> Here *Farr* with inbred rapture may resort,
> And see his ships glad sailing into port,
> With *Indian* treasures on the current ride,
> To crown the prospect and enrich the tide:
> What nameless raptures must his joys renew,
> With growing taste at once, and wealth, in view . . .
>
> From *Clifton*, by H. Jones

In his *Chronological Outline of the History of Bristol,* published in 1824, John Evans fortunately recorded something of Farr's early fascination with Blaise. 'This had been a favourite scene of Mr. Farr's shooting-excursions, when a school-boy; and, to the credit of his decision of character no less than of his fine taste, in being the first to appreciate the beauties of this spot, it should not be forgotten that he thus early determined, whenever he might possess the means and opportunity, to become its purchaser, and make it emulate, as far as its limits would permit, the charms of the far-famed Piercefield Estate, with the owner of which, the lamented Valentine Morris, Mr. Farr's family were on terms of intimacy. When the propitious era of maturity and competence arrived, Mr. Farr commenced his operations by laying out a walk around the wood, and opening the foliage at places of easy access for the most striking points of view.'[1]

In Piercefield then, across the Severn estuary, by Chepstow and poised above final dramatic meanderings of the Wye, Farr early identified with a precipitous and sylvan image that was to become his model for Blaise. Partly realised by him, this was to be taken up by Harford and developed through Repton's sophisticated re-interpretation. What were Piercefield's charms? What qualities did Farr attempt to emulate? There are many descriptions, Piercefield being one of the most eulogised pleasure gardens of the age. Words failed even hardened landscape critics. Shenstone, Wesley, that early appreciator of the picturesque William Gilpin, Marshall, Whately, Farington, and Joseph Banks all wrote of Piercefield and Arthur Young swooned at the very idea of views from Morris's cliff-top grounds: 'my pen drops from my hand', he managed somehow to write: the eyes of one's imagination would not be keen enough to take in this point, which the united talents of a Claude and a Poussin would scarcely be able to sketch.[2]

William Marshall, the well-known if anonymous author of *Planting and Rural Ornament,* wrote twelve pages in Piercefield's praise,[3] and George Mason, who considered that a desirable qualification for a landscape gardener was to have birth and education 'above plebian', wrote that though genius was the gift of nature, it required the sunshine of tuition to ripen it. He added a more analytical note about Morris's other Eden. The observer would not only admire each grand and picturesque composition as it presented itself, but be particularly satisfied with the total absence of fanciful accompaniments.[4]

Simple, natural, picturesque in detail, yet sublime in scale and breathtakingly beautiful, is the impression that descriptive topographers have left us of Piercefield. It was a relatively early example of its kind, having been created by a very young Antiguan-born heir. Valentine Morris (1678-1742/3), the father, left sugar plantations to his hospitable but reckless son and namesake, who acquired the use of Piercefield in 1753. He employed (in addition to local talent) Lancelot Brown to lay out one entrance[5] and enlisted the help of Richard Owen Cambridge (1717-1802), who had joked about Brown's ambitions, as well.[6]

Morris (1727-1789) overspent, was appointed Lieutenant-Governor of St. Vincent in 1772, and sold his beloved Piercefield to settle debts in 1784.[7] Prince Pückler-Muskau (1785-1871), another parkomane, commented that when taking the reciprocal view southward across the Severn estuary, in the general direction of Gloucestershire and Blaise, 'The grouping of this landscape is perfect: I know of no picture more beautiful. Inexhaustible in details, of boundless extent, and yet marked by such grand and prominent features, that confusion and monotony, the usual defects of a very wide prospect, are completely avoided.' Piercefield Park, which included the ridge of hills from Windcliff to Chepstow, was without question the finest in England, at least for situation. 'It possesses all that Nature can bestow; lofty trees, magnificent rocks, the most fertile soil, a mild climate favourable to vegetation of every kind, a clear foaming stream, the vicinity of the sea, solitude, and, from the bosom of its own tranquil seclusion, a view into the rich country I have described, which receives a lofty interest from a ruin the most sublime that the imagination of the finest painter could conceive, — I mean Chepstow Castle.'[8]

It is then possible that the Farrs and the Morris's became 'on terms of intimacy' through a common interest in sugar and in their respective estates there are similar associations of mood-provoking names like Lover's Leap, Giant's Cave and Druid's Temple. In Nash's Park Village East, London (suburban and later than Blaise Hamlet), stands a semi-detached pair of houses named, in the fabric, 'Wyndcliff' and 'Piercefield', and near Henbury is an area of land once called 'Wind Cliff', too. Perhaps Farr could actually see the place of his inspiration from battlements of Blaise Castle: perhaps this was one reason for its being built as it was.

Edmund Burke is said to have been Thomas Farr's guest at Blaise. Perhaps with Farr's guidance he savoured here the essence of the Picturesque, still to be formulated by Price. Certainly there was scope to exercise his appreciation of the Sublime and the Beautiful. John Wesley recorded in his diary a visit in 1783. The woods, which had been cut through in various directions on the side of the hill, were the most pleasant he had ever seen. And five years later, '. . . friends took me to Blaise Castle. Mr. F—. a person of exquisite taste, built it some years ago on the top of a hill which commands such a prospect all four ways as nothing in England excells.'[9]

Bristol merchants importing tobacco, sugar and wheat were deeply involved in American trade. Burke was elected as one of two Members of Parliament for Bristol in 1774 — the year before Thomas Farr became Mayor and a year of growing concern to observers of British policy in America. Burke wrote of Farr to the Marquess of Rockingham that the Mayor for the next year was his particular friend, and though not quite as alert as he wished and as the times required, he was wealthy, sound and very steady in his principles.[10]

Several Farrs are listed in a directory for 1775:[11] Thomas, merchant, Richard, alderman and merchant, and Francis Farr, mate of the *Blaze Castle*, are included. For the prominent and successful Farrs, at least, disaster was close. These were critical days.

Richard Farr and his sons, Thomas and Paul, partners in business, were in possession of numerous lands and properties when a meeting was held to consider the course of action to take concerning their bankruptcy at the Assembly Coffee House, Bristol Quay, on July 8, 1778. They owed 'several thousand pounds'.[12] Burke wrote to Richard Champion that news of the Farrs had filled him with grief, sincere grief, and that he wrote to Paul in consolation. He begged Champion to comfort Farr, and himself too, as Champion was also under severe financial strain.[13]

A Bargain and Sale of Estates summarises findings of the earlier meeting and goes on to confirm that Thomas Farr was indeed responsible for building the tower. He owned 'all that Building called Blaze Castle erected by the said Thomas Farr on or near the Top of the said Woody Ground called Blaze Hill and late in his occupation and used by him as a Summer or Pleasure House . . .'[14]

As it is so euphemistically phrased in *The New History of Bristol*, Thomas Farr was '. . . mayor of Bristol in 1775, and afterward resident in *London*'[15]: otherwise, 'Falling a victim to that mutability of human affairs, to which the mercantile world is especially liable, Mr. Farr, in the year 1778, was no longer able to indulge his taste for elegant retirement, and was constrained to sell this favourite retreat'.[16] Thus he shared one more experience with the lamented Valentine Morris.

Farr's tower, the subject of many prints and drawings, is frequently depicted soaring above the rugged cliffs, with an occasional undulating foreground cow contemplating space (Plate 13). Perhaps the most telling water-colour is one by J.M. Field[17] : telling, not only as a topographical work, but also as a mirroring of Repton's own impression of the tower on emerging from wild woods into the opening upon which the tower is set. This surprise by contrast was appreciated by Repton, who also found the first appearance of the castle most picturesque, 'because it presents the three turrets at once, and at this distance they appear of different heights. The form of this castle altho' not gothic, is well calculated for the situation, but it would give it more the character of a real castle at a distance if one of the round towers were elevated above the other two, and this I have shown . . . '[18] His advice was not taken.

Not all professional opinion favoured the tower: 'Prospect towers have a grand and imposing effect when judiciously placed in a woody eminence, or on the top of a rocky mountain,' John Claudius Loudon wrote. 'Very seldom, however, are they built in a suitable style of architecture: they are either of the most vulgar and common-place forms, as at Blaize Castle, Shooter's Hill, etc. or gaudy and affectedly uncommon, as at Clytho, Shuckborough, and numberless other places. These towers should always be designed in a style analogous to their situation'.[19]

Mylne recorded in his diary, January 1766, that he had 'Sent finished Drawings of . . . a Castle to Mr. Farr,'[20] and in the late Sir Albert Richardson's Collection of Mylne drawings are a plan and elevation inscribed, 'For a Tower near Bristol.' The plan is generally like that at Blaise Castle, although the elevation differs. The design is marked 'No. 3' and on it is also written 'Blaise Castle near Kingsweston' (Plate 14), which suggests that Mylne prepared several designs and that as this particular one was not taken up it has survived.[21]

For Repton, Blaise Castle — then far more widely visible than now — was an established local landmark around which to plan Harford's grounds, and 'The excellent taste displayed by Mr. Farr, and the peculiar beauties of his place on Blaise Hill, were celebrated in several poetical effusions . . .

> Here FARR, with willing heart, can frequent blend
> The connoisseur, the merchant, and the friend;
> At the rich genial board in each can shine,
> And make his converse lively as his wine.'[22]

Contemporary graffiti have tended to be less literary and not as appreciative of Farr's achievement. His castle has recently fallen into a depressingly ruinous state (Plates 15 and 16).

The Main Lodge

Repton's views on the architectural style necessary for Blaise Lodge have been outlined. There remain questions of who was responsible for the design, as built, and at what date the lodge was constructed. On the former there has been a little speculation; on the latter, '*c.* 1796' has been suggested.[1]

By the time Repton's *Theory and Practice* appeared in 1803, his relationship with Nash was unhappy. If Nash had been unfair to John Repton by denying him recognition, the possibly exploited Humphry could conceivably have reciprocated by denying Nash recognition for any help given with the Lodge (without publishing untruths), by stating, as he did, 'I, therefore, recommended the design, as a proper object to attract notice in the approach, which is one of the most interesting and romantic.'[2]

The *Red Book* demonstrates convincingly that he had it all worked out by February 1796 — months before the earliest date suggested for his entering into partnership with Nash.

The Tudor style accepted, what else does Repton's drawing in the *Red Book* tell us? One important thing: that while the elements he depicted were as to be built, they are shown in reverse — left to right (Plates 12 and 17). The octagonal tower is on the south of the drive: the square dwelling is on the north. Although it is unlikely that a blunder of such magnitude could have occurred, it is worth noting that this was no accident, as on Repton's own plan of the estate in the *Red Book*, small as it is, his earlier intention is confirmed.

If it can be accepted that the Lodge stands on Coombe Hill, there is little doubt that it was built in about 1801, as payments were made by Harford to one unnamed for a 'Lodge on Coombe Hill'[3] from May 1800, through 1801 and into 1802: i.e. several years after Repton planned his scheme, and after the Nash-Repton partnership had started. Nash could then, in theory, have influenced the final decision on the Lodge, and examination of cottage drawings from Nash's office shows frequent use of juggled and reassembled major components to produce variations on a design. On the other hand, regardless of when the Lodge was built, Repton might have had second thoughts of his own, practical, visual, or structural.

At this juncture a problem arises. It relates to this Lodge and to the two first-built Hamlet cottages — Double and Rose. Skilful wash drawings of all three are in the Repton Bequest.[4] The Lodge, apparently, is today much as built, complying as it does with Repton's illustration of it in *Theory and Practice*.[5] Nash charged Harford for fair drawings of (only) Numbers 1 and 2 — Double Cottage and Rose Cottage: and as the Repton Bequest cottage drawings are very close to working drawings in George Repton's *Pavilion*

Notebook (yet none of these, in some details, is as built), it could be supposed that the Repton Bequest Lodge drawing was itself a visualisation (Plate 18). It, too, differs from the finished construction.[6] However, this convenient theory collapses on discovering that the paper supporting the Lodge 'visualisation' (as, indeed, the plan of Double Cottage too) is watermarked 1830: that is, twelve years after George Repton had left Nash and about thirty years after construction of the Main Lodge at Blaise. It is possible then that these immaculate wash drawings were prepared from pre-constructional information for some form of publication, perhaps by one of Repton's sons.

Returning to the Lodge and to Humphry Repton for a final comment: 'I cannot help mentioning, that, from the obstinacy and bad taste of the Bristol mason who executed the design . . . I was mortified to find that Gothic entrance built of dark blue stone, with dressings of white Bath stone . . . Such, alas! is the mortifying difference betwixt the design of the artist, and the execution of the artificer.'[7] Paty had died in 1800.

In short, it has not been found possible to put forward here evidence that anyone other than Repton was responsible for the Lodge, but there remains the possibility that he might have been influenced by another in deciding on its final form — different in being left-to-right, but otherwise very much like his *Red Book* suggestion.[8]

Timber Lodge and the Root House

And next, within the centre of the gloom,
A shed of twisting roots and living moss,
With rushes thatch'd, with wattled oziers lin'd,
He bids them raise: it seem'd a Hermit's cell . . . [1]

Root houses, moss houses, hermitages, grottoes and arbours were closely related items of that whimsical architectural vocabulary which helped to articulate the romantic spirit as manifested in many eighteenth and nineteenth century English gardens. These characteristically gloomy and solitary refuges of the introspective, and fanciful playthings of affluent garden decorators, were in gothick, oriental, rococo, rustic or other styles — perhaps capriciously conceived and quirkishly contrived.

By the time Harford had bought the Blaise Castle estate there was a well-established tradition of building in this idiom. A master-designer of such garden shelters, Thomas Wright (1711-1786), had been working in the vicinity and was favoured with generous patronage at Badminton, where the park was in his charge.[2] His *Six Original Designs of Arbours* (1755), and *Six Original Designs of Grottos* (1758), illustrate delectable specimens, and later

Nash's office, in more chimerical moments, produced utilitarian buildings lightly touched by a kindred 'primitive' spirit. A thatched dairy shed for Cobham Hall, in Kent, sports a branching tree-trunk arcade[3] and a design for an anonymous and otherwise thatched garden building displays a primitive slate-roofed doric portico on one elevation and a seated rustic shelter — of semicircular plan and supported by six branching trunks — on another.[4]

One of the more intriguing minor bucolic deceits appearing in Repton's Notebooks is a rustic cow house for Lord Robert Spencer.[5] Vigorous, ruggedly betrunked and tattily thatched in a sweeping Chinese line, the design is difficult to dissociate, in spirit or image, from the celebrated illustration titling the section on 'Grottes et Hermitages' of Le Rouge's *Détail des Nouveaux Jardins à la Mode — Jardins Anglo-Chinois.*[6] The similarity is doubly interesting as that drawing was closely copied (if reversed — left to right — in the engraving process) from an English pattern-book, with about forty years separating the original 'Oriental Hermitage' in William Wrighte's *Grotesque Architecture, or, Rural Amusement*[7] from the pastoral caprice fancied by George Repton and John Nash and perhaps actually built by their patron, Lord Spencer, at Woolbeding in Sussex.[8]

Knight, of course, held his views: 'Rustic lodges to parks, dressed cottages, pastoral seats, gates, and gateways, made of unhewn branches and stems of trees, have all necessarily a still stronger character of affectation; the rusticity of the first being that of a clown in a pantomime, and the simplicity of the others, that of a shepherdess in a French opera.' Summarising his argument, he continues, '. . . for to adapt the genuine style of a herdsman's hut, or a ploughman's cottage, to the dwellings of opulence and luxury, is as utterly impossible, as it is to adapt their language, dress, and manners to the refined usages of polished society.'[9]

Francis Coventry, when writing in 1753 about upstarts, coxcombs and absurd taste in fashionable gardening, quipped, '. . . you are led into an old hermitage built with roots of trees, which the squire is pleased to call St. Austin's Cave. Here he desires you to repose yourself, and expects encomiums on his taste; after which a second ramble begins through another maze of walks, and the last error is much worse than the first.'[10]

Although, by the nature of their impermanence, such timber buildings of early date are difficult to find, it does appear that root houses of the more mysterious kind, such as those of Thomas Wright, preceded garden buildings of the Timber Lodge genre. Wright's *Six Original Designs of Arbours*, engraved on copper plates, was for the consumption of an eighteenth century élite. The dozen or so pages devoted to timber buildings in Loudon's *Villa Gardener* (1850), were aimed at a much wider public and printed in quantity.

Timber Lodge, deceptively, is strongly built, stone walls being inset with battens to bear planking, on which the outer rods and rustic timber-work are secured (Plate 20).

It is known that during Thomas Farr's ownership a Root House decorated Blaise, as J. Evans, in *A Chronological Outline of the History of Bristol*, recorded 'At the entrance of the wood was a neat rustic building, formed of roots and branches of trees.'[11] It has been suggested that Timber Lodge might be this place,[12] but that seems unlikely for reasons of style, structure and condition, at least. Repton makes no reference to it, so presumably (as it is sited right on his drive) it was nothing to do with him at that time. Even so, Timber Lodge has been firmly attributed to him by one writer, and dated 1791.[13]

So far as is known, there had been no identified record of what the real Root House looked like until a drawing by Grimm was found recently at the British Library. He made at least two visits to Blaise and drew views in the vicinity. But the most revealing is his drawing made in August 1789,[14] just before Harford purchased. It is of a large dome-shaped shelter with three arched openings, nodular columns and a topping knotty finial. Within, is a long bench seat; nearby is a rustic screen, with a decorated gothic window and other romantic traces (Plate 21). Written on the reverse side of the drawing is 'Root house in the pleasure ground of Blaise Castle.'

Evans recalls a pencilled inscription left in the unfortunate Thomas Farr's root house by an anonymous visiting punster :

> Farr I have roam'd, o'er many a foreign soil,
> And view'd the different beauties of this isle:
> They far excel what many pleasing call;
> But thy improvements, Farr! excel them all.[15]

It now appears reasonable to dissociate Timber Lodge from Farr, and to suggest that his Root House pre-dated Timber Lodge by many years. It disappeared from traced records well before 1840, by about which time a building additional to those mentioned by Repton in his *Red Book* had appeared in the vicinity of the drive. This might have been Timber Lodge as we know it.

Woodman's Cottage

Some distance beyond Timber Lodge is a parting of ways, a steep descent and what was, until the trees grew again, a first glimpse of the mansion. Repton, it will be recalled, intended that Woodman's Cottage (which stands at this once significant point on the drive) should, while serving a useful purpose, also be a focus of interest from Blaise Castle House, to be seen set within trees on a hillside glade. Repton had in mind aesthetic, associative and atmospheric landscape qualities.

It has not yet been possible to establish firmly a date of building, but there are clues. His accounts suggest that Harford, having topped out the mansion by October 1796, turned his attention to the grounds, and in 1797 he paid James Franks £2 2s. 0d. for quitting Still Acre before the year had expired.[1] Another transaction, also in 1797, concerned Thomas Daniel junior: 'allowed him for a piece of Land taken from Royals to build the Cottage in,' £2 0s.0d.[2] The Tithe Award names plot 501 'Ryalls', at which time (1841) it was occupied by a Thomas Daniel, owned by Harford, and adjacent to the Woodman's Cottage site, all of which suggests that the Cottage was built in about 1797. The likelihood is strengthened by a further entry: Stephen Powell was paid eighteen shillings 'for 18 Sheaves of Helm to finish Cottage', in that year.[3] The intended prominence of the building in Repton's scheme and the fact that to expose it to Harford's appreciative view demanded only surgery (not planting) would have favoured an early completion.[4]

Woodman's Cottage, as it now stands, is different in detail, enlarged, re-roofed and otherwise altered in appearance from the design suggested in the *Red Book* watercolour (as Plate 22). It is, though, essentially the same, similarly orientated and it emits smoke (Plate 23).

Repton adds a description of the proposed cottage in the *Red Book:* 'I think a covered seat at the gable end of a neat thatched cottage will be the best mode of producing the object here required, and the idea to be excited is "la Simplicité soignée." ' There are signs that such a penthouse has been removed.

Blaise Castle House

Despite having paid possibly £4,000 more than he wanted to initially,[1] Harford expanded his new estate in July 1794 with twelve acres of 'Rocky Woodland Ground' which ranged westwards and joined a similar piece called Goram's Chair, bought earlier, also from the Rooke family. Within another year fifteen acres more were added,[2] and the estate was further extended in August 1797 by the purchase of land on Coombe Hill.[3]

With 16 acres added by Skeet,[4] Harford's additional purchases of land would have given a new landscaping potential to the estate known to Farr, and some of Harford's negotiations had been entered into and purchases made years before Repton's first recorded visit. The house bought from Skeet was gabled and, if not rambling, hardly of fashionable appearance by late eighteenth century standards. Bearing in mind Harford's early concern about public footpaths near it, the possibility arises that he had the site for his new mansion in mind from the start. As the lands mentioned above were mainly unsuitable for agricultural use and were not, so far as is known, developed as commercial timber plantations, Harford might have envisaged the scenic possibilities of Blaise woods, acquired the necessary land, and later called upon Repton to realise the potential which he knew to be there. It could otherwise be argued that his additional early purchases were common-sense investments of surplus capital by an alert and able business man primarily expanding and simultaneously consolidating his newly acquired estate, which he later decided to improve as fashion suggested and as circumstances allowed.

Perhaps Harford was simply not enchanted by village folk and strangers passing close to his windows as they took a short cut to church, but whatever the reason, the facts remain that Harford bought the site, diverted the paths and, having done so, built his new house and demolished the old.

Churchgoers had been accustomed to cutting south-east from the Kingsweston Road across the park and 'over a small Iron Bridge across the Lawn belonging to and in front of the Dwellinghouse of the said John Scandrett Harford to the end of his premises home to the Churchyard Gate,'[5] and Harford lost little time in re-routing them to advantage. Undated notes[6] record his rough calculations made on pacing the place out: 'from Village and over the lawn beginning at bottom of second lane 636 steps', is typical.

A Special Sessions was held at Henbury on 17 August 1790 to consider turning the path. Two justices addressed their findings to the General Quarter Sessions at Gloucester on October 5, stating that the 'new publick footway is properly made and compleated fit for the use of the Public.'[7] A map prepared by J. Sturge explains it all[8] (Plate 24).

It will be recalled that the Patys — sculptors, masons, surveyors and architects — had long enjoyed an enviable reputation for the quality of their workmanship and there can be few provincial builders whose skill was recorded in published verse. In *Clifton,* a poem by Henry Jones, Thomas Paty's prestige was immortalised in lines reminiscent of Pope's earlier ones on Burlington:

> HERE buildings boast a robe, tho' rich yet chaste,
> The robe of judgement, and of ripen'd taste:
> Convenience here is mix'd with manly grace,
> Yet ornament but holds the second place.
> To human frames these structures seem akin,

With aspects fair, while reason rules within.
These domes discretion decks, and fancy cheers,
Palladio's stile in *Patty*'s plans appears:
Himself a master with the first to stand,
For *Clifton* owes her beauties to his hand.[9]

That was in 1766. William, one of Thomas' sons and co-partners, inserted a notice in *Felix Farley's Bristol Journal* on Saturday, 20 June 1789, on the death of his own brother, John. 'WILLIAM PATY, ARCHITECT and STATUARY, finds himself impelled by a recent domestic calamity, again to solicit a continuance of that patronage he had the satisfaction to receive from the Public, during a connection which subsisted many years with his late Father and Brother.'[10] Harford's future architect continued, 'To promise zeal and attention in the service of his employers, may be deemed superfluous; but he cannot help availing himself of this occasion, to offer his sincere acknowledgments for the protection he has been honoured with. June 19, 1789.'

With his catastrophies by then well behind him, William, the surviving son and partner, began work on the new Blaise Castle House on October 20, the foundation stone being laid by Harford on December 1, 1795. By the following spring large quantities of stone were being transported to the site.

Early in that same year, Harford had been drawing up a contract with one of the most important contributors to the building of his house. The Bristol carpenters and joiners Richard Jenkins and Joseph Lovell had submitted an estimate for carrying out their part of the work.[11] Confirmation that Paty was the intended architect is found many times in this draft contract, reference being made, for example, to the 'Plan, Elevation and Sections so drawn by the sd. Willm. Paty': and that he was in fact engaged is borne out by payments to him that suggest he was employed in his full capacity — as architect and mason.[12] If the final contract was on the same terms as this draft, it seems that Jenkins and Lovell were as good as their word on meeting deadlines. Roofing-in was to be completed by 29 September and Alice Harford states that there was a celebration dinner at the Blaise Castle Inn, with a gallon of ale all round, for the seventy workmen, in October 1796.[13]

By about mid-1798 bills for 'Household Furniture etc. for the New House at Henbury' were being settled and John Scandrett Harford's missing notebook recorded that the family 'Removed into new house at Blaise Castle on Wednesday, 17th Oct., 1798, to Tea.'[14] Then came the new stables. Payments began late in 1799, continued through the following year (when Paty died) and finished in mid-1801.

Blaise Castle House, started so late in William Paty's short life, may be seen as symbolising qualities readily associated with a prosperous Quaker banker of the time: substance, directness, dignity and security — qualities to be found also in Paty's town houses, such as those in Great George Street.[15]

Repton, who, in his *Red Book*, had recommended that the house should be slightly raised to appear as if standing on a small knoll, passed opinions on the design as well (Plates 25 and 26). Understandably not severely critical, he made them quite clear. He did not like the austere appearance. He wrote that mere masons, especially in areas where stone was plentiful, usually made a mess of the orders and that Paty was probably wise to have omitted altogether any columns and urns. And further, he, Repton, knew 'the difficulty of introducing columns according to the strict rules of architecture . . . yet lest I should be thought an advocate for discarding such ornament, I will insert at the end of this volume a sketch of the portico which my ingenious friend Mr. Collison suggested, and which might at any time hereafter be added to the south-east front . . .' Repton thereby gratuitously had his say and passed to 'Mr. Collison' any direct responsibility for slighting his patron's taste and the builder-architect's competence as a designer. Perhaps he already had Nash in mind when promoting Collison's ideas and was, indirectly, putting in a word for him when writing that 'In speaking of this building I must pay a just compliment to the skill of Mr. Patty for the attention given to the internal arrangement of the whole'. Nash had those square uncolumned Welsh country houses — Ffynone, Llysnewydd, Whitson Court and Llanayron — only a year or so behind him when work actually started on Paty's building, and just one clue has come to light to suggest that Nash might have been consulted on the design of Blaise Castle House too. J. Brewer wrote, 'This beautiful structure cannot be too highly commended, for the excellence of its proportions, and the exquisite simplicity of its design. The material is stone; and, where ornament is used, the Ionic order has been judiciously adopted. Mr. Paty was the architect employed, and he received, in his professional exertions, the assistance of Mr. Nash. Great praise is due to their conjoined efforts'[16] (Plate 27).

What weight can be given to Brewer's assertion? First, it must be noted that his is the only known early reference connecting Nash with Blaise Castle House and it was published well within Nash's lifetime. Second, on considering the exterior, would Repton (not an architect) have been so critical of the builder's inability to handle the orders if Nash had already been involved? Probably not: and especially so if the possibility of a partnership had been mooted. Unless either changes were made to the contract when it was finally agreed, or we do not accept at face value all that the draft relates, we are left with little doubt that Paty was responsible for the 'Plan, Elevation and Sections,' at least.

What evidence is there of Nash's hand inside the house? None of a documentary nature has come to light. While it would be imprudent to state that there is no influence, it does appear that the principal rooms and stairwell are Paty's. Yet there are also details at Blaise Castle House clearly not Paty's.[17] In the main these are decorative, and were probably added for J.S. Harford junior by Charles Cockerell. However, Collison's proposal for the south-east front was largely met when Cockerell inserted a picture gallery for the younger Harford in 1832-33[18] (Plate 27).

Cockerell, who appreciated that there were few 'who like Harford give their friendship & patronage at the same time,'[19] benefited from his patron's close connections with the cultural life of Bristol.[20] Their friendship lasted, and late in Cockerell's life the two men co-operated in producing a book on Michelangelo.[21] Perhaps their most fruitful venture was earlier, in the 1820s, when the then new master of Blaise met with Bishop Burgess (1756-1837) and Cockerell on one of the Harford estates, at Lampeter, in Wales. St. David's College building was to result. The Harford family contributed over twenty acres of land and a subscription, Burgess the driving force, and Cockerell the design. In Harford's enthusiastic letter to A.G.H. Battersby, addressed from Abergwili Palace and dated 20 December 1821,[22] he recounted events of the previous few days, and Burgess' elation on seeing Cockerell's first bird's eye view — produced on the spot. Cockerell himself recorded the response: 'this is magick, here is more done in a few days than many years have accomplished . . .'[23] A drawing for the College by Cockerell, with explanatory notes, has survived and is inscribed, 'First plan for St. Davids College Lampeter'.[24] Burgess got his College, Cockerell his commission[25] and Harford an Honorary Doctorate of Laws from Oxford for his efforts in promoting and raising funds for the building.

Cockerell, who seems not to have had a high opinion of Nash's work, wrote of Regent's Park that its architecture 'may be compared to the Poetry of an improvisatore — one is surprised & even captivated at first sight with the profusion of splendid images, the variety of the scenery & the readiness of the fiction. But if as many were versed in the Grecian rules of this science as there are in those of Homer & Virgil this trumpery would be less popular.'[26] Even so, Cockerell was later to move to and die at 13 Chester Terrace — the facade by Nash — trumpery, or not.

The Conservatory

There appears to be general agreement that John Nash was responsible for this building (Plate 28), but there has been uncertainty as to its date, opinions varying quite widely — from *c.* 1803 to 1811. The sources for attributing the Conservatory to Nash appear not to be recorded, which means that at least two facts have to be established — the author of the design, and the date when it was built.

Harford's accounts do not seem to help very much, although they do tell us that expenditure on hot-house plants resumed in 1803 after a period of abstinence and that William Thomas was paid £1 1s. 5d. for repairing the hot-house roof in 1811 (the two extreme dates already noted). He spent a lot on 'Hot-house and Greenhouse exotics' in that year, as he had done annually since 1805.[1]

A letter written by Harford to his sixth son, Alfred (1792-1856), when at Henry Wilkinson's Academy at Wandsworth, on 7th of October, 1806,[2] appears to go far towards answering the questions raised, but before referring to the most relevant part of this letter, some earlier passages are of general interest in that they throw additional light on the personalities of both John Harfords — the younger about to become of age: ' . . . long very long', the father wrote to young Alfred, 'I hope may it please Providence to spare his Life to us, when I Recollect his undissembled Piety, his Goodness of Heart, and mild and amiable disposition. I consider him as a pattern for us all, try to emulate his Virtues! and make him your Model. he dearly loves Alfred, and all his Brothers, and is sincerely anxious for their Welfare both temporal and Eternal; his Heart is truly devoted to the Cause of his Blessed Saviour and Redeemer, and from whence must flow that peace of Mind which attends the truly good'. Then, after some family news, John Harford senior continues '. . . The Greenhouse is now likely to be finished in the course of a few Weeks, to my great Joy, as it has been a very long tedious Job, the Pond for the Aquatic Plants and flowers is in the same good train, so that when we have the pleasure to go [over?] together [at] Christmas, I hope you will see [a] great [deal?] done.'

These observations appear to give us a date of completion — 1806. Then Harford adds a final touch in his next brief sentence. 'I expect Mr Nash here in t[he] course of this Month': and that all but answers the question of authorship.

Nash produced an elegant, stone-built, concave facade, extensively glazed and of seven bays, giving an arcaded effect. Once connected to the mansion by a wooden enclosure, the Conservatory helps visually to articulate the house, Dairy and trees. It also contributes a containing and sheltering influence over the intimate lower-level garden and pond, so much in contrast with the open sky and grand scale of verdant park-land and the secrecy of adjacent hanging woods.

When Nash was working on projects at Blaise he was also employed near Cirencester, at Barnsley Park, by James Musgrave. The resulting correspondence from Nash's office[3] includes details of work on the breakfast-room, library and drawing room and names some of Nash's craftsmen.

In a letter dated February 4th, 1807, Nash wrote that one Edwards (who had been his Clerk of Works at Goodwood and had been released by the Duke of Richmond's death), would serve him at Barnsley Park. Although the Duke had been perfectly satisfied with the man's abilities and conduct, Nash may not have been completely unsuspicious of his trustworthiness. With good reason, as it turned out, he advised Musgrave of his rule that Clerks of Works should never receive or pay money: ' "lead us not into temptation" is the best security for us all.' But within a month he had gone: 'the exactions which Edwards wanted to make has determined me to have nothing more to do with him', were the opening words of Nash's letter of the 20th: 'he is therefore discharged for ever from my service.'

A letter from Dover Street, posted to Musgrave on the same day as the relevant drawings and estimates, and dated 26 February, 1808, is of specific interest as it concerns the very handsome conservatory still standing at Barnsley Park. Nash, having advised that 'making the Columns and Entablature of Trellis Work instead of Stone saves only £100. 11.,' added that the building could serve a dual purpose in the summer when the plants were taken out and the doors removed. An open temple of those proportions would be a very beautiful object.

In the RIBA Collection are wash drawings, both attributed to J.A. Repton, for two other splendid green houses. One, rectangular in plan and with wreathed columns, is 'Very similar to the conservatory attached to the house at Sandridge Park, Devon, 1805.'[4] In the *Pavilion Notebook* are details, beautifully delineated, of a greenhouse very much like that wash drawing design, and annotated, 'Samuel Thornton Esq, Albury, Surrey', for whom Nash produced a bridge, no longer existing.[5] The other Repton Bequest drawing[6] is of a domed structure, more curvilinear and exotic in character. It might be considered akin to those earlier rationally designed greenhouses, so refreshing in their adventurous exploration of iron and glass: the kind perhaps encouraged by the scientific research of Thomas Andrew Knight,[7] to whom Richard resigned ownership of Downton Castle. The design drawn by Repton is, however, likely to owe its form more to ornamental than to rational considerations — to the development of which Loudon's ideas on flexible iron glazing bars are likely to have made a contribution.[8]

A new age of more scientifically calculated glass envelopes of exciting forms — acuminated semi-globes, domes and semi-ellipses — was about to open. Johnson, in his *History of English Gardening* (1829), sang the praises of Knight's younger brother: 'If the questions were put to me who is the most scientific Horticulturist now living? — who unites to a knowledge of the Practices of Gardening, the most perfect knowledge of the sciences that assist it? Which of living Horticulturists has conferred the greatest benefits on our art? I should quote Mr. Knight in reply to them all.'[9] Loudon refers to him in his *Encyclopaedia of Gardening,* [10] although by categorising the new designs as 'Not architectural', he appears not to have appreciated their qualities to the full.[11]

J.S. Harford junior's friend, Charles Cockerell, designed a conservatory for Harford's younger brother, A.G.H. Battersby, at nearby Stoke Park, in 1839. A drawing and model were made, but Cockerell gave up the commission on finding that he was expected to travel to and from Bristol on foot.[12]

The Dairy

Humphry Repton appears not to have been involved with the Dairy, although George was and his brother John might have been as well. There is an anonymous and undated drawing of it, attributed to John Repton, in the Repton Bequest[1](Plate 29). As it differs in small details from what exists and appears to agree very closely with working drawings in George's *RIBA Notebook*, it could be a visualisation; and if so, possibly by John, before his break with Nash. The two pages of drawings — a shaded elevation, cross-section (Plate 30), two plans and some details — in George's *RIBA Notebook* could then have been prepared on Nash's direction in order that his assistant could supervise the work. George's working drawings add cruciform finials to the dormers, and a conspicuous detail (the unusually angled dormer casement head) is seen in the 'visualisation' and in the Dairy itself. Yet this feature is not indicated in George's Notebook drawings (Plate 31).

What clues are there to the date of Blaise Dairy? Alice Harford reminds us that it was built on the site of the old house — the one occupied by Thomas Farr and vacated by John Scandrett Harford on moving to his new mansion — and in Harford's accounts there are entries for October 1799 and July 1800 concerning a transaction for materials from the old house made with John Griffiths, who brought stone for the new house and removed the old. While the range is narrow, there are differing opinions published on the date of building the Dairy: from *c.* 1803 to *c.* 1805 is usual. Presuming that there was only one such building on the estate at that time, an entry in Harford's accounts for 1804 appears to help: 'Pd for 12 dozn of Helm for thatching new Dairy @ 14/- a dozn. 8.8.0.'[2]

Pocock, writing at about the time that Blaise Dairy was built, shows a symmetrical decorative design — 'intended to combine the domestic uses of a Building of this description, with the pleasing gratifications to be derived from it in the Summer season.'[3] He then offers advice on siting. It should be 'placed on the North side of a Grove or Thicket, at a convenient distance from the House, and so situated as to be viewed from the South Windows. In the heat of a burning Summer so cooling, and refreshing an appendage, will, undoubtedly, be an agreeable object . . . This should be built of brick, and rough cast or stuccoed, and covered with Thatch'. He might almost have been writing Nash's brief.

'When the fashionable amusements of the town are relinquished for those of the country, there are few so interesting to the female mind as the dairy,' wrote John Papworth, in his pattern book, *Rural Residences* (1818), and he gives his views on an apt arrangement of the principal chamber. A glass door would lead to a marble pavement, 'and the tables for the vessels are designed to be composed of the verd antique Mona marble, supported by terms of the same material, surmounted by China vases; the dado and pilasters to correspond, finishing the walls by a verd antique architrave'. The compartments so formed would be filled with glazed tiles harmonising with the marble, and niches, designed to contain tripods, or urns, dedicated to the pastoral deities, would each sport a *jet d'eau*, 'as their lively, sparkling motion, joined with the coolness they impart to the air in warm seasons, make them fit ornaments for this species of building; and the variety of gently splashing sound which they produce, adds considerably to the interest created in their favour.'[4] Such a splendid arrangement is unlikely to have suited Harford's needs for Blaise. But even Papworth's vision, which he proposed should be realised so as to form an ornament to the shrubberies, fades when compared with the reality of the Queen's Laiterie at Rambouillet, built fifty years earlier, complete with grotto and stream.

A Cottage in Coombe Dingle

'JAMES FOSTER, many years Assistant to Mr. WILLIAM PATY, Architect, deceased, respectfully informs his Friends and the Public, that he intends carrying on the ARCHITECTURAL BUSINESS at his House, No. 24, ORCHARD-STREET: And hopes that by particular attention he shall merit the favors of those who may be pleased to honor him with their commands.' So ran an announcement dated February 26 in *Felix Farleys Bristol Journal* of February 28, 1801. Paty had died on December 11, as the same newspaper announced in a brief obituary two days later.[1]

On February 10, 1806, James Foster (*c.* 1748-1823) became a freeman of Bristol and was joined by his son, James (d.1836), in that same year. By 1826 James Foster junior had been joined by Thomas (*c.* 1793-1849), and shortly afterwards Thomas' apprentice William Ignatius Okely was added to their strength. The firm Foster and Okely was advertised in 1828.[2]

James Foster, the elder, remodelled Abergwili Palace — the Bishop of St. David's residence — just east of Carmarthen — from about 1803,[3] and J.S. Harford wrote from this address in 1821.[4] At Coombe Dingle, which lies beyond the southern extremity of the gorge at Blaise, our concern is only with James Foster and Son. In 1812 Harford entered in his rough cash book a payment to James Foster of five guineas 'for Drawing etc. for Cottage etc. at Coombe Dingle.' Additional information suggests that this cottage was built in the same year.[5]

Returning now to Paty: there were two branches of his business — architectural and statuary. While Foster was quick enough in setting up on his own account to continue the former (there being no obvious successor within Paty's family), the latter was bought separately by a London statuary named Henry Wood.[6] Perhaps knowledge of this possibility prompted Paty's craftsmen to act even more quickly than Foster. In *Felix Farley's Bristol Journal*, 27 December, 1800, an announcement opening 'WM. DREWETT (*Formerly Foreman to Mr. PATY, deceased*) In Connection with HENRY JONES and JOHN DUNN, Marble-Masons, Opposite the Tontine-Warehouses, near the Draw-Bridge, Bristol, RESPECTFULLY inform Gentlemen, Merchants, Tradesmen, &c. they execute Monuments, Chimney-Pieces, and every description of Ornamental Work, in Stone, with elegance and dispatch, and on the most reasonable terms', was made. The announcement concluded by advertising for an apprentice.

A William Drewett was active in Bristol by 1789[7] and one was still so in 1810; but these three masons (or perhaps some relatives) were in partnership earlier, and a Henry Jones was operating on his own account by 1794.[8] It was in 1810 that William Drewett supplied a memorial tablet to John Lloyd. This was placed in Carmarthen Parish Church[9] and nine years before that James Foster had provided one there to Richard Oakley.[10] But a Welsh connection is of longer standing than that.

It will be recalled that when Nash, early in his career, was climbing to fame from his adopted Carmarthen base, he undertook commissions to build country houses. These were characteristically enriched by elegant staircases. Between 1792 and 1796 he was building Ffynone for John Colby. This was such a house — entered by way of a vaulted vestibule which held from immediate view a semi-circular staircase. On June 3, 1794, Colby signed an agreement 'for the making putting up & compleating a Geometrical Stair Case with Moulded nosings & bracketted sophites of Painswick Stone'. Additionally, Colby agreed to the mason supplying paving of Painswick stone to cover the hall, 'or passage of communication to the different rooms on the parlour floor'. The other signatory was William Drewett, of Bristol, on behalf of Jones, Dunn and himself. The cost of supplying the staircase and paving was £84 12s. 6d., the stone being sent by sea from Bristol to Cardigan at Colby's expense. It was unloaded there under the supervision of Charles Jackson, who finished his work at Ffynone on 5 April, 1797.[11]

Here, then, we have a new, if very tenuous, link between Bristol, Paty and Nash sixteen months before Humphry Repton visited Blaise, and at the time Nash was working at Hafod for Johnes. Did Nash recommend Drewett? What is the link? At least, with this additional evidence, the possibility that Nash knew Paty by the time Harford was building Blaise Castle House is less remote.

The Druid's Temple

Here where once druids trod in times of yore
And stain'd their altars with a victim's gore
Here now the Christian ransomed from above
Adores a God of mercy and of love.[1]

Edmund Burke wrote of obscurity, dread and dark temples, of Druid ceremonies in the bosom of the darkest woods and in the shade of the oldest and most spreading oaks. He remarked on Milton's ability in heightening, or of setting terrible things in their strongest light by the force of a judicious obscurity.[2]

In the *RIBA Notebook* is a monochrome wash drawing of a Druid temple — three vertical megaliths supporting a massive capstone, under which is a low altar slab (Plate 32). Another vertical stone stands some feet from this group — the whole of which is assembled on a flat-topped mound backed by dramatically shadowed woody slopes. The drawing is inscribed 'Mr. Harford'.

Having worked at Hafod, Nash might well have known that Johnes had been in touch with Thomas Harrison (1744-1829), an architect of sufficient repute for Charles Cockerell to write that he had a spark divine. George Cumberland (1754-1848), who spent more than half his many years in Bristol, wrote *A poem on the Landscapes of Great Britain* (1780). He had met Johnes at Knight's London house and *An Attempt to Describe Hafod* (1796) appeared about three years later. Many letters passed between the two men and a considerable collection of those from Johnes to Cumberland is in the British Museum.[3] One (spring 1796) relates that Johnes had long been thinking of the 'Druidical Temple' for Cumberland's 'famous Knoll', and that he had recently met Harrison, whom he had long wanted to see. He sought the architect's advice and received a sketch. Stones of any size could be had, but only uprights would have to be brought from quarries on the Mersey, as very large local slates were readily available for covering. William Blake engraved the map that illustrates the *Attempt*. It marks 'Druid Temple' with a circle of stones.[4]

Even if Nash knew nothing of all this, it is possible that when building Cardigan Priory for Thomas Johnes' father, or Cardigan Gaol in 1793, he might have seen the real thing at nearby Pentre-ifan, now described in the *Ancient Monuments Handbook*: 'Here a very large capstone is balanced on the points of three tall uprights, and there are the remains of a crescentic forecourt of large upright stones.'[5] The form is very much like Repton's 'temple', although the now exposed setting is quite different from the one proposed at Blaise.

Relying on William Mason for adroit comment:

> . . . northward we turn,
> And lo! a pigmy Pyramid pretends
> We tread the realms of PHARAOH; quickly thence
> Our southern step presents us heaps of stone
> Rang'd in a DRUID circle. Thus from age
> To age, from clime to clime incessant borne,
> Imagination flounders headlong on,
> Till, like fatigu'd VILLARIO, soon we find
> We better like a field.[6]

Nash, given a site, could produce a building to fit and enhance it with confidence and sometimes a touch of genius as well. For enriching the gorge at Blaise, with its atmosphere and scale, the idea of a pre-historic decoration would appear fitting in terms of the terrifying and apt in its recognition of dark associations as established by local legends of Giant Goram, his Soapdish, Chair and Footprint. Echo Gate, Lover's Leap and the Robber's Cave are other evocative features. However, there is no reason to suppose that the idea of a Druid's Temple at Blaise was in the mind of anyone other than Nash and George Repton: neither has evidence suggesting that the place was ever built been found.[7]

We have knowledge of Harford's Quakerism, and letters, journals and memorials illustrate his piety. Whereas his taste was sufficiently liberal to embrace fashionable Tudor or Greek and rustic fancies too, his beliefs could not, perhaps, allow him to accept such an obvious symbol of paganism — a useless one, at that.

> The Druids now, while arms are heard no more,
> Old mysteries and barbarous rites restore:
> A tribe who singular religion love,
> And haunt the lonely coverts of the grove.
> To these, and these of all mankind alone,
> The gods are sure revealed, or sure unknown.[8]

A Cow House

Although no evidence is put forward here that John Nash or George Repton were responsible for designing a cow house for Harford that was ever actually constructed at Blaise, there is a design for such a building in Repton's *Pavilion Notebook*.

Four drawings — section, end elevation, front elevation, and plan, carefully placed and drawn — fill two pages, one of which is captioned 'Mr. Harford.' The drawings show a simple thatched construction with horizontally-boarded walls and feeding racks — accessible inside and out — running the greater length of the building.

As the design indicates that perishable materials should be used, it is unlikely that such a small structure, possibly in a fairly exposed situation, would have survived for 170 years, if built.

Richard Owen Cambridge, writing in the *World,* 13 June, 1754, reflected on former times, when the garden was made for fruit, the water for fish, and the park for venison; when the lord of the manor and his guests had nothing to do but sit down and gorge themselves with the products of each. 'I REMEMBER the good time, when the price of a haunch of venison with a country friend was only half an hour's walk upon a hot terrass; a descent to the two square fish-ponds overgrown with a frog-spawn; a peep into the hog-stye, or a visit to the pigeon-house. How reasonable was this, when compared with the attention now expected from you to the number of temples, pagoda's, pyramids, grotto's, bridges, hermitages, caves, towers, hot-houses, &c. &c. for which the day is too short, and which brings you to a meal fatigued and overcome with heat, denied the usual refreshment of clean linen, and robbed of your appetite!'

When Harford's guests had tasted all the landscape aperitifs he had prepared for their delight, they would, indeed, have arrived at his table exhausted. And he still held a rich dessert in reserve.

Notes to Chapter Six

Blaise Castle

1. John EVANS, *A Chronological Outline of the History of Bristol*, 1824, p. xxix.
2. Charles HEATH, *Descriptive Accounts of Persfield and Chepstow* (etc.), 1793, p. 7. An omnium gatherum of earlier writings on the district by Wyndham, Shaw Grose and others.
3. [William MARSHALL], *Planting and Rural Ornament*, 1796 (2nd edn.), i, pp. 286-298. A constructive criticism of the grounds, with suggested improvements, is included. Gilpin, in *Observations on the River Wye*, 1782, p. 40, found Piercefield to 'give a loose to the most pleasing riot of imagination'; but the views were not picturesque.
4. George MASON, *An Essay on Design in Gardening*, 1768. From 1795 edn., 'now greatly augmented', pp. 122-124. He barely knew Repton, but had heard from a most respectable person that he was a very agreeable companion.
5. Ivor WATERS, *Piercefield on the banks of the Wye*, 1975, p. 8, re the entrance nearest to Chepstow. He illustrates and discusses Morris's work at Piercefield, extending Ivor WATERS, *The Unfortunate Valentine Morris*, 1964. Piercefield is now known for its race-course, rather than Morris's gambling.
6. Elizabeth Wheeler MANWARING, *Italian Landscape in Eighteenth Century England*, 1925, p. 140.
7. Morris's departure — lamented by the local population — was recalled many times by accounts using emotional words to conjure dramatic scenes.
8. [Hermann PÜCKLER-MUSKAU] *Tour in England, Ireland, and France, in the Years 1828 & 1829*, 1832, ii, p. 192, 19 Dec, 1828.
9. *A Guide to Henbury*, 1970, p. 25.
10. George H. GUTTRIDGE (ed.), *The Correspondence of Edmund Burke*, 1961, iii, p. 208. See also Peter MARSHALL, *Bristol and the American War of Independence*, 1977, for an account of local events, Burke, Cruger, Champion, *et al.*

11. *Sketchley's Bristol Directory, 1775.*
12. Gloucestershire R.O. D2957 160 (21), 12 Oct 1780. *Commissioners in Bankruptcy to Samuel Munckley, William Gibbons, William James assignees.* Attested copy of Bargain of Sale of Estates.
13. GUTTRIDGE, *op. cit.*, p. 451 (31 May) 1778. Paul Farr had been a strong supporter of Burke, who frequently corresponded with him. Richard Champion was also a Bristol merchant.
14. Gloucestershire R.O. D2957 160 (21), p. 5 (see n.12).
15. *The New History, Survey and Description of the City and Suburbs of Bristol,* 1794, p. 111.
16. J. & H.S. STORER (del./sc.) & J.N. BREWER, *Delineations of Gloucestershire,* 1824, p. 104.
17. City Art Gallery, Bristol. K393, J.M. FIELD. Water-colour, 'Blaise Castle Henbury', 1827.
18. Humphry REPTON, *The Red Book for Blaise.*
19. John LOUDON, *A Treatise on Forming, Improving and managing Country Residences,* 1806, p. 409.
20. Howard COLVIN, *A Biographical Dictionary of British Architects 1600-1840,* 1978, p. 575.
21. I am indebted to Mr. Simon Houfe for identifying this drawing for me and for his interpretation of the inscription.
22. STORER, *op. cit.* pp. 104-105. Poem quoted, *Clifton,* by 'Mr. Jones'.

The Main Lodge

1. Dorothy STROUD, *Humphry Repton,* 1962, p. 72: *c.* 1796, *i.e.* at about the time of the *Red Book.*
2. J.C. LOUDON (ed.), *The Landscape Gardening . . . of Humphry Repton,* 1840, p. 251. At Avon County Library, Braikenridge xxx/57: Prospectus — *Specimen with Engravings plain* for the above book, which includes the two views of this Lodge and site (Plate 19). The work was to appear in twelve parts — 2/6 plain, 5/6 coloured.
3. Bristol R.O. 28048, F 9 (f.119), p. 152, £12 12s. 0d. to p. 206, Dec. 1802, 'To Lodge on Coombe Hill for balance'. £644 10s. 4d.
4. Made by Guy Repton in 1935. RIBA. JAR[3]/1,2 (K1/17/i, ii), Double Cottage, plan watermarked 1830; attr. to J. Repton. JAR[4] (K1/19), Rose Cottage; attr. to J. Repton. JAR[2] (K1/16), Entrance Lodge, watermarked 1830, attr. to J. Repton. The *Catalogue,* p. 121, notes: 'Record drawing of a design of the lodge . . . (designed by John Nash),' adding that it is possible that this lodge was designed by Repton while working under Nash, even though Nash is generally

thought to have been responsible for the other Blaise schemes. *Country Life*, 3 Sept. 1943, p. 429; while stating that Repton designed a Tudor gateway and [Woodman's] Cottage, the editor adds that Nash, apparently assisting Repton in the background, may have been responsible for the gateway and cottage.

5. And LOUDON, *op. cit.*, pp. 250-251.
6. Repton and Loudon both show a strong moulding running between floors across the facade, and a cruciform window above the door (both as built). Neither appears in the Repton Bequest drawing.
7. LOUDON, *op. cit.*, p. 261n. The maturing process has minimised this contrast.
8. Bristol R.O. AC/PL 80. Large scale elevation and plan of this Lodge. The facade is virtually as built, and includes Harford's arms above the door. This item is in the Ashton Court papers, but the possibility of another such lodge only a few miles from Blaise having been in mind seems remote. Repton worked at Ashton Court: STROUD, *op. cit.*, pp. 122-123; 165 (*c.* 1801), & Bristol R.O. AC/box 30.

Timber Lodge and the Root House

1. William MASON, *The English Garden*, 1781, Bk. iv, p. 35.
2. Eileen HARRIS, 'Architect of Rococo Landscapes: Thomas Wright', *Country Life*, 9 Sept. 1971, pp. 612-615. See also Howard COLVIN, *A Biographical Dictionary of British Architects 1600-1840*, 1978, pp. 933-934. Wright also worked at Stoke Gifford.
3. RIBA G.S.R.[6] (K1/25). Wash drawing attributed to G.S. Repton. Watermarked 1829.
4. *Pavilion Notebook*, See Appendix VII.
5. *RIBA Notebook*, f.22, *r.* See Appendix VII.
6. British Library. 34 F.11, 1776-87.
7. William WRIGHTE, *Grotesque Architecture, or, Rural Amusement; Consisting of plans, elevations, and sections, for Huts, Retreats, Summer and Winter Hermitages* . . . many of which may be executed with Flints, Irregular Stones, Rude Branches, Roots of Trees, 1767.
8. John SUMMERSON, *John Nash — Architect to King George IV*, 1949, p. 93.
9. Richard Payne KNIGHT, *An Analytical Inquiry into the Principles of Taste, 1808 (4th edn.), p. 224-225.*
10. *World*, 1789 (new edn.), 12 Apr. 1753, (No. 15), i, p. 92.
11. John EVANS, *A Chronological Outline of the History of Bristol, and the Stranger's Guide through its Streets and Neighbourhood*, 1824, p. xxx. Bristol R.O. 28048, F10, p. 198 (f.59), Dec. 1811, 'Henry Jones for thatching Root House', £1 9s. 8d.; which suggests that, though worth maintaining then, it had gone by 1824, or that Timber Lodge was thatched in 1811.

12. Max HEBDITCH, *Blaise Castle House Museum*, 1971, p. 22.
13. Georg GERMANN, *Gothic Revival in Europe and Britain*, 1972, p. 31 and fig. 12.
14. B.L. Add. MS. 15540, f.116. Reproduced by permission of the British Library.
15. EVANS, *op. cit.*, p. xxx.

The Woodman's Cottage

1. Bristol R.O. 28048, F9, p. 94(f.75), James Franks allowed 'for quitting Still Acre before ye year was expired,' £2 2s. 0d.
2. *Ibid.*, p. 96 (f.13).
3. *Ibid.*, p.94 (f.79), Dec. 1797: also F11/1, 31 Dec. 1797 (rough balance sheet).
4. The cottage also marks a vital pivot of the drive: and it does so in a strange way in that the drive approaches the cottage from behind. Repton's plan shows the drive sweeping below and in front of Woodman's Cottage, exposing it to view in the way one would expect — frontally, and above, to the left, on arriving.

Blaise Castle House

1. Bristol R.O. 28048, P43/3, copy agreement, Skeet-Harford. See Ch. 2, n.1. The spelling 'Skeet' is used, as this is how he signed his name. Alice HARFORD (ed.), *Annals of the Harford Family*, 1909, p. 50, refers to a draft letter of 7 July 1789 making a final offer of £11,000 which was £2,000 more than Harford first intended to give and £2,000 less than Skeet had asked. The deal, she adds, was accepted, and the conveyance dated 29 Sept. 1789. Skeet spent over £12,000 building at Bath at about that time. Bristol R.O. 28048, P43/4, is an undertaking to give possession of Blaise Castle Farm etc. to Harford 29 Sept. 1789.
2. Gloucestershire R.O. D2957/329 (26), 12 July 1794; 329 (28), 19 April 1795: conveyances and deeds.
3. Gloucestershire R.O. D2957/329 (31). Release in fee of land and cottages on Coombe Hill, 12 Aug. 1797.
4. Bristol R.O. 28048, P43/3, 20 July 1789.
5. Gloucestershire R.O. Q/SRh 1790 D.
6. Bristol R.O. 28048, P43/22-23.
7. Gloucestershire R.O. Q/SRh 1790 D. The path had been completed by 21 Sept.
8. Gloucestershire R.O. Q/SRh 1790 D/1.
9. Henry JONES, *Clifton*, 1766.
10. For an account of the Patys' building activities see Walter ISON, *The Georgian Buildings of Bristol*, 1952, pp. 39-43: also Andor GOMME, Michael JENNER,

Bryan LITTLE, *Bristol: an Architectural History*, 1979. The following notice appeared in *Felix Farley's Bristol Journal*, 9 May 1789: 'Monday died, aged 77, Mr. Thomas Paty, architect and statuary of this city; whose amiable character, pure integrity, and skill in his profession, rendered him an ornament to human nature; and made an impression on the minds of his friends and relatives that will endure, as long as the firmest marble shall record his name.' A week later John and William announced their continuance of the business. Within a month, John was dead.

11. Gloucestershire R.O. D 2957/160 (25). See Appendix II. Bristol R.O. 28048, F11/1: the first entry of expenses located for the 'New House at Henbury' is for £160, Aug. 1795.
12. Bristol R.O. 28048, F11/2. Stone for the house, probably from Bath, was apparently unloaded on the Avon, near Shirehampton: F11/1, 24 June, 1796, 'Pd James Franks for halling 5 barge load of stones from Lamplighters Hall', £11 0s. 0d.
13. HARFORD, *op. cit.* 1909, p. 53. See also Bristol R.O. 28048, F11 re payments to Jenkins and Lovell.
14. *Ibid.*, p. 56: p. 54 refers to Harford's small red notebook marked 'J.S.H., 1795'. It contained minute particulars of the new house, but a protracted search for it has proved fruitless. The author would still appreciate advice on its whereabouts.
15. Nikolaus PEVSNER, *The Buildings of England: North Somerset and Bristol*, 1958, p. 436, notes that a number of houses in Great George Street were by Thomas Paty. Confirmation that Harford's house is that one now numbered 25 can be found in the deeds, which state that he bought the property on 21 Dec. 1801 from Philip Prothero.
16. J. & H.S. STORER (*del./sc.*) & J.N. BREWER, *Delineations of Gloucestershire*, 1824, p. 105. 'Consultant' rather than 'assistant' would probably be more applicable to any professional employment of Nash if Paty had already been engaged.
17. I am grateful to Mr. Gordon Priest for drawing my attention to similarities in carving at Blaise Castle House and 25, Great George Street.
18. Max HEBDITCH, *Blaise Castle House Museum*, 1971, p. 17, reproduces a rejected drawing, perhaps by Cockerell, for the picture gallery.
19. David WATKIN, *The Life & Work of C.R. Cockerell*, 1974, p. 170.
20. *Ibid.*, p. 49.
21. *Illustrations, Architectural & Pictorial, of the Genius of Michael Angelo Buonarroti*, 1857. Explanatory notes on the architecture are by Cockerell.
22. Bristol R.O. 28048, C69: C80/5, obituaries etc. J.S.H. junior, 1866.
23. WATKIN, *op. cit.* pp. 148-150, discusses these events at Lampeter.
24. RIBA. CRC [J 10/15].
25. Built 1822-27.

26. WATKIN, *op. cit.* p. 69.

The Conservatory

1. Bristol R.O. 28048, F9, p. 226 (f.27): F10, p. 198 (f.59): F4 (f.31), showing regular payments of £130 0s. 0d. *p. a.* 1805-12.
2. *Ibid.*, M 6.
3. Bodleian Library. Mss. DD. Wykeham-Musgrave C53. The correspondence dates from mid-1805 to Autumn 1808. Nash also designed an existing lodge at Barnsley Park.
4. RIBA. Repton Bequest, JAR [10]: watermarked 1810.
5. Terence DAVIS, *John Nash — The Prince Regent's Architect*, 1966, p. 105. E. MALDEN (ed.), *Victoria History of the County of Surrey*, 1911, iii, p. 74, states that Samuel Thornton (1755-1838), who was an M.P. and governor of the Bank of England, lived at Albury Manor from 1800-1811.
6. RIBA. Repton Bequest, JAR[9].
7. President of the London Horticultural Society.
8. One, curvilinear, of note, was erected for Mrs. Beaumont at Bretton Hall, Yorkshire, in 1827. J.C. LOUDON, *Encyclopaedia of Cottage, Farm, and Villa Architecture*, 1833, pp. 980-981, gives an account of the remarkable building of iron and glass. In the writer's collection is a marked catalogue of its sale, dated Monday 23 April 1832. The 'Far Famed Dome Conservatory' is here twice referred to as having been 60 feet in diameter, 45 feet in height, and to have cost £15,000 — smaller, though more expensive, than stated by Loudon. The ms.-marked price is 540 gns., which secured also an engine house with 4 tons of lead on the roof, very capital steam boilers and a dwelling room. See Kenneth LEMMON, *The Covered Garden*, 1962, p. 141.
9. George JOHNSON, *A History of English Gardening*, 1829, p. 271.
10. J.C. LOUDON, *An Encyclopaedia of Gardening*, 1835 (new edn.), pp. 567-605, gives a detailed account of the history, construction and principles of moveable and fixed frames and hot-houses, which includes references to Knight's work. J.C. LOUDON, *Villa Gardener*, 1850 (2nd edn.), pp. 465-496, gives additional information and illustrates a variety of designs — none curvilinear.
11. J.C. LOUDON, *Encyclopaedia of Cottage, Farm, and Villa Architecture*, 1833, p. 980 (1961); illustration 1732, p. 981.
12. David WATKIN, *The Life and Work of C.R. Cockerell*, 1974, p. 178n, and Pl. 80.

The Dairy

1. RIBA. Repton Bequest, JAR *delin.* [1].
2. Bristol R.O. 28048, F9, p. 242 (f. 155).
3. W.F. POCOCK, *Architectural Designs for Rustic Cottages*, 1807, Pl. 1.
4. John PAPWORTH, *Rural Residences*, 1818: quoted from 2nd edn., 1832, pp. 89-90.

A Cottage in Coombe Dingle

1. Howard COLVIN, *A Biographical Dictionary of British Architects 1600-1840*, 1978, pp. 315-316, gives an account of the Fosters' building activities: pp. 626-627, of the Patys'. *Felix Farley's Bristol Journal*, 13 Dec. 1800: 'Last night died, at his house in College-Place, Mr. William Paty, and [*sic*] eminent architect, of this city:— His death will be greatly regretted by the public in general, but particularly by his friends and acquaintance [*sic*].'
2. Clare CRICK, *Victorian Buildings in Bristol*, 1975, comments on and illustrates work of the Fosters and their successors.
3. COLVIN, *op. cit.*, p. 315.
4. Bristol R.O. 28048, C69, 20 Dec. 1821, to his brother A.G.H. Battersby, re his visit, with the Bishop and Cockerell, to the site for St. David's College, Lampeter.
5. Bristol R.O. 28048, F19, cash book for 1812-1815. £99 0s. 0d. was paid to William Lee 'in full for Masons Work at Cottage etc. in Coombe Dingle'.
6. COLVIN, *op. cit.*, p. 908.
7. A monument to Mary Teast (d. 1766) in Henbury church, signed Drewett (1790).
8. *Matthews's New Bristol Directory*, 1793-94, p. 49. Henry Jones, Mason, 16 Denmark Street; Jones, Dunn and Drewett, Marble Masons, 'under the Bank.' George Jones, mason, was at 16 Denmark St. in 1775.
9. Rupert GUNNIS, *Dictionary of British Sculptors 1660-1851* (n.d.), p. 133.
10. *Ibid.*, p. 156, adding *fl.* 1795-1825; and that James Foster 'took over the yard on his master's death in 1801.'
11. National Library of Wales. Spence-Colby Papers, 1882, 1223, 1236. Drewett and partners' bill is dated 19 Nov. 1796. It included 15 straight flyers, £10 0s. 0d.; 10 winders, £9 0s. 0d.; a centre winder, £1 16s. 0d. Jackson was paid £5 12s. 0d. for his services.

The Druid's Temple

1. Barbara JONES, *Follies and Grottoes,* 1974, pp. 227-245, investigates the 'Cones, Bones and Druids' cult. The verse quoted was engraved on a tablet at Bishop Law's Banwell Folly (*c.* 1830).
2. Edmund BURKE, *A Philosophical Enquiry into the Origin of our Ideas of the Sublime and Beautiful,* 1759 (2nd edn.), III, 'Obscurity', p. 99-101.
3. B.M. Cumberland Papers, Add. MS. 36491-36516. Elisabeth INGLIS-JONES, *Peacocks in Paradise,* 1971, pp. 117-119; Cumberland met Johnes at Knight's Whitehall house, 1793-4. Johnes invited him to (re-)visit Hafod, which he did, breaking his journey at Downton Castle.
4. Herbert VAUGHAN, 'Some Letters of Thomas Johnes of Hafod (1794-1807)', *Y Cymmrodor,* 1925, pp. 200-213, includes a selection of extracts from the letters: p. 203, 'I should imagine ten or twelve very large Upright Blocks would be sufficient.'
5. Cyril FOX, *Ancient Monuments . . . South Wales and Monmouthshire,* 1955 (3rd edn.), p. 18; Pl. 1. With acknowledgements to the author and Her Majesty's Stationary Office.
6. William MASON, *The English Garden,* Bk. iv, 1781, pp. 23-24, writing on 'false taste'. 'Villario' is a reference to Pope's *Epistle to Lord Burlington,* 80-88.
7. *The Gentleman's Magazine*, 1835, ii, pp. 437-438, obiturary Nash; his drawings included one of 'Druid's Temple at Blaize Castle' and one of a bridge for Mr. Johnes of Hafod.
8. Nicholas ROWE (1674-1718), from his translation of Lucan's *Pharsalia,* i; quoted from Alexander CHALMERS, *The Works of the English Poets,* 1810, xx, p. 23.

Cow house, from a plan and elevations by George Repton inscribed 'Mr Harford'

7 *Blaise Hamlet — 'Smiling Village'*

'We have still to notice a very pleasing feature of this demesne. The grounds attached to the mansion are adorned with a lovely group of cottages, known by the name of BLAISE HAMLET. These cottages are ten in number, and were erected about the year 1810, by the late John S. Harford, Esq. father of the present proprietor, as retreats for aged persons, who had moved in respectable walks of life, but had fallen under misfortunes, preserving little, or nothing, in the shock of adversity, but unblemished character. The buildings evince no ostentation of charity, and would seem designed as elegant, though humble, places of voluntary retirement, rather than as the refuge of the needy, bestowed by the hand of neighbouring affluence.' So wrote J.N. Brewer, a few years after Harford's death.[1]

With more than one hundred and sixty years between ourselves and the construction of the Hamlet, we can see what its creator might well have sensed at the time, but could hardly have expected as a future judgement. Sir Nikolaus Pevsner considers this group of cottages to be the *ne plus ultra* of picturesque layout and design.[2]

It has been seen that Harford frequently added land to his estate. His purchase, the subject of a conveyance dated 11 April 1807 (whether or not then intended for the Hamlet) was, in part, to be used as its site. For £1,000 was bought 'All that Close Piece or Parcel of Land called Greens containing by Estimation Six Acres (more or less) situate lying and being in the Parish of Henbury . . . '[3]

With some understanding of the chronology of events through about forty years of development at Blaise, and with a sense of the quality of the aesthetic climate in which Harford, Repton and Nash lived and worked, we must face up to one important question about the creation of Blaise Hamlet: who, or what, inspired the vision of it? Accepting, for the moment, that Nash was indeed architect of the scheme, what more specific influences might have guided his imagination and judgements? What might he have seen, read, discussed, planned, or even built, that could have led to such a concept? Perhaps, up to a point, we can now answer some of these questions.

It will be recalled that eighteenth century estate villages such as New Houghton, Nuneham Courtenay and Milton Abbas, were different in nature from that at Henbury, where Harford made no attempt to uproot tenants or raze existing dwellings. He did not rehouse the wilfully displaced in identical cottages formed into a processional way at his gates. While such formal arrangements might have been considered by some of their promoters to suggest a high degree of social enlightenment, fashionable taste, or affluence, and even demonstrate an awareness of agricultural or architectural improvement, they might be seen through other eyes to have exemplified inhumanity, arrogance, greed, conspicuous extravagance and conceit.

Admittedly, Harford did not build his estate cottages inside the walls either, and it can hardly be argued that he built a real 'village' anyway, as the Hamlet lacks those ingredients usually associated with traditional rural settlements in England, such as a church, school, inn, vicarage, shop and manor. These components contributed variety of architectural form, broken building lines and scale to the village scene. They accommodated traders, artisans, labourers, professionals and gentry — a cross-section of society following its several pleasures and occupations. Harford's was a detached virgin site. However, it was within an established village context that the Hamlet was built, and comparisons remain broadly valid, master and tenants, incidentally, still being housed according to their respective stations.

When William Gilpin set forth on a tour in 1772, the brand-new brick cottages at Nuneham must have appeared rather harsh. While in general terms he, like later picturesque enthusiasts, could not accept regimentation of cottages in principle, he doubted even if such a genius as Nash could appear and almost condoned the linear solution: 'The village of Nuneham, through which the road passes, was built by Lord Harcourt for his cottagers; and with that regularity, which perhaps gives the most convenience to the dwellings of men. For this we readily relinquish the picturesque idea. Indeed I question, whether it were possible for a single hand to build a picturesque village. Nothing', he continues, 'contributes more to it, than the various styles in building, which result from the different ideas of different people.'[4]

Harford's 'village' is not only modestly tucked away, but can even be difficult to find. No blatant self-advertising is apparent here. The poor are not paraded under an impressive display of decorative gables, neither is their condition — their need — lightly shrugged off. The sophisticated cottages are well built, of various designs, irregularly placed and generously spaced. Yet they are not so dispersed that isolation is encouraged and either visual or community cohesion lost. There is space enough for withdrawal, yet interdependence is favoured within the group, which, architecturally speaking, demonstrates a firm grasp of spatial understanding handled with accomplished ease. The concept is painterly, too. Limited colour, a multiplicity of contours and forms, varied surfaces, broad harmony and engaging detail are all disciplined and contribute positively to a unified, spirited and confident whole, each major element retaining its identity within the assemblage.

Blaise Hamlet may also be seen as different from precursors in that its materialisation was, in its own right, a significant creative act. We are reminded of Price and his *Essays*, in which he devoted a dozen pages to the analysis of visual qualities and details that contribute to the traditional picturesque English village. Before censuring the symmetrical approach Price posed the problem: 'As human vanity is very fond of new creations, it may not be useless to observe, that to build an entirely new village, is not only a more expensive undertaking than to add to an old one, but that it is, likewise, a much more difficult task to execute it with the same naturalness and variety of disposition; and that it is hardly possible to imitate those circumstances of long established habitation, which, at the same time that they suggest pleasing reflections to an observing mind, are sure to afford delight to the painter's eye.'[5]

Price then condemns the Nuneham Courtenay (1760) solution — uniform houses in two parallel lines, evenly spaced, flanking opposite sides of a straight road. He continues: 'Such a methodical arrangement saves all further thought and invention; but it is hardly necessary to say that nothing can be more formal and insipid.'[6]

Goldsmith, in the *Deserted Village* (1770), had also decried such sweeping change and the suffering that demolition of an existing community, to place it elsewhere, could entail.[7] In 1783 Crabbe's verse, *The Village*, expressed his feelings about the rural poor being uprooted and of the cottager's poverty being blatantly exhibited alongside riches:

> When plenty smiles — alas! she smiles for few —
> And those who taste not, yet behold her store,
> Are as the slaves that dig the golden ore —
> The wealth around them makes them doubly poor.[8]

Price continued in his writing: 'The characteristic beauties of a village, as distinct from a city, are intricacy, variety, and play of outline: and whatever is done, should be with a design to promote those objects. The houses should, therefore, be disposed with that view, and should differ as much in their disposition from those of a regularly built city, as the trees which are meant to have the character of natural groups, should from those of an avenue. Wherever symmetry and exact uniformity are introduced, those objects which produce a marked intricacy and variety must in general be sacrificed.'[9]

In the early years of the nineteenth century — half a life-time after Gilpin had begun to record his responses to the picturesque — Loudon, then still in his twenties, imagined the best way to set about creating an artificial village was to apportion a suitable amount of ground, either side of a public road, to each villager and to allow him to build his own house. This would result in irregularity of building and individuality in the laying out of gardens. A condition would be that some larger fruit or forest trees would be planted near, or on the plot. 'Unfortunately, however, most villages built by proprietors are so stiff and formal as to be entirely destructive of picturesque beauty, without exciting any idea sufficient to compensate the want of it.' Perhaps Loudon had the Milton Abbas deceit in mind when he continued, 'As such villages contain cottages generally two stories high, two families are obliged to lodge in one house; and this at once destroys the native liberty of the cottager, and probably may introduce some of the corruptions of great towns in place of rustic innocence and simplicity.'[10] Loudon considered that such villages deserved no praise, unless for their novelty when first erected, no matter how laudable a proprietor's intentions.

Much of Loudon's earlier experience was in a Scottish context. He expressed strongly his views on independence: all proprietors ought to prevent too great a familiarity between villagers, ' . . . and to enable them to conceal as much as possible their little domestic arrangements from the prying eye and flippant remark of their more independent neighbours.' This ought to be an indispensable rule.[11]

It is likely that very shortly after committing his opinions on estate village design to print, Loudon had an opportunity to put theory to the test at Great Tew, in Oxfordshire, where Colonel Stratton had demolished the house and engaged the Reptons to advise him. Although a *Red Book* had been produced and John Repton had drawn plans for the house, neither proposal went ahead. As recently as 1974 it was written in the *Buildings of England* that the village was unforgettable, with thatched cottages engulfed in gardens in a valley encircled by trees: Great Tew had all the cosiest ingredients of the picturesque — a calculated effect, brought about by improvements made to existing cottages and by planting great clumps of trees. It is possible that Loudon influenced the scene. And the years of his managing the estate coincided exactly with the planning and building of Blaise Hamlet. However, it is likely that Thomas Rickman (1776-1841) was at least in part responsible ten years later.[12] Great Tew, so recently the subject of praise, is now the scene of tragic decay.

Quite apart from earlier eighteenth century writings which related to matters concerning painting, architecture and gardening, and works (such as those already referred to) on the theory and practice of picturesque landscape, a literature concerned with the village itself was emerging. Price had his considered opinions to add on cottage settings: 'Trees, whether single or in groups, whether young or old, are obviously of the greatest use in accompanying buildings of every kind; but there seems to be a much closer union between them and low buildings. Cottages appear to repose under their shade, to be protected, sometimes supported by them; and they, on the other hand, hang over and embrace the cottage with their branches: it seems as if they could never have been separated from each other; and there would be a sort of cruelty in dividing them.'[13] The benefits were mutual. By the contrast of its form and colour, the cottage could enhance the peculiar beauties of vegetation.

So far, the views expressed by Gilpin and Loudon seem very broadly sympathetic to the concept of Blaise Hamlet. But there is a particularly close affinity with these passages quoted from Price. They must have been very much in his mind at the time Harford and his architect were discussing the Hamlet as the amended text of his final edition of 1810 would have been in preparation at about that time.

Mention of an earlier meeting between Nash and Price in Hafod days has been made, and evidence of a further connection between the two men, beyond the transient and purely social, is found in Repton's *RIBA Notebook*, where drawings (just a few pages from those for the Dairy at Blaise) of a patently picturesque cottage prettily contrived for 'U. Price Esq' are to be found. Even if a continuing, though perhaps intermittent, association between Price and Nash cannot be taken for granted, it is unlikely that Nash was unfamiliar with Price's views on village design. Loudon, too, knew Foxley and wrote appreciatively of Price's planting and developments there.[14]

Before leaving his *Essays* we should look at Price's observations on introducing smaller-scale decorative plants on cottages themselves. He considers favourable situations, the visual benefits of plant forms seen against irregularly shaped buildings, and the quality of closely-trimmed hedges. On writing of the desirability of climbing plants on buildings he observed: ' . . . but what I principally allude to, are porches, of which so many models may be taken both from real buildings, and from pictures. Wherever honeysuckles, vines, jasmines, grow over them, they attract and please every eye'.[15]

Moreover, Price believed that there was no scene where neatness and picturesqueness, where simplicity and intricacy could be so happily united as in a village; or where they might be so well contrasted without any affectation or impropriety.[16]

What other influences, possibly more distant in time or place, might have been significant? While the idea of an architect planning to group rustic buildings — such as in a *ferme ornée* — might not have developed far beyond a number of aristocratic fancies in eighteenth-century France, one cannot say with certainty that architectural inventions of the kind like those built at Chantilly, Rambouillet and l'Hameau were entirely without influence. Sir John Summerson has commented on the many books by French authors in Nash's library.[17]

Although there is no known record of Nash having visited France before 1814 (that was after the building of Blaise Hamlet),[18] he could have known of such celebrated buildings, despite the war years, by way of spoken, written or pictorial descriptions of them, before actively considering the possibility of designing village groups himself. Then there was his close connection with Pugin, the refugee.

The inventive Nash, if invited to build a miniature village at Henbury, must have leapt at the chance. He had behind him a familiarity with genuine humble dwellings set in rich romantic landscapes extending from his early days in Wales, a long-standing fascination with designing minor rustic buildings, and an undeniable connection with some of the picturesque theorists and practitioners themselves. He would have known his client's tastes: the client would have been familiar with his chosen architect's predilections. And a philanthropic client with pockets as deep as Harford's might well have offered at that critical moment in Nash's career, when visualising and theorising could satisfy no longer, an opportunity too tempting and potentially fulfilling for Nash to decline, however busy he might have been with his plans for Regents Park, a mansion at Rockingham, additions at Preshaw and Parnham, and possibly other commissions too. Unfettered by existing buildings at Henbury or by lack of funds, but liberated through an enlightened client's concern for his retainers' well-being, the time was ripe to create the *ne plus ultra* picturesque village.

But one vital detail of information is still missing. Between Harford's decision to build at Greens and his architect's pegging out the field, someone had to envisage the form the grouping should take. Why are the cottages withdrawn? Why are they not near the mansion gates? Why are they arranged around a plot? Was this also Harford's idea? No. In short, it was indeed Nash who supplied the notion, and Cockerell left us the long-awaited explanation.

He wrote, 'Nash has always original ideas. he recommended to Mr. Harford to build his alms Houses in a picturesque manner & in a retired spot & not in a row. he says the pride which is natural to men & makes them ashamed of receiving alms is an honorable one & should not be crushed. the bounty you afford should not be dashed by stamping these paupers with their mark of indigence. nor is it well to tarnish a benevolent motive with the blazon of a coat of arms & an inscription seting forth the liberality of the Founder. he built therefore irregular cottages with all those little penthouses for beehives, ovens & c. & irregularities which he found in peasants' cottages & they are so beautiful that it is a sight visited from Clifton & I have always called it Sweet.'[19] And we shall find that Nash himself expressed such sentiments — in similar terms — years earlier, about another cottage-building scheme with which he was involved.

Price's stated aim in discussing villages as he did was an attempt to redress a balance. Goldsmith had described with feeling the ravages of wealthy pride. Price suggested that they were no less hostile to real taste than to humanity. Those who were not moved by Goldsmith's words to repent and mend their ways would perhaps be restrained from destroying a village and, through Price's *Essays*, 'might even be induced to build one, in order to shew their taste in the decoration and disposition of village-houses and cottages.'[20]

Had it not previously come about elsewhere, possibly through the action of a reformed village desolator, Price's ideal was to be largely realised at Henbury through Harford's patronage and Nash's sympathetic inspiration. With the completion of Blaise Hamlet, Harford's architecturally enterprising reign was all but at its close. His most widely acclaimed achievement was to become an influential model.

> O Sons of Wealth, who these fair scenes survey,
> Warn'd by the bright example, go your way,
> Intent to emulate the lofty prize,
> Virtue's rich portion in her native skies![21]

Notes to Chapter Seven

1. J. & H.S. STORER (*del./sc.*) & J.N. BREWER, *Delineations of Gloucestershire*, 1824, p. 108.

2. Nikolaus PEVSNER, *The Buildings of England: North Somerset and Bristol*, 1958, p. 468.
3. Gloucestershire R.O. D2957/160(30), 11 April 1807, Conveyance: Charles Brooke and others to Harford.
4. William GILPIN, *Observations, Relative Chiefly to Picturesque Beauty, made in the year 1772*, 1786, i, p. 22.
5. Uvedale PRICE, *Essays on the Picturesque*, 1810, ii, pp. 345-346.
6. *Ibid.*, p. 346.
7. Mavis BATEY, 'Nuneham Courtenay: an Oxfordshire 18th-century Deserted Village', *Oxoniensia*, xxxiii, 1968, pp. 108-124, traces the elimination of the village, reconstructs its plan and comments on passages from Goldsmith. Mavis BATEY, 'Oliver Goldsmith. An indictment of landscape gardening', Peter WILLIS (ed.), *Furor Hortensis*, 1974, pp. 57-71, develops her account. The same author, in *Nuneham Courtenay Oxfordshire*, 1970, p. 19, quotes the verse of William WHITEHEAD, *The Removal of the Village at Nuneham*, 1771. He did not, as did Goldsmith, disguise the scene of his attention.
8. (CRABBE, ed.), *The Life and Poetical Works of the Rev. George Crabbe*, 1847, p. 116. Edited by the poet's son, the work includes many notes and interpretations. Crabbe's village was desolated by the sea.
9. PRICE, *op. cit.*, ii, pp. 346-347.
10. John LOUDON, *A Treatise on Forming, Improving, and Managing Country Residences*, 1806, i, pp. 145-146.
11. *Ibid.*, p. 146,n.
12. Jennifer SHERWOOD & Nikolaus PEVSNER, *The Buildings of England: Oxfordshire*, 1974, pp. 624-625; also Howard COLVIN, *A Biographical Dictionary of British Architects, 1600-1840*, 1978, p. 692, and John GLOAG, *Mr. Loudon's England*, 1970.
13. PRICE, *op. cit.*, ii, p. 351.
14. LOUDON, *op. cit.*, *e.g.* ii, p. 563.
15. PRICE, *op. cit.*, ii, p. 354.
16. *Ibid.*, p. 348.
17. John SUMMERSON, *John Nash — Architect to King George IV*, 1949 (2nd edn.), p. 254.
18. Howard COLVIN, *A Biographical Dictionary of British Architects, 1600-1840*, 1978, p. 579.
19. David WATKIN, *The Life and Work of C.R. Cockerell*, 1974, pp. 80-81.
20. PRICE, *op. cit.*, ii, p. 345.
21. J. ANTROBUS, *Clifton; or, Thoughts and Scenes*, 1834, p. 22.

8 *'New Cottages at Henbury'*

It is now necessary to consider in rather more detail some source material already referred to which records the laying out, building and appearance of the cottages at Blaise Hamlet.

Harford's accounts, George Repton's *Pavilion Notebook*, correspondence with Harford about the cottages, and an inventory of defects, between them, give us many new facts about the building of Blaise Hamlet. Examination of them will make possible a new understanding of the course of events and of the respective contributions of Nash, George Repton & Harford to the realisation of plans for the cottage group. The Notebook drawings and letters to Harford which came from Repton's pen in Nash's office 170 years ago can now be considered together and in relation to the buildings themselves for the first time since their origination.

The Harford Papers include four ledgers, eight journals and seven cash books. Together, they span about thirty five years from 1780. Not all the accounts are John Scandrett Harford's. Ten of these items are books kept by his father — Edward Harford (1720-1806). Some of the books have roughly entered details. Others were little used. It is with John Scandrett Harford senior's books — covering between them from 1793-1815 — that we are especially concerned.[1] They record, on a monthly basis, domestic expenditure under headings such as folio 168, 'Expences in Gardens', folio 31, 'Hothouse and Greenhouse Exotics', folio 119, 'Lodge on Coombe Hill': and Harford allocated folio 170 to 'New Cottages at Henbury' or, as was sometimes entered, 'To Cottages at Greens'.

What follows below is an attempt to interpret this new evidence, so far as it helps us to understand the process by which Blaise Hamlet evolved. Because of its importance and the possibility of future re-interpretion, the correspondence between Harford and Nash's office has been transcribed in its entirety under Appendix IV.

It is evident from the letters that work had started on designing the cottages by August 1810, although the first entry under folio 170 was made some months earlier. Expenses were, after that date, recorded on a monthly basis, although in the ledgers and journals the exact nature of purchases or services paid for are not often disclosed, any more than are the recipients necessarily identified. Such is the case for the first Cottages entry of March 1810: to cash paid, sundrys, £6 13s. 0d., possibly for site clearing or fencing off that part of Greens to be used for Blaise Hamlet. By December 1812 costs had mounted to more than four thousand pounds,[2] Nash's expenses and fees totalling a little over two hundred and thirty pounds.[3] As his son observed, Harford's books were methodically kept over many years, although the last-found entry for the cottages made three months after his death were in a less patient hand, as had been the case from December 1813.

One other surviving record of importance kept by Harford is his last rough cash book — the one which referred to the cottage in Coombe Dingle.[4] It yields information about the embellishments of Blaise Hamlet and other matters too in newly revealing detail. Some points of interest will be noted in due course.

On turning to George Repton's *Pavilion Notebook*,[5] we find that Nash's assistant prepared over twenty pages of drawings, including plans, elevations, sections and details — some, or all — for every one of the nine Hamlet buildings. Coverage — cottage by cottage — is uneven. For some, such as that to be named Rose Cottage, four pages of carefully delineated and heavily annotated designs were prepared. For Circular Cottage, there were only two. Yet on those small pages Repton was able to give three elevations, a ground-floor and a chamber plan drawing, uncramped.

As will be demonstrated, there was an important element of impromptu in the final visual form that the cottages were to assume. Details, perhaps not of prime importance to their occupants, were to prove crucial to an overall realisation of Nash's village picturesque. For example, some of the *Pavilion Notebook* drawings have been altered and minor amendments to details have been pencilled in, but out-houses and pents, essential to the total varied outline effect, might not be shown at all in these drawings. Chimneys are modest in height and of a standard design. As built, they might be the most conspicuous, as well as the most memorable feature. However, it must be borne in mind that the *Pavilion Notebook* drawings, like one side of Harford's correspondence with Repton, were the communicator's possibly incomplete record of what had been sent to the partner in an exchange. Neither the letters received from Harford by Repton, nor the drawings Repton sent to Harford from which the builder worked, have yet been found. There might well have been variations, intentional or otherwise, in the material received by either party and additional plans or instructions might still be unknown to us.

Although the eight surviving letters (dated from August 1810 to December 1812), sheets of notes and an undated site plan are not all that passed between Nash, his office and Harford,[6] a sequence of events can be traced through them, and the very first letter Repton addressed to Harford from 29 Dover Street opens with a statement that appears, once and for all time, to answer largely a point that we set out to resolve: 'I expect to receive the designs for one or two of your Cottages from Mr Nash by tomorrow or Saturdays post, when I will lose no time in drawing them out, and forwarding them to you.'

It is immediately clear that Nash was designing at least these two cottages and subsequent correspondence discloses that others were also from his hand. As we already know from Cockerell's recollections, the decision on irregular placing was Nash's and on one of his two visits he pegged out the site. The second visit charged for is likely to have been in October 1811, for the purpose of inspecting the work and drawing up an inventory of defects for all the cottages, which were, by that date, approaching completion.[7]

Repton, in his first letter, continues: 'I shall be obliged to you to inform me if you wish to have shaded drawings of all the Cottages like those you have already received',[8] and by this same date, in the correspondence if not the drawings, Nash's ideas about the imposing chimneys, as perhaps suggested to him by Price's writings, were already beginning to take form. The fair drawings supplied were of Rose and Double cottages — the same subjects, incidentally, as two of the Repton Bequest drawings (Plates 40 and 47). They cost Harford five guineas the pair.[9]

The extent to which the individual cottages changed from the *Pavilion Notebook* drawings is conveniently recorded for us by an excellent folio, probably published in or shortly after 1826, with fine lithographic views of each cottage, drawn skilfully on the stone by J.D. Harding (1798-1863), from originals by Hugh O'Neill (1784-1824)[10] (Plate 48). *Nine Lithographic Views of the Cottages, Composing Blaise Hamlet* goes further than presenting us with these large lithographs alone, as the folio also includes a ground floor plan of each cottage (Plates 43, 44 and 45) and a plan of the whole village site[11] (Plate 34). We now have reference to the cottages as they stand, to their appearance and plans soon after they were built, and (through the drawings in Repton's *Pavilion Notebook*) to Nash's earlier intentions as well. This graphic information, when expanded on by the Repton-Harford letters and the 1811 inventory of defects, gives a picture of how individual designs evolved in the mind and on the ground as the scheme took shape.

Nash was probably accustomed to complaints of soaring costs and

Harford's mild observation when it came to settling up is unlikely to have caused the architect to lose much sleep. 'I have been looking into the Account of the Expenditure of the Cottages etc done for me and find that though the original Estimates did not amount to £2,000 that I have already expended upwards of £3,000'.[12] Nash charged 1½% on the £407 7s. 0d. estimate for Double Cottage[13] and Harford, having deducted some non-building costs, settled for 5% on £3,000 — £150 0s. 0d. — plus the £81 7s. 10d. for fees and expenses.

Having decided on the layout, Nash left for Ireland, probably to supervise the building of a splendid domed country house for Lord Lorton of Boyle, at Rockingham, in County Roscommon. As a result, all the correspondence with Harford known to have survived is by George Repton, who interpreted Nash's instructions and generally supervised the operation, apparently by remote control.

Owing to the great distance Nash was from home,[14] there were delays and frustrations that sometimes tried Harford's patience. Apparently he left a 'figured plan' with Harford, but had insufficient information with him in Ireland to communicate unambiguously where to place some of the cottages on the site. What was Harford to make of a drawing captioned 'Second Cottage from the top North side looking South East',[15] for example? He might have guessed, but could still have been uncertain, that it was number 3.

By September, matters were getting under control again. Harford sent Repton copies of two plans for him to forward to Nash, although Nash had already, as it happened, written direct to Harford for one of them.[16] His letter had apparently miscarried.[17] Nash was perhaps not so much in doubt about his own intentions, but just lacking the vital numbering to make those intentions utterly clear to Harford.[18] Despite the resulting confusion when it came to relating designs to the site on the ground, the drawing up by Nash of the overall plan need not have been quite as haphazard an operation as is sometimes supposed, especially if he had made site notes and drawings as well (Plate 35).

Harford's draft letter of September 1st. 1810 tells us two more important things. By that date the first two cottages were nearly ready for tiling. Harford had already 'fixed' for their chimneys. We also read that the general plan, as numbered by Nash, had been brought down from London to Harford by none other than 'Foster', who might well have discussed it in Nash's office, or have even been briefed on it. So the possibility of a third architect being involved at Blaise Hamlet arises. The suspicion is confirmed by an entry under December 1812 in Harford's rough cashbook: 'By New Cottages etc. p'd Jas Foster Architect in full' £16 5s. 6d.:[19] not a large sum, but enough to account for about three hundred pounds worth of building. What was Foster's role? Not a leading one; but in the long absence of Nash and probable non-appearance of Repton, he might well have acted as Harford's local consultant, or have undertaken supervision of work resulting from the October 1811 inventory of defects. Bearing in mind that a special visit by Nash cost Harford as much as £33 4s. 0d. a time,[20] such a fee would have been well invested.

It will shortly be necessary to consider some cottages in greater detail, but first a number of important common components can be discussed to advantage in more general terms. There are the chimneys, privies and pents; and of these, perhaps the most remarkable are the towering stacks. Yet very important too are the porches, wash-houses and lean-tos that cascade asymmetrically from the main eaves to be buried in bushes and vines, almost to the ground, giving diversity of form on all sides, every individual configuration varying from view to view. Both features, in the main, were additional to early proposals and probably contributed to the increased costs. In Repton's drawings most ovens and coppers were crammed into the kitchens and under stairs. Some were later relocated, to be drawn in less carefully on Repton's miniature plans.

Harford became anxious as matters got under way: 'I observe', he drafted on 18 August, 1810, about a plan he had received, that 'there is a room appropriated for a Cellar and Pantry which is [an unnecessary?] one and not wanted as in the other plans the Pantry is taken out of the Scullery and if this mode is adopted it will very much lengthen out the Building and enhance the expence'. Repton replied to Harford on August 23: 'in answer to what you mention in your letter that the Pantry and Cellar in the first designs you received were placed in the Cottage itself — if we make them all so it will very much injure (if not entirely destroy) the picturesque effect of the different Cottages where so much depends upon the leantoos and Sheds etc to make a variety in their form — more particularly where the number and scale of the rooms are so similar and the pantry and Cellar projecting from the Cottage is not more expensive than if it were in the body of the building where you must still occupy [*word missing*] space, and must increase the Upper Rooms'. And there, to judge by visible results, the matter rested. Repton had his say, Nash his way. Harford, apparently unprotesting, paid the bill and Price, presumably, would have acclaimed the wisdom of their united decision.

Chimneys, like the complexities of roofscapes and the multiplicity of porches, were the subject of close consideration by Price in his *Essays*: 'The forms of chimnies are not less to be attended to in village-houses, than in those on a larger scale; and in some respects still more so: for although any poverty of form gives greater offence when mixed with the beauty and splendour of architecture, yet, in low houses, the good or bad effect of chimnies is more immediately striking, as they are nearer the eye, and larger in proportion to the building.'[21]

Lamenting some tall and thin single chimneys which produced the most mean and wretched outline he had ever seen, Price continued: 'The opposite extreme in some of the old stone chimnies, which are built as massively as towers, is more suited to the lover of painting; who might in particular cases, be induced to build a chimney of that kind, where something of a massive character seemed to be wanting in the composition: a new, but by no means unentertaining way of considering every part of a building.'[22]

Repton, in his first letter to Harford, on August 9th, suggested putting into practice in the cottages at Blaise just the advice that Price was re-publishing: Mr. Nash had asked him to say that he considered the chimneys to be a great feature in the cottages. It is worth re-stating that the chimneys shown in Repton's drawings are comparatively inconspicuous and all of one design: so unimportant, it would appear, that they were completely omitted from some drawings. Repton went further. Nash recommended Harford have moulded bricks made for them. They would very much increase the effect. Transported with enthusiasm, Repton concluded his opening missive: 'should you wish it I will send you 2 or 3 different designs for them,' and he developed his theme a week or so later by sending the greater number and suggesting to Harford that rather than select just one he might use them all in different parts of the village: 'you have so many opportunities of using them', he observed. Again, Harford complied.

This letter of 18 August is devoted entirely to chimneys, which would produce, in Repton's estimation, a very picturesque effect: 'their character requires they should be very high — even more so than I have described upon the enclosed drawing.' Repton would even have sent another half dozen designs if Harford wanted to have every cottage in a different style, but there is no evidence that he took up the offer. Here, Harford drew the line, either his aesthetic or his economic sensibilities deciding the matter.

It appears that moulds for the ornamental bricks were eventually made under Repton's supervision, as the architects' account includes a charge for 'Mens time and Materials making Moulds for the ornamental Chimney Stacks, and packing case for the Same 3. 14s. 10'.[23] W.J. Pountney, reminiscing in *Old Bristol Potteries* (1920), wrote that he was uncertain of the exact date of the cottages, but he did know that the chimney-pots and ornamental bricks for the chimney-stacks were all made at the Westbury Pottery.[24] Pountney was of a pottery manufacturing family and it was his father who directed William Fifield to paint a series of views of the cottages between 1820 and 1822, which he did at Temple Back Pottery.[25] The Harfords collected the ceramic plaques on which these views were painted.

There are many minor and some important differences between the plans in *Nine Lithographic Views* and those in Repton's *Pavilion Notebook*. The inventory of defects lists numerous alterations — some small technicalities concerning copings, pigeon rests and mouldings, and others of real significance to the final appearance of a cottage. Apart from the chimneys, most of the latter result from decisions made about sanitation. Harford's observations on the location of coppers and ovens in some of the cottages and Repton's reply pointing out the importance of lean-to extensions to picturesque appearance have been referred to already: not that there would have been much room to launder and bath, or to enjoy the home-baked produce anyway, had some of the original intentions been carried through.

Despite the relative luxury of such facilities, installations were not to be lavish. The inventory opens with general directions: 'The Coppers and Ovens can have but little spaces allowed for them. the gardner must therefore enquire and find out the smallest sized coppers and ovens that will be sufficient for the sort of people who are to live in the Cottages and let them be built accordingly':— [1]* consumer research at grass roots level. Specifications for the earth closets are more exacting: 'NB all the Bogs to be 4 feet diameter & 6 or 7 feet deep & to be [stoned?] & domed over except where the shoots from the privys enter them and to be kept as far from the body of the building.' —[3]

Nash employed four different solutions to the problem of privies. One was to contain them (more or less) within the general plan already shown on Repton's drawings, as at Numbers 2 (Rose Cottage) and 7 (Oak Cottage). This meant change of space use, or enclosure of previously open lean-tos. Numbers 3 (Dial Cottage) and 6 (Vine Cottage) had extensions attached to them individually. The third solution, at 8 and 9 (Diamond and Jasmine), was to provide an extension on the north side of the latter. Numbers 4 and 5 (Circular and Sweetbriar) were distinguished by a free-standing semi-detached block, 'to be back to back close in the hedge . . . to be 6′ 3 high to the eaves & hipped all round the walls of 9 inch Brickwork'. —[11]

Provision of a copper and oven probably meant more expense again for Harford at Number 2. Repton's plan shows an oven, or copper, tucked almost impossibly under central stairs. The inventory required the west-side open lean-to to be converted into a walled enclosure, which had to be widened for the greater part of its length by a foot to contain the fixtures. This demanded

* For convenience of reference, the inventory, which is transcribed under Appendix IV, has paragraphs numbered. They are identified in the text of this book thus:– -[1], -[2], etc.

adjustment of the eaves line. —[2] Altering the position of ovens and adding coppers might require the relocation of flues and building of additional chimneys: and adding lean-tos and constructing privies could result in important changes to rooflines and eaves-levels as well. Whereas such modification of the utility areas might be of relatively little significance to the external appearance of, say, Number 9 — Jasmine Cottage —, changes made as a result of the inventory were of considerable importance visually to some others. For example: 'The privy of No. 6 (Plates 57, 58 and 59) to be built at the NW corner of the scullery building by the extension of the NW wall and the continuation of the roof so far that the Eaves may be 6:3 high over the privy — and the seat placed in the angle and the bog so formed that the shoot of the privy may go into it'. —[14] Improvisation was exercised with great confidence all round: 'the Copper and oven to be in the scullery behind the stairs & a Chimney stack made for it unless the old flue can be made use of with safety to the stairs.' —[15] Harford must have wondered where it would all end, as it was further required for this same cottage that a penthouse 'be put over the South West window . . . composed of the continuation of the lower course of Eaves tiles of the penthouse over the seat and the addition of another (lower) course of Tiles underneath supported by 4 brackets as shewn by the Sketch on the plan.' — [22] Vine Cottage, without its third great chimney and canopied front window, would hardly have the personality and impact that it has. Vigorous improvisation is evident in conjuring the final cottage form. Better facilities resulted, agreed: but some exuberant compositional touches also emerged at this very late stage. It was through the creative aspects of this process — intuitive and innovatory — that the painterly attitude necessary to fulfil the painterly dream was to demonstrate itself to visible effect.

These late inventive improvements resulted in an articulation of forms realised with rare assurance and panâche — all in close spiritual compatibility with the philosophical writings of Price and relating to practical every-day needs of tenants and client, even if not always essential to them or agreeable to his pocket.

Having been provided with their coppers, the cottagers would have needed an adequate supply of water to ensure their use, quite apart from other daily needs. Number 5 — 'Sweetbriar' by 1826 — was also known as 'Omega' (1822, 1825) and sometime as 'Pond' Cottage. Ashmead's (1826) plan shows a pond in the extreme north-east corner of the village site, but this is unlikely to have been the main source of supply after the builders had left. Almost certainly the permanent source was outside Number 3, Dial (or Spring) Cottage, named after the sundial — a feature of the envisaged scheme, mentioned by Nash in his bill of 1812, and the subject of an entry in Harford's rough cash book, which records under 1812: 'p'd Wm Watkins for a Sun Dial £5. 5. 0.' (Plate 50). In the same year an obelisk was provided by Charles Melsom for £15 10s. 0d. and a copper vase to go with it was purchased from R & [N?] Bush for a further £2 5s. 0d.

No suggestion as to who might have built the cottages at Blaise Hamlet is known to have been put forward elsewhere, but this same source reveals at last the names of those Harford paid. John Dunn, who measured, received £42 2s. 0d., James [Hoare?], for plumbing, was paid £45 4s. 3d., the smith £5 14s. 0d. and Benjamin Ford, carpenter, £165 16s. 0d. James Tillett provided stone tiles, Hutchins & Co. the bricks. Also in 1812, £401 12s. 0d. was paid to the mason (builder of the Coombe Dingle Cottage), William Lee.

Once completed, the Hamlet (having nestled cosily into its naturally undulating niche and the pensioners into their snug, sophisticated retreats) became so much an object of picturesque curiosity that none of the numerous Bristol guide books published in the next sixty years was likely to pass it by without benediction or polite applause. Then, from late century, the Hamlet withdrew quietly from the searchlight of public attention to doze peacefully out of one world war and nearly through the next, in the meantime inconspicuously deteriorating behind secretive walls. Then, suddenly, in 1943, it again captured national notice through a flurry of articles in glossier periodicals on its purchase from Mr. Donald Hughes of Bristol by the National Trust.[26] The Corporation of Bristol had declined his offer to sell them the Hamlet for £2,325.

Rather naively, in that architecturally indeterminate period between neo-Georgian and post-Brave New World, the *Illustrated London News* asked if Harford's almshouses might not serve as models for new cottages to be built after the war. Modernised within, they would be eminently suitable for country districts.[27] Prophetic Nash's Hamlet might have been, but this gem was no answer to the massive problems of post-war rehousing. Bristol was to turn its engineering genius and productive capacity to a more realistic solution of that ever-urgent problem.

Sir Nikolaus Pevsner, having praised Blaise Hamlet as the ultimate in picturesque village perfection, put the cottages into a contemporary perspective by remarking on another less flattering of their influences: that they were indeed responsible for some of the worst sentimentalities of England.[28] A million creeper-clad tea services, crazy-paved china toast-racks, inter-war *culs-de-sac* and diamond-glazed semis testify to this. Even if Blaise Hamlet was not totally responsible for the image of suburban noddyland, it is likely to have played a significant part in its promotion (Plate 36).

Prefacing the second edition of his *Rural Architecture* (1826), Peter Robinson considered the pros and cons for cottagers — the tenants of such scenic dwellings: 'Erected with care, and with some attention to form, it [the cottage] becomes an object of interest in the picture; vistas are opened to admit of occasional peeps from the pleasure ground, and a morning is frequently dedicated to visit the thriving family.' Paternalistic curiosity passes to social psychology: 'The attention of the landlord is met by the assiduity of the tenant, and neatness and even elegance is the result. The woodbine is trained with care round the window, every unseemly object is kept out of sight, and the good wife, anxious to please her benefactress, and grateful for the attention paid to her, is ever on the watch for the morning visit, and consequently always in order.'[29] James Harding, as well as drawing up the stones for *Nine Lithographic Views*, illustrated Robinson's book; and in 1830 the latter produced his own work on village architecture, illustrative of Price's *Essays on the Picturesque*.

In view of these coincidences of draughtsman, topic and date, the Introduction to *Nine Lithographic Views* also makes interesting reading: "The Air of Comfort diffused over these little Dwellings; the play of Light and Shadow produced by their Projections and Recesses, which afford shelter to a variety of beautiful Creepers; the highly Ornamental and varied Character of the Chimnies; and the Beauty of the surrounding little Gardens, glittering throughout the Summer with Flowers of the brightest hues, and guarded from the intruding hand by Hedges of Sweet-Briar, suggest the most pleasing Images to the Fancy, and shed a romantic and poetical Character over this favoured Asylum. The only Rivaly [*sic*] we could hear of, as existing among its Inhabitants, was,

> 'Who should first
> The welcome spring salute, whose borders shew
> The earliest bloom, the sweetest proudest charms
> Of Flora.' "

Harford, the Introduction continues, set out to provide a comfortable place for the elderly who had sufficient means to maintain themselves 'when relieved from the expense of House-Rent', and 'it was his delight, as long as his health permitted, to visit a spot in which he had been the means of centering so much happiness.'

Brewer's description in *Delineations of Gloucestershire* (1824), gives a fair account of the Hamlet as a second contemporary topographer saw it. 'A terrace-walk, of a wavy outline, leads along the front of the buildings, and encloses a lawn that called for no operation of art, but was left undulating by the hand of nature. Ivy, woodbine, jessamine, and various simple flowering plants, cling to these tenements of peace, and impart to them a beautiful and appropriate dressing. As a picturesque object, this hamlet is, indeed, a gem of prodigious value to the domain. — It is a just principle, in arranging the ornamental buildings planned by the landscape-gardener, that utility should be blended with display; and hence we find, in many pleasure-grounds, that even the mimic-ruin conceals a shed, subservient to some use of pasturage or rural husbandry. How much superior are the devices here practised! since the smiling village, that adds to the picturesque attractions of the territory, at the same time forms a memorial of the founder's exemplary benevolence.'[30]

Although Loudon advocated simple natural ornaments such as house leak and sweetbriars for cottages in preference to ostentatious or unregional ornaments, he was rather sceptical about the seductive qualities of thatch — an object of admiration by those who had little experience of country life, and sometimes, even then, copied by townsfolk in suburbs for effect. 'Such cottages have, perhaps, the gable end covered with ivy, the chimney tops entwined with Virginian creepers, and the windows overshadowed by roses and jasmines. The ivy forms an excellent harbour for sparrows and other small birds . . . In June, as soon as the young birds are fledged,' he warns (presumably from hard-won experience), 'all the cats in the neighbourhood are attracted by them, and take up their abode on the roof of the house every night for several weeks; the noise and other annoyances occasioned by which we need only allude to. We say nothing of the damp produced by the deciduous creepers and the roses . . . [and] that loathsome creature, the earwig, which, in autumn, whenever the windows are open, comes into the house in quantities, and finds its way into every closet, chink, piece of furniture, and even books and papers.' But worse is to come: 'All cottages of this kind harbour snails and slugs in the ivy, and spiders under the eaves . . . and wherever there are spiders, there are also abundance of flies.'[31] He continues with sinister references to slugs that get so fat they cannot escape from the pantry, earwigs in bed, swarms of beetles, cockroaches, then fleas. It was John Evans who recounted in 1824 that Nash intended that the cottages at Blaise should be 'clothed with the ivy, honey-suckle, jasmin, and other ornamental shrubs, even to the chimney-tops.'[32]

Perhaps life, even in the Hamlet, was not quite perfect for its residents after all; and elsewhere, deep in rural England, cottage life in the nineteenth century was not necessarily as cosy as a twentieth-century romantic might imagine it to have been. Conditions could be deplorable. Disease, squalor and poverty were norms in many families. Lack of efficient sanitation combined with unprogressive habit and overcrowding to make diarrhoea, typhoid, dysentery and early death commonplace. John Woodforde's *The Truth about*

Cottages (1969) tells a grimly fascinating and disillusioning tale of the darker side of rural existence. It appears that provision of coppers and ovens was at least unusual and even an earth closet something of a rarity until comparatively recent times, and from the evidence of pattern books it is clear that most earlier architects' designs in print for the prettiest of dwellings passed sanitation almost completely by, although it must be conceded that while George Repton's *Pavilion Notebook* plans show no lavatories at all, every cottage did in fact have its own privy, copper and oven by the time Harford, Nash, Repton, Foster and William Lee had completed their task. Exceptional, the standards appear to have been; but with such a team might one expect less?

Peter Robinson's appreciation of rural life was not one-sided. He knew enough about life as it was actually lived to consider current evils of rural existence. In the fourth edition of his work (1836) he delivered a homily on cottage pride and the importance of concerned patronage in raising the aspirations of the destitute, straitened and indigent mass: 'the habits of the Cottager himself are thus improved and rendered more pleasing than those of his neighbour who resides in the less inviting dwelling; from the latter we turn with disgust; the muck heap at the door, and the idle children wallowing in their own filth, are not very tempting objects to the patroness, who delights in decency and good order . . . The little gardens will be trimmed with attention, the woodbine and ivy will be trained round the mullioned window, inviting a nearer approach, and the interior will present a well-arranged system of comfort and cleanliness. The pleasure arising from occasional visits to the aged dependant, will be repaid by new attention on her part, and the dwelling will eventually become a little picture of pride and satisfaction to both parties, produced by feelings flowing from different sources.'[33]

Moral blackmail might even give way to well-intentioned bribery. *The New Annual Register* for 1789 records that at Nuneham the cottagers celebrated a *Fête de Vertu* in August. It was an annual entertainment considered admirable in its calculated promotion of good behaviour and industry among the villagers, prizes being awarded to those inhabitants best behaved throughout the year, and to those girls and women who spun best on the day of celebration. The occasion opened with a church service beginning with the distribution of prizes for good conduct, and this was followed by a 'very excellent sermon, or rather charge,' to the persons immediately concerned. A dinner preceded the spinning contest, this feast being rendered doubly agreeable to the guests by the amiable affability of their noble patrons. Umpires then judged the spinning. Prizes were duly awarded. Then the evening wound up with a dance.

The young Harcourt, reluctant earl and 'gentle executioner' (as Walpole dubbed him), while retaining a love for gardens, moderated in his maturity those excessively revolutionary views he affected during his close discipleship of Rousseau, who was once his father's prestigious, if fleeting guest. One small and perhaps painful step in Harcourt's transmogrification was recorded for us by Farington, in 1801. August 12: 'At *Nuneham* I was told that Lord Harcourt no longer has the annual Spinning feast which during several years was given at Nuneham House to people belonging to the village, and prizes to those whose industry and moral conduct was most remarkable. Such as were fortunate enough to obtain prizes had a star printed over their doors and the letter M (merit) also marked.' Farington had seen two or three such signs in some of the doors. But this happy manifestation of generous and enlightened philanthropy came to an abrupt and undignified end, though not because Harcourt deserted his paternalistic beliefs. It was in consequence of some rudeness having been committed that Lady Harcourt was thrown down. His Lordship returned to common custom after that, by holding an old-fashioned annual harvest feast.[34]

Who, anyway, were these rustics; what were their needs? Let Loudon, who must have written many thousands of words about matters with a direct bearing on the cottage-dwellers' lot, explain. Few could have been better equipped than he to offer an informed opinion on these contemporaries of his. 'The wants of man in the lowest stage of society are comparatively few: they are only those of simple nature; and nature, always consistent with herself, affords obvious and simple means of resource. The part acted by the cottager in the great drama of life, though important when viewed collectively, is nevertheless, as to the operations of the individual, scarcely discernible.' Having put the rustic firmly in his insignificant nook, Loudon then really cut him down to proper size. 'The first and last time that we see him is in the field or in the highway at hard labour; when he is no longer capable of toil, he retires under the shelter of his cottage, and leaves the world as obscurely as he came into it.'[35] Here then, is the *raison d'être* of our quest.

So, were the real interests of such an un-noticeable section of society even remotely connected with the dozens of pattern books and many learned works published on the aesthetics and construction of rustic cottages? Was the talent, industry and money poured into all this earlier activity usually intended to benefit the impoverished inhabitants of such picturesque delights as found their way from fashionable architects' drawing boards on to the pages of elegant publications and into real three-dimensional form on country estates? Loudon was concerned that conditions should be improved.

A spendthrift prince might leave a trail, even if cottagers could come and go without trace. Pückler-Muskau, having left Piercefield, wound his way to Bristol, visiting Blaise in December 1828, to see 'an interesting establishment called "The Cottages." The proprietor, Mr. Harford, has endeavoured to realise the "beau idéal" of a village.' And he found that a beautiful green space in the midst of the wood was surrounded by a winding road: 'on it are built nine cottages, all of different forms and materials . . . each surrounded with different trees, and enwreathed with various sorts of clematis, rose, honeysuckle, and vine. The dwellings, which are perfectly detached though they form a whole, have separate gardens, and a common fountain, which stands in the centre of the green, overshadowed by old trees.' The perceptive prince adds details which illuminate his account: 'The gardens, divided by neat hedges, form a pretty garland of flowers and herbs around the whole village. What crowns the whole is, that the inhabitants are all poor families, whom the generous proprietor allows to live in the houses rent-free. No more delightful or well-chosen spot could be found as a refuge for misfortune: its perfect seclusion and snugness breathe only peace and forgetfulness of the world.'[36]

Harford's father had, as has been mentioned, faced problems when keeping the curious public from Blaise woods, and young Harford had to bring additional restrictions into force. Even the prince was frustrated: 'Voi che venite — di *entrare* lasciate ogni speranza,' was his comment when refused entry by a churlish porter into Repton's landscaped grounds — a forbidden paradise — on that closing Sunday of the traveller's eventful year.[37] On April 23, 1834, instructions had been written for Richard Tainton — possibly a cottager, perhaps even the churlish porter himself — 'Never to admit Strangers, only their own Friends, after the Hours specified', to the Hamlet, trades people and tenants excepted. Tainton was to have a register of those who might be admitted at other times.[38]

Hints for the Cottagers have also survived, from the same year. They were advised: 'To commence the day with a portion of the Bible, & a Prayer: To lock the Gates after them always, excepting between the hours of 12 & 5 — on pain of forfeiting their Keys: To employ Tainton to keep their Gardens & to mow the Village Green.' The notes, apparently in John Harford junior's hand, conclude with an appeal to tenants to keep their gardens very gay with common flowers and to maintain their cottages in good repair — as they would have found them on entry.

The occupants had their moments, no doubt, as celebrity, aesthete, tripper and the more genuinely curious filed through the gate to parade themselves and circum-perambulate the daisy-powdered green: and none perhaps was more celebrated than the one thought worthy of mention in a journal by Harford in 1845. 'Queen Adelaide (Qn. Dowager) accompanied by her Sister the Duchess of Saxe Weimar, Prince Edward, & the 2 Young Princesses of Saxe W. attended by Lords Howe & Denbigh etc. lately visited Kingsweston, & Blaise Castle. I received her Majesty on Kingsweston Hill, & conducted her through the Evergreen Drive — first to The Cottages — & then to the House.' Harford had arranged that Henbury church bells should peal from the moment the Queen's carriage reached Kingsweston Hill, and he was much pleased with her truly amiable demeanour. Nevertheless, she wasn't so enthused (or was she just spellbound?) as to alight from her carriage either at the cottages, or even the house, excusing herself by remembering that time was pressing hard. But her sister did actually walk round the green, and even went upstairs in one of the cottages: '& Mr. Coles, hearing of the Queens love of Jasmine gathered a pretty nosegay of it which was presented to her.' Harford was well pleased with the final act of this village drama: 'She then drove up to our House where Louisa was standing in the Portico ready to receive her & was presented to her by one of the two Lords in waiting . . . She expressed herself as delighted with our Grounds — as were also all the rest of the Party.'[39]

These cottages were indeed justly deserving of that public interest which they excited: 'Each, is in itself, a truly picturesque object, and by means of the skill displayed in their mutual Contrast, Shape, and Collocation, they form, from various Points of View, most pleasing Compositions, and offer a variety of subjects for the Pencil.'[40] Artists, untutored and professional, came in true Gilpin and Syntax tradition and the drawings and prints that flowed in such numbers found their way to countless Sunday albums, as to collections and museums at home and abroad (Plates 2, 59 and 63).

Before Blaise Hamlet had been completed the concept had already blossomed to metropolitan scale in the mind of Nash. The Crown Commissioners had recommended and the Treasury approved his Regents Park plans.

If we accept as accurate the closing lines of introduction to *Nine Lithographic Views*, Blaise must have meant much more to Nash than we might otherwise have supposed, bearing in mind later glittering commissions at Brighton and elsewhere. For, we are told, he entered with lively interest into the project, and had often been heard to say that no palace he ever planned had imparted a pleasure comparable to that which he derived from this humble employment of his talents and ingenuity at Blaise Hamlet.

As Peter Robinson suggested might prove to be the case, the patron also found reward. Of this, his son's Memoir leaves us in little doubt: 'In a particular manner he loved to stroll around the sweet little village, which he had recently erected, and he met there in every Cottager the beaming expression of gratitude to a kind Benefactor: he witnessed the happiness he had given birth, and the blessing thus bestowed upon others returned with a large increase into his own bosom.'[41]

Notes to Chapter Eight

1. Bristol R.O. 28048, F4, 1804-1815, ledger, J.S.H: F9, 1793-1804, journal of J.S.H: F10, 1805-1815, journal of J.S.H: F11/1, 1793-1804, rough journal of J.S.H: F11/2, loose papers: F12/1 1813-1814, rough journal of J.S.H: F12/2, loose papers: F19, 1812-1815, last cash account book of J.S.H.
2. *Ibid.*, F4/1; F10.
3. *Ibid.*, P52/9, 22 Nov. 1812; P52/10, 2 Dec. 1812; see Appendix IV.
4. *Ibid.*, F19, 1812-1815.
5. Art Gallery & Museums & the Royal Pavilion, Brighton, Appendix VII.
6. *E.g.* Bristol R.O. 28048, P52/5, a letter from G.S. Repton to Harford, in which Repton mentions that he has received a letter from Nash saying that the latter had written to Harford for a figured plan. Neither letter mentioned is with the Harford Papers. Then there were the drawings. Appendix IV.
7. *Ibid.*, P52/8, Oct. 1811. Appendix IV. The document is not signed. Nash charged for two personal visits. We shall find that one was for pegging out the site and that no visit was charged for Repton on Nash's bill. It is conceivable that George Repton met Nash at Blaise, but there is no suggestion of this in the correspondence. While it could be taken for granted that Nash would have inspected the work and drawn up the inventory, it is also worth noting that it appears to be in his hand and not Repton's. There are letterforms and spellings characteristic of Nash when writing to others at about this time.
8. *Ibid.*, P52/1, 9 Aug. 1810. Appendix IV.
9. *Ibid.*, P52/9, 22 Nov. 1812. Appendix IV.
10. *Nine Lithographic Views of the Cottages, Composing Blaise Hamlet* (n.d.), T. Bedford, 23 Broad Street. Drawn on the stone by J.D. Harding from sketches by O'Neil[l]. Plates are dated 1826 — two years after O'Neill's death. He worked in Bristol from about 1820.
11. Plan by G.C. Ashmead, Surveyor, Bristol. Ashmead's plan (1826), numbers the cottages clockwise, from Oak (1) to Vine (10). Nash's plan starts at Double (1) (only), moving again clockwise, via Vine (6), to Jasmine (9). His numbering is

used throughout this account.

12. Bristol R.O. 28048, P52/10, 2 Dec. 1812. Appendix IV. Not all of the sum was for building.
13. *Ibid.*, P52/9, 22 Nov. 1812. Appendix IV.
14. *Ibid.*, P52/2, 15 Aug. 1810. Appendix IV.
15. *Ibid.*, P52/6, 1 Sept. 1810. Appendix IV.
16. *Ibid.*, P52/5, 23 Aug. 1810. Appendix IV.
17. *Ibid.*, P52/6, 1 Sept. 1810. Appendix IV.
18. *Ibid.*, P52/7 (n.d.), a plan outlining each cottage and numbering them all.
19. *Ibid.*, F19, 1812-1815.
20. *Ibid.*, P52/9, 22 Nov. 1812. Appendix IV.
21. Uvedale PRICE, *Essays on the Picturesque*, 1810, ii, p. 349.
22. *Ibid.*, pp. 350-51.
23. Bristol R.O. 28048, P52/9, 22 Nov. 1812. Appendix IV.
24. W.J. POUNTNEY, *Old Bristol Potteries*, 1920, p. 266.
25. *Ibid.*, p. 113.
26. *Sphere*, 14 Aug. 1943, p. 218: *Country Life*, 3 Sept. 1943, p. 429: *Illustrated London News*, 11 Sept. 1943, pp. 300-301: *The Architect and Building News*, 17 Sept. 1943, pp. 168-169: *Field*, 9 Oct. 1943, p. 378.
27. *Illustrated London News*, 11 Sept. 1943.
28. Nikolaus PEVSNER, *Buildings of England: North Somerset and Bristol*, 1958, p. 469.
29. P.F. ROBINSON, *Rural Architecture; or, a series of Designs for Ornamental Cottages*, 1826 (2nd edn.), quoted from the reprinted Introduction (4th edn.), 1836. He was also author of *Designs for Village Architecture, being a series of Designs illustrating the Observations contained in the Essay on the Picturesque by Sir Uvedale Price*, 1830.
30. J. & H.S. STORER (*del./sc.*) & J.N. BREWER, *Delineations of Gloucestershire*, 1824, pp. 108-109.
31. J.C. LOUDON, *The Suburban Gardener, and Villa Companion*, 1838, p. 115.
32. John EVANS, *Chronological Outline of the History of Bristol*, 1824, p. xxx.
33. ROBINSON, *op. cit.*, 1836 (4th edn.), Design XV, for a quadrangular almshouse in the gothic style, as built at Highgate Archway.
34. James GREIG (ed.), *The Farington Diary*, 1922, i, pp. 310-311, 12 Aug. 1801.
35. John LOUDON, *A Treatise on Forming, Improving and Managing Country Residences*, 1806, i, pp. 124-125.
36. [Hermann PÜCKLER-MUSKAU], *Tour in England, Ireland, and France, in the years 1828 & 1829*, 1832, ii, pp. 204-205.
37. *Ibid.*, p. 205.

38. Bristol R.O. 28048, C81, 23 April 1834.
39. *Ibid.*, C55, p. 21, 1845.
40. *Nine Lithographic Views of the Cottages, Composing Blaise Hamlet* (n.d.), Introduction. Apart from this high quality folio of larger lithographic views with plans, perhaps most popular of all the views published were sheets of nine (3 × 3) miniature portraits of the cottages. There were numerous editions and variations of this arrangement, the cottages appearing in different sequences and over various individual names, according to the edition. At Blaise Castle House is an original wash drawing from which at least one such lithographed edition was possibly made.
41. Bristol R.O. 28048, M24/1.

At Circular Cottage, Blaise Hamlet, 1973

9 'These Tenements of Peace'

He pass'd a cottage with a double coach-house,
A cottage of gentility!
And he own'd with a grin
That his favourite sin
Is pride that apes humility.[1]

The final chapter will carry our inquiry further afield, first returning to Wales, then to Herefordshire, Salop and Cheshire in quest of Nash's cottage building activities which might lead to the identification of other ventures by him in village design.

But before embarking on such expeditions it would be timely to examine rather more closely some features of the Blaise Hamlet cottages and in the course of doing so make a preliminary sortie to the Isle of Wight, where some rustic creations very much in the spirit of those at Blaise were built to Nash's design.

The Henbury Cottages, sited as they are, invite critical inspection. They must read not only as a group, but satisfy individually and stand up to scrutiny of detail. Repton's notes about construction accompanying his drawings for Rose Cottage are of sufficient consequence to be transcribed verbatim.[2] He required the walls to be faced in rough stone, irregularly set, with the quoins tooled and joints good. Their rugged texture contrasts with the precise line and pattern of moulded brick chimneys — at some cottages so close to the viewer's eye.[3]

On comparison of the Notebook drawings with Harding's renderings in *Nine Lithographic Views*,[4] and then Repton's delineations with the buildings as they stand, further disparities are revealed. Double Cottage, seen from the green, is virtually as envisaged, yet several changes had been made behind the scenes by the time it was built. Repositioning the ovens and privies not only necessitated modifications to the west elevation, but allowed for relocation of the stairs and other internal adjustments[5] (Plates 38, 39, 42 and 43). The inventory required that alterations to the dormer should be made in order that it would comply with the plan — which had, as it happened, been lost. And Nash complained that the diamond glazing was badly done. Quite apart from workmanship the scale was coarse.[6] The ten-inch brick tiles which Repton considered suitable for the kitchen, scullery and pantry floors may sometimes be found edging gardens or paths, while the stone-coloured paint he had in mind for exterior woodwork would have muted minor features in the interests of overall harmonious colour-tone control.[7]

Of all the dwellings comprising Blaise Hamlet, Circular Cottage is most widely known and it was possibly Nash's favourite design as well. Under a bonnet of thatch, its trim, cosy bee-hive image and miniature scale are redolent of the picture-book English cottage ideal (Plates 52 and 53). When George Repton left Nash's office he followed his father in working at Sarsden, proposing extensive changes to the Oxfordshire house. The church was also to be altered, a new rectory designed and a substantial thatched cottage with tree-trunk columns was remodelled.[8] A shaded drawing of a trimly thatched cottage captioned 'Keepers House Sarsden'[9] (Plate 54) is similar to Circular Cottage at Blaise: and yet another rendering on this happy theme can be seen in a Herefordshire lane.[10]

Repton's *Pavilion Notebook* drawings for Circular Cottage indicate that thatch was intended here from the start. Penthouse eaves, the inventory adds, were to be 'horizontal and level with the top of the lintel the Eaves of all the thatch to be cut level or nearly so in the under side.'—[24], —[25]. Vital to the appeal of Oak Cottage as its recently replaced thatch is now seen to be, Repton's drawings for it offer no hint that either it, or Jasmine, should be roofed in this way (Plates 60, 61 and 62).

A special contribution made by Oak Cottage to Blaise Hamlet is its trunk-flanked porch, set between cruciform windows — devices which earned the sobriquet 'Cross Cottage' for a time.[11] The components of this elevation were also much favoured by Nash. Diversely reassembled from design to design, they appear elsewhere, as on the west front of Jasmine Cottage, only two doors away, but turned from general view (Plates 67 and 68). Another version was designed for H. Vernon,[12] and a fourth was drawn for George Ward, one of Nash's wealthy neighbours on the Isle of Wight[13] (Plate 64).

Here Nash had been building his own maritime equivalent of Knight's Downton Castle exterior since the days when Harford, also reaping the rewards of his endeavours, was constructing Humphry Repton's drive through the woods at Blaise. Nash, his bankruptcy behind him, had invested in property and built at East Cowes a seat of sufficient distinction to place him among the élite of his day. His Castle (Plate 69) was in easy reach of delectable landscapes. As the painter John Hassell (d. 1825) explained in his *Tour of the Isle of Wight* (1790),[14] this island and its vicinities were allowed 'to yield a rich assemblage of all those beauties that enchant the eye.' Its scenic pecularities offered an abundance of winning settings for patternbook cottages in romantic taste: an opportunity the gentry did not entirely overlook.

Lesser works by Nash, and others possibly influenced by his style, proliferated nearby. Villas, a market and guildhall, an institution, cottages and lodges, all engaged his skills. George Repton drew a finial and chimney for Barton Farm, possibly the place that Nash mentioned to Farington in 1821, a month before the diarist's death. This property Nash valued at no less than £30,000 which, he said, was equalled by his East Cowes estate. He had an extra £7,000 per annum as well. He and Mrs. Nash had adopted Miss Pennethorne, her niece, and Nash intended to give her £10,000.[15] Grand sentiments, indeed, when only months earlier he was in debt to the tune of eight-hundred-thousand or even a million pounds, the painter Westall had heard. Nash was at a stand in money matters.[16] He had no family, but could fall to low estate without repining. He was indifferent to his fate. He could live or die. And when, years later, he did so, he was in debt; and it was said that creditors intended to 'arrest' his corpse.

The ubiquitous Pückler-Muskau visited Nash several times, valuing as he did the instruction he received; and he appreciated John Adey Repton's ability sufficiently to employ him at his Muskau estate. The German prince wrote in 1827 of Nash that he was said to have an enormous fortune: 'He has a beautiful country-house, and no artist is more handsomely lodged in town.'[17] This opinion Farington was in a position to confirm, having measured the vista in East Cowes Castle from the end of the dining room to the end of the conservatory by pacing it out to be 120 feet. 'The Dining Room is 30 feet by 20 and 15 feet high. I also measured the Terrace and found it 227 steps.'[18]

Susanna Eleanora Watkins (1768-1847), widow of the Reverend Thomas Watkins (1761-1829), was staying at Vernon Lodge near Ryde in the summer of 1835. Transported by the landscape wonders of the isle, she drove to visit places of picturesque repute, though finding little of interest at West and East Cowes. They had nothing remarkable to offer, 'but Mr. Nashs Castle surpasses anything for Scenery, I have ever seen,' the well-travelled lady from a remote border country estate near Brecon entered in the closing pages of her journal. Nash had just died. His house was empty, and Mrs. Watkins has left for us an all too brief impression of what she saw: 'when the Drawing room door is opened, and you catch the Coup d'Oeil of the Conservatory at one end, and the Magnificent Scenery of this beautiful Island on the other it seems like fairy Land.' In terms of sheer luxury, scale and setting, East Cowes Castle must have been a dazzling spectacle compared with Penoyre, begun by her husband in 1799.[19] The Castle was 'on Sale and happy must anyone be to become its possessor!'[20]

What, one asks, took Mrs. Watkins to Nash's mansion. Was it temporarily open to view? Did she have a special interest in the architect? Perhaps she had known Nash's name from childhood. It is even possible, although there is no evidence on which to base such a suggestion, that Thomas Watkins engaged Nash to build the first Penoyre — Welsh for Golden Head. For Susanna had been a Miss Vaughan, the daughter of Richard Vaughan, of Golden Grove,[21] and it will be recalled that it was John Vaughan of Golden Grove who slipped the *rouleau* of guineas into Nash's bag at the opening of what was to prove the remarkable career that brought him to die here — at East Cowes Castle.

John Lloyd Vaughan Watkins (1802-1865), Thomas's younger son, inherited the estate and built a grand new Penoyre to the design of Anthony Salvin (1799-1881), formerly a pupil of Nash and architect responsible for additions made to Hafod after Thomas Johnes' time. Lloyd (as his family knew him) was to join that celebrated band which numbered Thomas Farr and Valentine Morris in its ranks. By the time Kilvert happened upon it Penoyre was, as it is again today, a sorry sight.[22]

South-east of Nash's embattled mansion, beyond Osborne and Ryde, lay the estate of Edward Simeon at St. John's, which proves to be the scene of another familiar pattern of events, Humphry Repton having preceded Nash in working there.[23] *A New Picture of the Isle of Wight* (1813), advises that 'The taste of Mr. Repton has here been most conspicuous; giving to this estate an ornament beyond what a more laboured and costly edifice would have conferred, and thus furnishing an additional gratification to the numerous annual visiters to the island, whose amusement and convenience it appears to be the liberal wish of Mr. Simeon to promote.' William Cooke then describes this delight: 'Within a handsome railing and gateway the avenue commences, between two charming cottages of stone; whose thatch is disposed in a pleasing manner, and in front thrown forward over a rustic porch, formed by natural trunks of trees.'[24]

Having commented favourably on the manner in which the jesamine and rose entwined around the windows and intermixed with the clematis or virgin's bower that climbed those rustic pillars to adorn the thatch they supported, Cooke tells us more of these cottages themselves, which contained within an eighteen-foot square a sitting-room, bedroom and pantry. One building served as a lodge — the comfortable residence of a cottager who attended Simeon's gate. The other was an occasional retreat for visitors, complete with a rustic seat under the porch, 'where a few books, some neat suitable furniture, and the pleasing novelty of the situation, must give a charm that a fastidious taste can hardly fail to allow.'[25]

The *Pavilion Notebook* includes two pages of drawings for cottages either side of a gate, which not only agree closely with this written description, but also correspond with an engraving illustrating Cooke's text, even to details of the palings and design of the gate (Plates 70and 71). Also, barely visible, is a feeble perspective: sufficient evidence in all to leave little doubt that Nash's office was associated with these novel lodges and that George Repton drew them at least seven years after his father had been active at St. John's.

On returning to Blaise Hamlet, we shall see that the assertive placing of Diamond Cottage (Plates 34 and 37) has been contrived to hold Jasmine Cottage completely from view on entering the green. As Nash's plan unfolds just one more half-anticipated pleasure is introduced in a way reminiscent not only of Knight's lines on taste cautiously revealing its store, but also of Pope's, addressed to Lord Burlington a century before Blaise Hamlet was built:

> Let not each beauty ev'ry where by spy'd,
> Where half the skill is decently to hide.
> He gains all points, who pleasingly confounds,
> Surprises, varies, and conceals the bounds.[26]

However natural the village setting might once have been, and despite their vernacular origins and the architectural conceits employed in designing the cottages, they do not deceive. John Thomas Smith was one artist deeply appreciative of rustic cottage charms, although the kind about which he was moved to write were hardly of the pattern book breed. The genuine order captured his interest; hovels, cots and shacks which acquired their picturesque qualities by way of age, use, adaptation, fortuitous appendages, poverty and dilapidation rather than buildings from the drawing boards of smart London architects. Smith's earthy vision was closer to that of the Northern school of landscape painting — to Ruisdael, Cuyp, Hobbema and Both; the more rugged, with knotty oaks and rutted tracks —, than to the calculated perfections of Poussin, or the luxuriance of Claude.

Smith (who listed John Constable and Colonel Johnes among his subscribers), published his *Remarks on Rural Scenery* in 1797, accepting (as believed by Robinson and illustrated by Nuneham) that in poverty nothing would excite benevolence more than cleanliness and neatness, yet rejoicing in what we might esteem a far more profitable subject, 'the neglected fast-ruinating cottage — the patched plaster, of various tints and discolourations . . . the weather-beaten thatch, bunchy and varied with moss — the mutilated chimney top — the fissures and crevices of the inclining wall — the roof of various angles and inclinations — the tiles of different hues — the fence of bungling workmanship — the wild unrestrained vine, whose "gadding" branches nearly deprive the chambers of their wonted light — the paper-pasted casement, with here and there a whisp of straw stuffed through a broken pane — the decayed bee-hive and the broken basket — the fragment of a chair or bench — the slatternry of tubs and dishes scattered about the door — the mischievous pranks of ragged children — the intrusion of pigs — and the unrepaired accidents of wind and rain — '[27] But unlike Nuneham, such ramshackle hovels offered far greater allurements to the painter's eye.

Although they have roots in a common culture which has exerted strong influence on their respective forms, the carefully considered and sanitary Blaise Hamlet cottages are far removed from the subjects of Smith's exultation.

Unhappily, it is not likely that Blaise Hamlet will ever be seen again as Nash and Harford knew it, even if every cottage were to be restored to its original state. Prince Pückler-Muskau, in his description of it, remembered this *beau-idéal* of a village scene from times before housing estates and motor roads had been allowed to encroach within yards of the cottage boundaries. He knew Blaise Hamlet as a beautiful green space in the midst of the wood — a setting essential to the completeness and tranquillity of these tenements of peace.[28]

Notes to Chapter Nine

1. Robert SOUTHEY, 'The Devil's Walk', *The Morning Post,* 6 Sept. 1799.
2. Appendix III.
3. RIBA. JAR *delin.* [4] (K1/19), (no dated wmk.), and Repton's Notebook drawing for Rose Cottage (Pl.47), show the stack placed symmetrically astride the roof apex, the former drawing with two shafts, the latter with three. It was actually built against the main west wall, asymmetrically. *Nine Lithographic Views* shows both two and three shafts in different views.
4. *Nine Lithographic Views of the Cottages, Composing Blaise Hamlet* (n.d.).

Unlike the plan P52/7 (in the Harford Papers), Ashmead's (1826) shows cottage garden boundaries and a key numbering and naming the cottages (Pl.34, 35).

5. Reece WINSTONE, *Bristol as it Was,* 1967, Pl.88 (1866), shows the right window only under the penthouse, as built. Later, a second window was inserted. RIBA. JAR *delin.* [3] (K1/17, ii), perspective (Pl.40), shows Double Cottage with one window placed centrally under the pent, but the accompanying plan (wmk. 1830) shows the window to the right.
6. Bristol R.O. 28048, P52/8. See Appendix IV:-[26],-[27].
7. Appendix III.
8. 'Cottage Ornée: Sarsgrove House, Oxfordshire', *Connoisseur,* Dec. 1956, pp. 222-225. RIBA. GSR [33] (K2/14, i-iii), Sarsgrove Cottage; plan and two perspectives, one wmk. 1829.
9. RIBA. GSR [32] (K2/12, i), no dated wmk.
10. See Chapter 10, Dewsall Lodge.
11. Avon Reference Library. Braikenridge, i, p. 264.
12. *RIBA Notebook.* Possibly at Hilton Park, Staffordshire.
13. *Pavilion Notebook.*
14. John HASSELL, *Tour of the Isle of Wight,* 1790, i, p.vi. He imitated closely Gilpin's work, especially in his illustrations.
15. James GREIG (ed.), *The Farington Diary,* 1928, viii, pp. 301-302: see also John SUMMERSON, *John Nash — Architect to King George IV,* 1949, pp. 87-90: 273-274 gives details of Nash's death, will, burial, etc. W. PAGE (ed.), *Victoria History of Hampshire and the Isle of Wight,* 1912, v, p. 274, states that Nash bought the manor of Ningwood in 1806. Nash's widow devised it to John Pennethorne and his sister Anne.
16. GREIG, *op. cit.,* viii, p. 275, 27 Feb. 1821.
17. [Hermann PÜCKLER-MUSKAU], *Tour in Germany, Holland and England, in the Years 1826, 1827 & 1828,* 1832, iv, p. 85, 14 July 1827. An abridged edn., by E.M. BUTLER (ed.), *A Regency Visitor,* 1957, includes a biographical essay on the astonishing life-style of the prince.
18. GREIG, *op. cit.,* viii, p. 302.
19. C.P. FENDALL & E.A. CRUTCHLEY (eds.), *The Diary of Benjamin Newton,* 1933, p. 18; Penoyre (earlier 'Pennoyre'), records a very handsome ground floor of four rooms, one of which had a circular end, and another was a complete circle.
20. Author's colln.
21. Elsie PRITCHARD, *Penoyre,* 1969, gives an account of the family and estate.
22. William PLOMER (ed.), *Kilvert's Diary,* 1938, i, p. 215, 25 Aug. 1870. Penoyre was empty and for sale Aug. 1977.
23. Dorothy STROUD, *Humphry Repton,* 1962, p. 106, states that H. Repton

worked for Simeon *c.* 1798 and she raises the question of Humphry's possible contribution to Nash's own estate on the island at about that time.

24. William COOKE, *A New Picture of the Isle of Wight*, 1813 (2nd edn.). An engraved plate dated 1812 shows the 'Lodge or Cottage Entrance to St. John's': another, facing p. 74, depicts the seat of Edward Simeon. See Howard COLVIN, *Biographical Dictionary of British Architects, 1600-1840*, 1978, p. 681.
25. COOKE, *op. cit.*, pp. 77-79.
26. Alexander POPE, 'Epistle IV,' *Moral Essays*, 1732, quoted from the edition of 1767, ii, p. 281.
27. John Thomas SMITH, *Remarks on Rural Scenery; with twenty etchings of cottages, from Nature; and some observations and precepts relative to the Pictoresque*, 1797, pp. 8-9.
28. [Hermann PÜCKLER-MUSKAU], *Tour in England, Ireland, and France, in the Years 1828 & 1829*, 1832, ii, p. 204, 21 Dec. 1828. Of the four vols., i & ii are of this title: iii & iv as in n.17.

From a plan and elevations by George Repton for a cottage at 'Spring Grove'

10 *The Village Picturesque – An Early Vision Realised?*

MAN is a changeful creature at his best;
He builds, and plants, and then he goes to rest;
And never shall return; no, never, never. —
When time on earth is gone, 'tis gone for ever.[1]

One of our aims has been to investigate the possibility of Nash having projected or actually built a picturesque cottage group before he embarked on his commission at Blaise Hamlet. Apart from close relations, or even identical twins of the individual cottages being scattered about the countryside, was there really no precursor of the whole?

The Park Villages are well known.[2] In some respects they did relate to Blaise Hamlet, and they might have done so far more closely in style of building also had one of Nash's proposals come about (Plate 72). The Park Villages differ in that they were suburban developments built about fourteen years after the Hamlet, and our concern is with rustic precedents for Blaise rather than with its successors.[3]

Only one shred of evidence that Nash might have had an earlier opportunity to plan a picturesque village has been recorded and even that might not bear on events before 1810. In 1829 Nash's speculative enterprises and his alleged unsatisfactory handling of public funds were, as has been mentioned, the subject of questions in the House. The report of a Select Committee had exonerated him,[4] but such was the hostility that Nash felt it necessary to make his side of the case known, which he did in his privately printed *Statement*, of 1829. He mentioned the Park Villages, regarding them as 'a source of occupation and amusement' in his old age and added, 'It happened to me to have formed in another part of the Kingdom a village such as I in this instance contemplated.'[5] This could, of course, have been at Henbury. Yet the possibility that Nash had another project in mind cannot immediately be dismissed.

George Repton's *RIBA Notebook* has long been accessible and its contents have been listed in print for many years,[6] so any obvious clues it might contain are likely to have been detected already by others. However, the *Pavilion Notebook* is virtually unknown. It is, therefore, just possible that some cottage designs, uncaptioned or for anonymous clients, drawn up intermittently and previously unidentified, could have been for one client or site and comprised a coherent group.

Whereas Harford's cottage designs in the *Pavilion Notebook* are named as being for him and contained within a limited spread of pages, some others, widely dispersed (perhaps through both Notebooks), prove to have been made for three clients, all with long-standing connections with Nash and with mainland country estates in their possession. They are John Edwards of Rheola, near Neath, in South Wales, John Matthews of Belmont, near Hereford and George Legh of High Legh, in Cheshire.

Repton's drawings for any one of them might, because of their number or variety, have been compactly sited and have contributed to, or in one instance even comprised, a small estate village.[7]

The fact that many pages of the *Pavilion Notebook* after the 1818 drawings are unused could well be accounted for, as that was a momentous year for George. The news of his secret marriage broke. This was to a woman several years his senior, though (Farington recorded on New Year's Day) despite being nearly forty, she owned only to being thirty-six. She was no picturesque dairy maid either, but Lady Elizabeth Scott, daughter of the Lord Chancellor of England, no less. Lord Eldon, her father, was not amused[8] and Nash was, or affected to be, much offended by Repton. Farington put it like this: '. . . Eldon's daugr. . . . having resided much with Mr & Mrs Nash in the Isle of Wight, Repton, who also frequently became an inmate there, had much intercourse with Her. — Mr & Mrs Nash are gone to Paris, it is supposed to be out of the way at this time'.[9] Humphry probably died well satisfied with his talented son's recent conquest. In due course all was forgiven, and Repton, who stayed on some time with Nash, continued to practise 'in a desultory way'.[10]

One commission executed by George Repton at about the date of parting was for the Aberystwyth Assembly Room, built only yards from Price's eccentric Castle House of thirty years earlier. An embattled romantic symbol of Nash's misty past, this must have made a quaint contrast to his assitant's crisply modelled and urbane classical rooms, within whose stuccoed walls John Scandrett Harford junior was to find one door closed against him in a highly favoured life. Here, in 1849, he addressed disappointed Conservative supporters after his Parliamentary election defeat.[11] He failed twice before abandoning such ambitions, his earlier contest having been in 1842.

There is a drawing of the extant Assembly Room in the Repton Bequest, but attention must be turned from that to the elevation of another building in Wales appearing early in the *Pavilion Notebook*. It depicts a simple dwelling with an angular bay rising through both floors (Plate 73) alongside a short verandah. The accompanying plan shows the return side to include the door and porch. It is inscribed 'Farm house for Mr Edwards — in Wales'.[12]

Under 'Rheola Families', Phillips' *History of the Vale of Neath*[13] gives biographical information on Edwards, Nash's collaborator and possibly a relative, who was implicated in charges that the Select Committee investigated. He came from and was buried in Lambeth and shared with Nash the handsome double town-mansion at 14-16 Regent Street, on which both Farington and Pückler-Muskau commented. It is said that it cost them £39,000 — a very substantial sum.

John Edwards (1772-1833) came into the Rheola estate, which it is believed was bought for him around 1800 by his father, also a John Edwards (*c.* 1738-1818), from Lambeth.

It is easy to relate George Repton's drawing to the existing west front, as at a glance they fit (Plate 74). But, on considering plans and measurements, close comparison is frustrated, not only in relation to the altered interior, but to the façade and details as well. Presuming that the design Repton drew was actually constructed without amendment, possibly very little of that building remains visible today.

We must next look at the Repton Bequest perspective and plan of a substantial cottage, on the mount of which a caption states that it was at Blaise Hamlet[14] (Plate 75). First it must be said that although it is not impossible that such a design was submitted to Harford, no such building was constructed at Blaise Hamlet. Further, it is unlikely that once the Hamlet as a whole had been envisaged a building of this plan and scale would have been considered. However, a house to this same design was constructed a decade later. And it still stands, shorn of its west-facing bay window, the log-columned loggia infilled and the north end built on to, half a mile east of Edwards' house at Rheola[15] (Plate 76). Although the Bequest drawings give no indication of the steeply sloping Rheola site, they comply, even to the placing of bushes, with Repton's drawings for a Steward's House — those same drawings of October 1818 in the *Pavilion Notebook* (Plates 77 and 78). It is possible then that this dwelling was the last cottage to be supervised for Nash by Repton before their professional association ended.

There is a further set of *Pavilion Notebook* drawings for a farmhouse, typically Nash in general and more specifically so in showing diagonal chimney shafts, dormer windows, a stone porch and a canopy with paired supports set over a seat (Plate 79). By mid-century a new main road and drive had been constructed south of Rheola House, alongside the old Neath Canal. Today, a stone-built lodge of 1860s character stands at their junction and although it bears no obvious resemblance to the farmhouse elevation Repton drew, it has a pair of diagonally set chimneys and, at the front, a pent roof — just as in the farmhouse elevational drawing which Repton made (Plate 80).

The prime intention of this excursion into South Wales was to establish whether or not Nash produced for Edwards a picturesque village on the Rheola estate. Without exploring further Edwards' enterprises there, or the relationship between the two men, we are obliged on the strength of present evidence to find that no such group was constructed. The buildings so far identified are well dispersed and of varying character and scale. While the house itself was greatly enlarged by stages, the minor buildings amount to no more than one might find added to any developing estate of those times.

Although a large aluminium factory has invaded Edwards' valley his influence here can still be strongly felt. It was also sensed by William Weston Young in 1835. He versified his feelings thus:—

> I paint the scene before me, e'er a stone
> Was laid in yonder building, now so fair.
> I knew its master when he stood alone,
> And mark'd his progress up to wealth and care;
>
> But now he's gone, and all the beauteous scene
> Is lost to him, who plann'd it in his thought:
> He liv'd to catch a view: death came between;
> He pass'd, and all to him is now forgot.[16]

Mention has been made of John Matthews (1755-1826) and of a connection between him and Farington. Dr. Matthews, having resigned his position at St. George's Hospital, London, retired prematurely to Clehonger, near Hereford, and by 1790 had built Belmont, overlooking the Wye, to the design of James Wyatt.[17] Characteristically for an educated landowner of his day, Matthews became Colonel of the local militia and served as a justice and M.P. while following in parallel another familiar if more self-indulgent path as gardener, writer and patron of architectural arts. In the pursuit of these pleasures his marriage to an heiress in 1788 might well have played a significant part. Less characteristically for one of his station, he became a mayor, senior alderman for twenty years and was father of fourteen children, one of whom he had taken to London in 1794 on the breakfasting occasion with Farington already alluded to.[18]

In that same year Knight published his *Landscape* and Matthews, it is believed, was the anonymous author of *A Sketch from the Landscape* (Plate 6), a poem which defended Brown and attacked Knight's published views. Knight took advantage of the opportunity offered by his 1795 edition to deny publicly ever having read, let alone pillaged, Mason's *English Garden*. Rather remarkably, he had hardly even heard of it. Not without some justification, Knight chastised his adversary's satire: a bungling attempt, it was; 'a sort of doggerel ode . . . this contemptible publication', which opened with these promising lines:

> BOLD KNIGHT, who salliest forth in rhymes
> Against the monsters of the times,
> From REPTON up to BROWN, that thick sot;
> Well dost thou these enchanters maul,
> Like any AMADIS DE GAUL,
> ORLANDO, HUDIBRAS, or QUIXOTE . . .

It concluded:

> Now peering with prophetic eye,
> I see BROWN'S thread-bare genius fly ---
> Like tail-burnt dog, he seeks his den!
> Rollers are sunk, scythes break, clumps fall,
> REPTON *and Co.* shall, one and all,
> Cry, 'Chaos comes again!'
>
> Triumphant KNIGHT! to give thy name
> A passport to immortal fame,
> What shall the grateful world agree on ?
> . . . Thy statue of Colossal size,
> In ductile yew, shall nobly rise ---
> (Think not thy modesty shall 'scape us)
> The *God of Gardens* thou shalt stand,
> To fright improvers from the land,
> A huge and terrible *Priapus*.[19]

Over and above his literary achievements Matthews was greatly respected locally. A contributed obituary observed that his death had excited 'a greater degree of public regret than we have ever before witnessed': his genius embraced every department of classical and elegant literature. His poetical effusions were of that peculiar grace and felicity never to be forgotten 'and the scenery of our highly favoured county has borrowed additional charms from his tasteful hand.' Perhaps picturesque thatched cottages clustered around his gates, or tree-trunked lodges punctuated the boundaries of his estate, for we are also told that his possessions became discernible at a glance.[20]

Probably so, a hundred and fifty years ago. But detection on the ground today of those architectural embellishments drawn for Matthews by Repton has not proved so simple. Perhaps they were never even built. The *RIBA Notebook* yields three proposals — a cottage of uneasy articulation, a Tudoresque gatehouse-like building in a wall and a 'gymnastum' of single cell and Grecian form which, like the 'gatehouse', cannot be found. Neither can the cottage be placed with confidence. The *Pavilion Notebook* offers two more possibilities — a semi-detached pair of cottages(Plate 81) and 'No. 2 Spring Grove' (Plate 82); and had it not been that a Brother of Belmont Abbey chanced to photograph an isolated whitewalled dwelling in 1939 the latter might well have passed unrecorded. Twenty five years later, ruined, vandalised, derelict and soon to be burned, it was photographed again. The cottage, though altered, complied in every important way with Repton's drawings for Spring Grove (Plate 83). Similarly, a snapshot of Belmont post office appears to account for the pair, removed without trace early in 1967[21] (Plate 84).

There, if one relies on the Notebooks alone as a guide, Matthews' architectural ventures with Nash might rest. However, it appears that he built at least two cottages more.

Lake Cottage (once Woodman's Cottage) is set inconspicuously and low behind a hedge, opposite the post office site and a turning to Belmont House. Ornate chimneys have been replaced and its decorative thatch is believed to have been a victim of steam-waggon sparks. Inspection suggests that the roadside front once contained an open porch (possibly with a neatly fitted seat and tree-trunk columns) and arrow-slit windows opening in flanking walls, this now familiar assemblage being topped by a dormer set in a roof of forty-five degree pitch (Plate 85).

Price's Foxley is only six miles distant and Repton's drawings for him (Plate 87) share with Lake Cottage as it was a five-columned loggia[22] (Plate 86). Although the lakeside cottage was very much like Oak Cottage at Blaise Hamlet, it was even closer to one for H. Vernon — adjacent to Price's cottage drawings in Repton's book.[23]

Dewsall Lodge is prominently poised at a bend in the lane, two miles south of this miniature lake. While its presence demands attention, the full truth of its probable ancestry might not immediately register, as it now presents a 'black-and-white' image (Plate 88). Transform the colour and texture of this brick-built cottage with natural stone rubble; replace new chimneys with a diagonally-set pair; reinstate a horizontal axis by replacing the sweeping curve of its low-set penthouse, and Circular Cottage at Blaise Hamlet will re-appear: and also, for that matter, the Keeper's House at

Sarsden (Plates 53 and 54).[24]

Matthews' reputation as an exemplary landowner, his literary activites, and the likelihood that Nash provided at least six cottage designs for him (two very much akin to those at Blaise), are clues enough to encourage the thought that another Hamlet might have distinguished the Belmont estate. But we must continue our search elsewhere — northwards, to Shropshire — for more positive evidence of his early involvement in village design, as it appears that in the main Matthews' cottages were on scattered sites. So we turn next to an estate near Shrewsbury, where the second Lord Berwick employed both Nash and Humphry Repton on improvements more grandiose and sweeping than those undertaken by the Herefordshire squires. We must also leave for the moment Repton's Notebooks, as these prove not to be our guide at Attingham Park, where George Steuart had provided a lofty classical mansion for the first Lord Berwick shortly before his death in 1789, and for which Humphry Repton submitted a *Red Book* to his son, Thomas Noel Hill, nine years later.

Re-routing public ways that passed through private estates was common enough practice at the time for Harford, Edwards and (as will be seen) Legh all to have done so to improve their parks. The second Lord Berwick, about four years after seeking Repton's views, and having returned recently from Italy 'with his luggage full of works of art and his mind full of the romantic landscape paintings which he had been studying',[25] set about further improving the estate left to him by his father.

In April 1802 a Special Sessions was held at Atcham (bordering the Park) and Berwick's offer to provide a new public road in place of the one that wandered across his grounds to Upton Forge was accepted.[26] As a result, he enjoyed a new degree of privacy, free from the gaze of curious trippers and rustics. They in turn, although no doubt losing a source of much gossip and entertainment benefited as Berwick had stated they would by a new road, 'more Commodious to the Publick' and a hundred yards shorter than the old.

Berwick's thinly veiled altruism allowed him simultaneously to improve further his main entrance, which earlier had been to the east, towards Tern Bridge. Repton had criticised it. It was all too close. His proposed remedy — to build two lodges near Tern Bridge and allow the road to pass between them — had been at least in part acted upon, so that the stranger would be led to believe that he passed through the park, not on the outside of it.[27] At least one lodge was built and a previously unidentified drawing of it attributed to John Repton may be seen in the Repton Bequest.

The approach developed from Atcham village was happily placed to take advantage of John Gwynn's handsome bridge over the Severn, by which travellers might pass from Shrewsbury to the mansion, leaving Atcham and the main road behind them on passing through the screen, which Nash provided by about 1807.

It is at this point — the intersection of Watling Street, Berwick's carriage drive through his park, the new public road, and Atcham village street — that we must now look more closely.

Before Humphry Repton's arrival the roadside adjacent to the existing main gates at Atcham was flanked to the north by houses. An undated map (apparently of late eighteenth century origin) shows about nineteen buildings here, a 'New Road to Berwick' breaking the row to run across what is now the Park, to Attingham Hall (Plate 89). A note reads, 'this Road & all the Houses on this side of it thrown into the Lawn.'[28] By 1793 the row had been depleted and between the surviving buildings and the *Mytton and Mermaid Hotel* (opposite to them) the main road emerged from Gwynn's bridge, to open suddenly into a triangular space, rather like a village green[29] (Plate 90). This feature appears on the Quarter Sessions plan of 1802 as well.

Accounts show that Nash was being paid by Berwick from 1800. In 1802 he designed a superbly sited Steward's house at nearby Cronkhill and by 1803 he was Berwick's principal architect. Work on the new art gallery, also to Nash's design, was all but completed by 1807.[30]

In that same year an estate plan[31] records significant changes around the 'village green.' Only one building survived on the north and part of the verge had been planted. But most intriguing of all the changes was that a circular plot, also planted, had been created in the centre of the 'green'. It was like an island coppice in the middle of the road: this at a time when what is now the *Mytton and Mermaid Hotel* was known as the *Talbot Inn* (Plate 91). By 1846 the Tithe Map had been drawn. It confirms these earlier impressions as the Apportionment describes plot 305 — the island coppice — as 'Wood in Road'.[32] It was in the ownership of Lord Berwick.

All these changes, and others south of the main road, could pass as interesting enough though typical of their time when considered through maps alone. Yet today few can fail to notice the three-light gothick window facing Gwynn's bridge on the north end of a cottage terrace (Plate 95). It is a sophisticated device, both generous in character and well placed to catch the visitor's eye. However, its fuller significance could only be appreciated after examination of seven painted panels, depicting rustic cottages, which were found recently at Attingham Hall. One portrays a general village scene and the others include individual portraits of cottages prominent in the group — which also shows a small wood encircled by a road.[33] Beyond are several pretty cottages cunningly disposed, displaying abundantly those details that we have come to associate with Nash's cottage work (Plate 92). Thatch, peaked dormer windows, angular bays, porches, pents, a gable-end pigeon-loft, loggy columns and open lean-to sheds all decorate rustic buildings of similar scale and entertaining in their varied forms. On the right hangs a sign charged with a belligerent beast — possibly a talbot heraldically displayed.

An inn at 'Addingham', Sir John Summerson has noted,[34] was designed by Nash at an unknown date. In relation to the cottage terrace the *Talbot* would have stood just about where the hanging sign is shown in the general view of the village.

The individual 'portraits' show the cottages on a larger scale and in more detail, so they tell us more. One — of the terrace — is a key to the possible site (Plate 93). Take the overall proportions, chimneys, dormers, fenestration, mullions, transomes and doorways for a start. All of them relate closely to the row now opposite Attingham gates (Plate 94). Differences between the terrace as depicted and the building as it stands can reasonably be accounted for: but one more important comparison must be made. On the end of the terrace in the painting, shadowy as this passage is, can be seen a gothick-windowed bay, facing (as it were) Gwynn's bridge. It is very much like the one to be seen there today[35] (Plate 95).

Finally, on the back of the panel showing a round-towered riverbank cottage — a sort of peasant's edition of Cronkhill — is a paper label inscribed in a Nash-like hand. It reads, 'Cottages & Village belonging to The Rt. Honble Lord Berwick at Attingham'. Then, to this unequivocal caption is added, 'J Nash 28 Dover Street Piccadilly' — his temporary address before moving to number 29, early in 1800.

While there is no reason to presume that when Nash wrote to Lord Methuen at Corsham in September 1799 of his plans to call at Attingham and Downton Castle[36] he had any intention of discussing with Berwick the possibility of creating an Atcham Hamlet, it could be that such a vision was in his mind's eye or already under discussion. Inspired, but possibly disappointed by earlier experience, he could have been seeking a client like Berwick who was wealthy, landed, and enthused by painting, park-making and the picturesque.

Be that as it may, on the evidence presented it is apparent that Berwick and Nash were at one point seriously considering a composed cottage group at the entrance to Attingham Hall. It is possible, too, that Repton had his part to play in their plans. But even if, as yet, there is no firm evidence to suggest that such a scheme as the panels depict was ever completed, it is reasonable to suppose that at least a start was made, either by conversion, or by rebuilding the terrace from scratch. Close by are some other cottages showing a professional touch[37] and later road improvements might have swept more away, as they have the island coppice.

Whatever the full facts might eventually reveal, Nash's Dover Street address suggests that he had formed detailed plans for the village redevelopment a full decade before the building of Blaise Hamlet. That he might have offered Berwick painted visualisations of what was proposed is borne out by a letter Nash wrote to George Legh in connection with his estate near Knutsford, fifty-odd miles distant, perhaps earlier still.

By 1797 Humphry Repton was preparing his *Red Book* for Lord Berwick, who kept his landscape gardener waiting a week for an appointment at Attingham. This caused Repton unanticipated expense. By the time he eventually arrived at High Legh, the seat of George John Legh (1769-1832), this second client had departed. So Repton celebrated his own forty-fifth birthday with the aid of a bottle of the absentee's claret, completed his tasks about the estate, and borrowed enough money to see himself home. During that journey in his jolting post-chaise he wrote a most interesting letter — the first of a series between himself and Legh, in which lively correspondence Nash was shortly to join.[38] In this final excursion an attempt is made to interpret what those letters imply.

Humphry wrote of the two days just spent with Nash surveying the High Legh estate and he recorded for Legh their opinions on aspects of it such as fencing and planting, and offered advice on how to improve the approach to his stables. But the most significant topic to us, and the only one we can pursue at the moment, is that very one sought since our enquiry began. Legh had invited Repton and Nash to give their opinions on laying out a village to the west of High Legh Hall. Before Repton posted his letter at St. Albans on May 5, one of his sons who was travelling with him transcribed a copy for Nash in order that he would be fully informed on the recommendations Repton had made on behalf of them both.[39]

Repton, no stranger to this part of Cheshire, had on the 10th of October 1791, signed a *Red Book* which had been hastily prepared for Legh so that decisions might be made before he set forth on travels abroad.[40] The essence of Repton's analysis and the remedial treatment he suggested for this narrow estate was in some ways similar to the advice he was later to give Lord Berwick on Attingham Park. In both, the highway passed too close to the house. Scenic deceits should be employed to present 'the idea of the high road passing thro' the park and not skirting it.' Besides, a man of Legh's standing should not have a house so sited as 'to convey the idea of those Mansions which spring up like Mushrooms near great Cities, and which are more the habitation of sudden

Affluence, than the Antient dwelling of Family Inheritance.'

Few families in England could lay better claim to such a distinction, as already by the twelfth century it had been established here long enough for two distinct branches to have emerged — the (Egerton) Leighs of West Hall and the (Cornwall) Leghs of East Hall, or High Legh Hall, as the Georgian rebuilding was known. With two manors, two mansions, two squires, two chapels, two inns and an intricate intermixing of land ownership developing over many centuries, landscape improvements presented particular problems at High Legh: problems not diminished by the two Halls being only a few yards apart.[41]

Repton recommended that the east-west, Knutsford-Warrington road should be diverted away from the house, from immediately north of the already existing Village Cross and *Red Lion Inn* to some twenty yards to its south. In a hollow between these two routings a new gate could be opened into Legh's pleasure garden for travellers from the north and for servicing the house. As Repton put it: 'at this gate a porters lodge may be hereafter placed with great propriety, and utility'. By 1797 the road had been diverted and a lodge was all but complete. Opposite was a small rough green on which 'the Rugged Cottages' — a blacksmith's, and to its north a building sometime called Partington's — stood. West Hall drive and Legh's chapel gate both opened on to the north of this little green (Plate 98).

It was round about this site, the scene being substantially set by established ingredients and the implementation already made of his earlier scheme that Repton, with Nash and George Legh, attempted planning a picturesque village.

Legh knew what he wanted, up to a point. It was for the two professionals to calculate visual effects, devise detailed plans, estimate costs and advise on how to realise the envisaged ideal.

Repton's 'post-chaise' report and the correspondence that ensued give us something more than an understanding of the general course of events. Some insights into the partners' professional procedures, attitudes and relationships are gained too. Nash, who appears generally to have gone along with Legh's views, was remarkably uninhibited in expressing his opinions about the client's estate. To take one instance; in letter dated 24 June 1797, in a passage advising Legh on his existing fencing on either side of the road, his 'obliged obedient humble servant' felt able to say of Legh's hurdles that they were the ugliest grotesque things he had ever seen. Repton, on the other hand, while showing that he could be inflexible and tenacious about views that he held, could also be excruciatingly polite. When writing to Legh, he was usually prepared to gloss over differences of opinion he had aired with his partner.

Nash, in contrast again, was not above scoring over Repton in similar circumstances, thereby putting his partner in a disadvantageous light.[42]

Repton's firmly held opinion was that no new buildings should be constructed on Legh's boundary east of the green. The new Lodge and long-existing chapel presented no problems, but Legh's pleasure grounds should be kept private, and they should be seen to be so. For this reason the *Red Lion* was a totally unacceptable intrusion. It should be demolished and rebuilt south of the cross roads. Repton went further. Not only should there be no cottages east of the green, but those already on it should go as well. Yet only two new ones could be built on what land remained fronting the green and they would not by any means meet the owner's needs. What was more, West Hall would gain in prominence by such an arrangement at George Legh's expense. 'Without much vanity', Legh replied in his draft letter, 'I think it is not advisable to give the property of others close to you more consequence than it has.'[43] Repton had misunderstood. Legh wished to meet his neighbour's request that the green should be enlarged to the west and that enough land should be given from adjoining Egerton-Leigh territory to allow for new building on that side. Legh, having explained this to Repton, had to 'lay it down as data to go on that there should be Cottages on each side of the road — '[44]

Repton accepted, probably with relief, the notion of an extension. He replied with apparent nonchalence, 'the larger the area of the Village Green — the more airy & cheerful it will make it — '[45] But he stood firm about not building to its east. By early in 1798 Nash had been persuaded. On sending their plan at about that time he explained that Repton wanted the appearance of an extensive boundary there and 'a cottage on that side would certainly interupt besides the unpleasant intrusion of a cottager under your pales — to this reasoning good in itself we had only to oppose the want of Cottages — of course being convinced I gave way — '[46]

The inn and blacksmith's shop were key buildings in the proposal and they would be prominently set. About them and the green eight cottages, two of them doubles, would be scattered — not in confusion, let it be understood, but in accordance with principles of picturesque intricacy. Travellers would easily see why each cottage was so placed. Clearly, despite the early date, this was to be no Nuneham or Milton Abbas arrangement: something far more in the spirit of Price's picturesque was in mind. Careful planting would remedy the 'nuisance' of cottagers entering into the view of the village: a precaution betraying attitudes clinical, if not cynical and far removed from the popular concept of an English village green animated by reminiscing rustic worthies and jolly ragged peasants. No crones would gossip at these wicket gates.

Clumps would intercept cottages and screen back gardens. Judiciously planned plantations would direct the fascinated traveller's eye to perceive these enchanting cottages unfolding — one by one — to his view: to be glimpsed through the elegant stems of carefully ordered trees.

Perhaps such principles were to guide Nash's hand when designing Blaise Hamlet, years later. Is this why only Double Cottage, focal point on entering, has a door facing the green? Certainly, in the case of High Legh, Nash thought in terms of an art object for the personal delectation of the owner and visitors. There is no hint that philanthropic considerations entered into the reckoning at all at this stage.

For those so fortunate as to leave by way of the lodge a different order of visual pleasures was in store. Held from view as far as the exit from Legh's drive, the new inn, cottages and blacksmith's shop would, as one, burst into the beholder's view. Even the forge would be so placed that at night it would enliven the village scene. Let Nash explain: 'we turned the smiths shop to look up the road so that the fire may illuminate the whole length of road and give a chearfulness at night to the whole village'.

Although Nash's letter closed on a note of hope that Legh would find their village to be what he expected, the client's response to the detailed proposal remains unkown. We must therefore turn to indirect evidence of it and speculate on whether or not this imaginative scheme was ever adopted in principle and put into effect.

Quite early in the *RIBA Notebook* is a perspective drawing of a sizeable and highly picturesque building which complies with plans and elevations appearing there later of an 'Inn to be built in Cheshire' for G.J. Legh (Plate 99): plans which do not agree, as it happens, with the written description made by Nash of intentions in 1798.[47] The *Pavilion Notebook* contains drawings for a blacksmith's cottage and, among others, designs for a lodge and school-house too. All were for Legh, and as the book is dated 1805, we must conclude that the drawings were all made some years after the High Legh village proposals: and nothing suggests that any were built to comply with the plan Nash and Repton submitted to Legh[48] (Plate 100).

Was the idea abandoned because of Repton's intransigence? Did the partners press their own ideas too hard against Legh's? Whatever the reason Nash, typically it would now seem, fostered a long-lasting connection with the owner: not that he was conspicuously backward in opening opportunities for himself anyway. The case of (Repton's?) nearly completed lodge by the green illustrates this well. From the start Nash ridiculed its appearance, as in his letter of 24 June: 'I am sorry to say I do not like the lodge but it may be helped by the form of the Piers and a little change in the outer form to give it less the appearance of the small octagon tea Caddies.' And if Legh wished Nash to redesign the Lodge, he would need the working drawings: 'It may be done now at a little expence as the building is but just coverd in and no Stucco done'. Later, having pointed up a small difference which had arisen with Repton, Nash closed with a parting shot at the miserable lodge: 'it is incorrigible — and so like the small oblong octagon tea cadies that I wonder you can bear it'.[49] Then, in January 1798, his campaign of attrition met with total success. On hearing of Legh's intention to demolish the new building, Nash wrote, 'I congratulate you on that determination'. Then he delivered his *coup de grâce*: 'and I should recommend that in future no lodge be seen but only a handsome Archway and the lodge a mere leantoo building against the wall':[50] and who better to design one, Legh might well have asked himself, than Nash? Perhaps he was even tempted to have a painted visualisation of the proposed handsome archway, as Nash had already offered to depict the cottages: 'much of the effect of this village will depend on the detaild form of the cottages — if you wish me to make them out, it will be necessary for you to inform me . . . the expence of working drawings compleat will be 3 Gns. each Cottage. if a painting of each Cottage such as you have seen 3 Gns each'.[51] And which cottage paintings had Legh been shown? Were they Lord Berwick's, for Atcham, one wonders, especially as two similar panels, passed down through a Pennethorne, very recently came to light? Although there is nothing to connect the paintings with High Legh, it is of interest to find that one shows a Nash-like cottage and the other a stone entrance arch with a cottage lodge attached to one side[52] (Plate 101). Although the arch is grander than the one Nash suggested it would hardly be unique if in this case an architect's idea had matured by the time it was presented for the client's further consideration.

High Legh is now only a relic of the place it once was. The combined agencies of further nineteenth-century road works, war-time military occupation, the demolition of both mansions, recent removal of the Village Cross and clearing for a housing estate have transformed almost beyond detection the exact chosen spot on which three men considered creating their perfection of the village picturesque twelve years before the promise was fulfilled by one of their number at Blaise (Plate 102).

Yet, despite the sweeping local changes, John Nash, George Repton, their patron George Legh and John Scandrett Harford would have responded to the Chaplain's House standing in a rich shrubland setting.[53] Built as a schoolhouse for the Misses Legh, its front is almost a duplicate of Double Cottage at Blaise, and drawings for it in the *Pavilion Notebook* are adjacent to those of Harford's version — quite different in plan (Plates 39, 42, 103 and

104). This suggests that Nash's connection with Legh endured, a suspicion confirmed by a letter to him from East Cowes Castle, of 6 July 1810: 'I herewith send you the working drawings of the School Cottage and also of the blacksmiths Cottage. I have not the least doubt that you will like them if they are correctly executed', Nash advised his client reassuringly: 'nor can they be formed better for œconomical building'.[54] By the same token then, we can take it that Legh's needs for the blacksmith had not been fully met by this time, although a smithy was built (perhaps it was this one) at some time, well west of High Legh Green.

Nash told Legh that he was seeking to advance his assistant: 'Mr George Repton who you know was brought up with me is to receive a Moiety of all Cottages farmhouses & picturesque buildings — my object in this is to promote him and any Commissions you can recommend to us in that way will advance my views with regard to him.' Nash then adds another interesting sidelight on Repton's career in this postscript to the letter about the School-house: 'he also has commenced general Architect but his commission with me at present extends only to these sort of buildings I recommend him to you as deserving of patronage and I have no doubt of his acquitting himself to your satisfaction.'

Written at just the time that work was under way at Blaise Hamlet, this letter, seen in isolation, might highlight again the question of authorship of the cottages there. However, we now know that George Repton awaited designs from Nash before he was able to forward working drawings of them to Harford at Blaise. Although the extent of any personal contribution to the designs is unknown, we can now take it that by mid-1810 Nash considered his assistant a capable architect, if still acting under direction as a member of his staff.

Even if plans for Legh's picturesque village never materialised, in the minds of the partners and on paper the whole idea was all but complete at the point where this revealing correspondence ends. Nash and Repton were in general agreement not only about the placing of cottages, but also on details such as planting, palings and footpaths. As at Blaise Hamlet, where Cockerell's notes provided our answer, we are faced again with the vital question — who conceived the idea of this picturesque village? Was it Repton, or Nash, or Legh?

Bearing in mind Cockerell's explanation, the Attingham panels and Nash's enthusiastic letter of explanation to Legh, it might well be considered likely that the inspiration came from Nash. Repton, in his 'post-chaise' letter (which it will be recalled was copied for Nash), suggested that the recommendations had been jointly arrived at: 'both Mr. Nash & I shrink from the idea of a row like almshouses — or the appendages of a manufactory . . . we should like to make the doors open on the sides or back of the houses that the fronts to the gardens & Turnpike might be kept neat'. But even weeks later Nash gave Legh a quite different slant on the matter and again took the chance to score at Repton's expense. 'Mr Repton suggested the putting them [the cottages] in a Row but I must step out of the slippers and inveigh against so alms house an idea.'[55] Although he could have been writing quite truthfully, doing so in this way might be considered unprofessional. Was Nash, so early in their partnership, sowing seeds that were to grow into the Reptons' discontent?

We could possibly accept Nash's explanation that the picturesque village concept was his; that, as he suggests, there was some disagreement on the matter of informality or alignment of cottages and that for the sake of presenting a unified opinion Repton toed Nash's line. But we must look further back still, before Price's *Essay* even, to 1791 and Repton's *Red Book for High Legh*. In his recommendations about this very same approach he advised Legh on its potential. This might be an object of great beauty: 'The whole village may be so picturesquely ornamented as to mark that it belongs to the person whose name it bears'.[56] Or, as Legh later had to remind his landscape gardener when drafting that ruling to bring him back into line, the 'Principle I wish to be acted on is to make the Green of High Legh a Village & surely this was the idea that first struck you as mentiond in yr Book.'[57]

Notes to Chapter Ten

1. William Weston YOUNG, *Guide to the Beauties of Glyn Neath,* 1835, p. 22.
2. For accounts of developments at Regents Park see Anne SAUNDERS, *Regent's Park,* 1969 and John SUMMERSON, 'The Beginnings of Regents Park', *Architectural History,* xx, 1977, pp. 56-62.
3. I am grateful to Sir John Summerson for drawing my attention to the plan reproduced here as Pl.72, with acknowledgements to the Public Record Office. Crown Copyright. MPE 911.
4. *Committee — Report from the Select Committee on Crown Leases,* Reports and Committees, 1829, III. See John SUMMERSON, *John Nash — Architect to King George IV,* 1949 (2nd edn.), pp. 248-252; p. 278.

5. John NASH, *A Statement*, 1829. This is a privately printed document. I am grateful to Sir John Summerson for permission to quote from his notes taken from a copy of it.
6. John SUMMERSON, *John Nash — Architect to King George IV*, 1949 (2nd edn.), pp. 281-282.
7. It is acknowledged that these select clients need not be the only candidates: also that G. Repton need not have been engaged on some schemes and that Nash might have been involved with yet others before G. Repton joined him.
8. SUMMERSON, *op. cit.*, p. 154, who comments on the match and Eldon's 'terrible wrath'.
9. James GREIG (ed.), *The Farington Diary*, viii, p. 159, 1 Jan. 1818. See also Dorothy STROUD, *Humphry Repton*, 1962, pp. 162-163.
10. SUMMERSON, *op. cit.*, p. 154. Farington confused J.A.R. with G.S.R.
11. Bristol R.O. 28048, C41/4, 1-8 Oct. 1849. John S. HARFORD, *Address Delivered in the Assembly Room of Aberystwith*, 1849.
12. 'Welsh Country Homes, LXVII. — Rheola', *South Wales Daily News*, 25 March, 1911, p. 9; an anonymous illustrated article describes the dwelling John Edwards bought as 'little more than a cottage — a small, double-fronted house of two storeys, with a little entrance hall and rooms to right and left. It is probable that for some years he only used it as a summer residence.'
13. D. Rhys PHILLIPS, *The History of the Vale of Neath*, 1925, pp. 420-423.
14. RIBA. GSR [26] (K1/18, i, ii): plan and perspective in wash mounted with the shaded drawing of Rose Cottage (K1/19). The inscription 'George Stanley Repton Blaise Hamlet (Glos)', is by an unidentified hand on the joint mount. The house has been considerably altered and added to at the north end. The loggia has been filled and the bay window, which looked towards Rheola House, has recently been removed.
15. This need not (to judge by other cases) have been the only house built to the same design. Looking towards Nash's dining room there was, from at least 1815, a cottage happily sited by the woods. Now totally ruined, it had diagonally-set chimneys and a bay window.
16. YOUNG, *op. cit.*, p. 22. He considered 'Bryn-awel' a 'pretty object'.
17. Hereford City Library. 2282, p. 115 (item 95), *Belmont*, aquatint, I. Black (*del./sc.*), Ackermann, 1 Sept. 1800: PC2328, *View of Belmont*, watercolour, J. WATHEN (*pinxt.*), 1791: also PC2267, etc. The front of the house is now very Gothic.
18. GREIG, *op. cit.*, i, p. 68, 31 Aug. 1794. Matthews married Elizabeth Ellis (*c.* 1757-1823).
19. [John MATTHEWS, attr.], *A Sketch from the Landscape, a Didactic Poem, addressed to R.P. Knight Esq.*, 1794. The publication has also been attributed to George Huddesford (1749-1809), an exhibitor at the R.A. who 'dabbled in

painting' and was once a pupil of Reynolds. In a 'Postscript' to *A Sketch*, its author defends Brown against 'Mr. P.'s' recently published attack.

20. *The Hereford Journal*, 18 Jan. 1826.
21. Partly screened by a hedge and covered with snow, the cottages photographed — which appear to have been altered and added to — cannot be positively matched with the drawings, although there are several comparable features. I am grateful to Brother James Oakley, now of Llanarth Court, for his help.
22. Hereford Library. 914.224(1944); a lithograph, *The Lake, Belmont, Herefordshire*, 1821. See detail Pl.86.
23. RIBA. GSR[47/f.39*v*.&f.40*r*.], cottage for U. Price: [47/f.40*v*.&f.41*r*.], cottage for H. Vernon.
24. I am grateful to Mr. & Mrs. Bryan Turner of Dewsall Lodge for their help and to Mr. Percy Pritchard for producing his early photographs of the cottage.
25. Dorothy STROUD, *Humphry Repton*, 1962, p. 107. J.C. LOUDON (ed.), *The Landscape Gardening and Landscape Architecture of the Late Humphry Repton, Esq.*, 1840, pp. 224-230; Attingham.
26. Salop Record Office, Attingham Collection, SRO. QR210/66-68, 26 April 1802. Quarter Sessions order redirecting the highway, and plan. Crown copyright.
27. John CORNFORTH and St. John GORE, *Attingham Park, Shropshire* (n.d.), p. 17: the *Red Book for Attingham*, 1797-98.
28. Salop Record Office. Attingham Collection, SRO. 112 (n.d.).
29. Salop Record Office. Attingham Collection, SRO.112, 1793: Plan of Cronkhill, Chilton and Atcham etc.
30. CORNFORTH and GORE, *op. cit.*, pp. 4, 7.
31. Salop Record Office. Attingham Collection, SRO.112, 1807; plan of the Attingham Estate.
32. Lichfield Joint Record Office. TP4; Tithe Map and Award — Atcham, 1846.
33. These paintings are on wood, about 7″ × 10½″ and executed cleverly in oils. They were found at Attingham Hall by Mr. Merlin Waterson. The seven panels are all reproduced in Nigel TEMPLE, 'In search of the Picturesque: a recent discovery at Attingham Park', *Architectural Review*, Aug. 1976, figures 11-16. I am grateful to the National Trust for making the panels and photographs of them available.
34. SUMMERSON, *op. cit.*, p. 288.
35. Significant relationships between the paintings, the existing terrace and Atcham village plan were established and recorded independently by the author in July 1972.
36. STROUD, *op. cit.* p. 96.
37. Notably the brick-built Post Office and a cottage to its east. A blacksmith's shop

is depicted on one panel. There was, on the evidence of maps, a smithy on a site approximating to that suggested in the general village view, towards the church.

38. John Rylands University Library of Manchester. Cornwall-Legh Papers (uncatalogued). There are six early letters referred to in this account: Appendix VI (below) places them in an order, although some are undated. Number [1] Repton to Legh, 4 May 1797: [2] Nash-Legh (copy) 24 June 1797 ('Rcd. August 5th'): [3?] Legh-Repton (draft), (n.d.), [14 Aug. 1797?]: [4] Repton-Legh, 26 Sept. 1797: [5?] Nash-Legh (n.d.), [Jan. 1798?]: [6] Nash-Legh, 2[1?] Jan. 1798.

39. John Rylands University Library of Manchester. Cornwall-Legh papers, Letter [1]. Re Humphry's birthday: this is generally understood to have been on 21 April 1752; his baptism on 5 May. Repton celebrated entering his 45th year on 2 May 1797.

40. I am grateful to Mr. C.L.S. Cornwall-Legh for allowing me to quote or reproduce material from the *Red Book for High Legh*. Repton was concerned more about his literary style than his opinion being influenced by haste. The latter must always be formed on the spot.

41. Raymond RICHARDS, *The Chapels of the Blessed Virgin Mary and St. John at High Legh, Cheshire*, reprinted from the *Transactions of the Historic Society of Lancashire and Cheshire*, 1949, is an account of the chapels and some other aspects of this remarkable estate and its occupants.

42. *E.g.* Whereas Repton appears to have swallowed his pride in writing to Legh that a garden building would best be converted to a hovel or shed (Letter [1]), Nash was in open disagreement with him when writing to Legh (Letter [5?]): '. . . I am sorry to say I shall not have Reptons concurrence for he is determined it should be a Temple — but I think with you it should be an hovel'. Nash at times agrees with Repton, against Legh's views.

43. John Rylands University Libary of Manchester. Cornwall-Legh Papers, Letter [3?].

44. *Ibid.*

45. *Ibid.*, Letter [4].

46. *Ibid.*, Letter [5?].

47. *Ibid.*, Letter [6], in which rooms, their purposes and dimensions are given.

48. *E.g.* Cheshire R.O. EDT 203, 1848-49, Tithe Map and Apportionment which, while marking the lodge and cross, indicates no cottages at all round the green. The *Red Lion* has gone. Its foundations served until recently as a rock garden. Also, during 1886-88, E.G. WHELER, Agent at High Legh, compiled a substantial bound and illustrated record of changes which occurred in his time. Further realignments of roads had been made 'about the Year 1854 . . . whereby the grounds of both Halls were enlarged and several cottages pulled down.' I am most grateful to Mr. C.L.S. Cornwall-Legh for protracted loan of this record and for permission to quote or reproduce material it contains.

49. John Rylands University Library of Manchester. Cornwall-Legh Papers, Letter [5?].
50. *Ibid.*, Letter [6], which mentions Legh's friend 'Mr Pit'. In the Cornwall-Legh Papers is a sheet, dated 1799, headed, 'Plan and Elevation of a Cottage at Tunbridge Wells', apparently in Nash's hand. It is endorsed 'Pitts Cottage'. William Pitt consulted Repton about Holwood House, Kent, in 1791. No cottage complying with the circular plan design has been traced and no guides consulted name Pit[t]. I am grateful to Miss Jean Mauldon for local research conducted on my behalf.
51. *Ibid.*, Letter [5?].
52. I am indebted to Mr. Peter Silsby for contacting me about these paintings and for his permission to reproduce them.
53. I am grateful to Mr. Hugh Lucius & Baroness Lucius for their co-operation.
54. John Rylands University Library of Manchester. Cornwall-Legh Papers, 6 July 1810.
55. *Ibid.*, Letter [2].
56. See Appendix V.
57. John Rylands University Library of Manchester. Cornwall-Legh Papers, Letter [3?]. See Nigel TEMPLE, 'Marginalia', *Architectural Review*, Sept. 1977, pp. 133-134.

Likeness of a cottage once at Spring Grove, Belmont, near Hereford

Appendix I

Letters by Humphry Repton to persons unnamed.
University of Bristol Library DM 180/3,4

Harestreet by Romford
Nov. 6: 1794.

My dear Sir,

I have long wish'd to send you my answer to Mr. U. Price's attack, but have not known where to direct it — till Miss Nicholls inform'd me; — She with Mr & Mrs. Nicholls are now at Harestreet, &, tho' not absolutely well in every respect, yet I am happy to find them in excellent spirits with little other symptoms of indisposition except the effects of a recent Cold — but I will leave to your Charming correspondent the subject of their health etc — while I congratulate you on the pleasure you must have had in your Western tour. Lord Eliot told me you had been in Cornwall and tho he said none of the family were there, he hopes you got a sight of my red book for Port Eliot — it is one of which I am not a little vain — because it has had the sanction & approbation of three persons whose judgment I much revere — Mr. Windham — Mr Pitt. & Mr. Pole Carew — the latter has a place at Antony on the St Germain river it is under my direction; & that Red book is my Chef d'oeuvre —. I often regret that Sheffield place is almost the only place of consequence on which I did not deliver my opinion in a Red book — but I was consulted there before I had become a book maker (in M.S. I mean) for as to making printed books I have had so much anxiety — expense & trouble in getting my first volume thro the press, that I fear I shall never have courage to attack a second. My plates are all done — & almost all the letterpress but such are my engagements that I cannot see the Sheets as they are printed off, & am therefore obliged to submit their correction & revisal to an Editor by profession — tho a thousand things would occur to the Author which will not strike the Editor.

The work will, however, soon make its appearance; but I have been obliged to defend myself from the false & I may say malicious attack of Mr: Knight with whom I have lived in some habits of intimacy & had no reason to suspect this contumelious treatment of my profession — especially as I am actually endeavouring to raise it in the Scale of Polite Arts. but, however I may feel hurt or express those feelings in Confidence to my friends, I hope the publick will see that I coolly defend myself & my predecessor & you & every lover of Landscape gardening as distinguished from Landscape painting — with arguments — with facts & an appeal to experience — I have letters on this subject from Gilpin — Mason — Mr. Windham etc etc part of one from the Latter I have transcribed in my letter to Lord Sheffield & I wish at your leisure you would have the goodness to let me add a letter of yours to the Curious collection of M.S.S. which I am proud to possess on the Subject of this Controversy —

Lest my letter should exceed its due weight I will inclose the pamphlet in a seperate Cover & hope to make this more valuable to you by a letter from Miss Nicholls — Believe me very cordially dear Sir

Your obed humble Servant
H. Repton

Harestreet by Romford
Feby. 13. 1796.

My Dear Sir.

At my return from Oxfordshire I have just met your letter which I am truely ashamed should have been necessary, but I hope e're you recieve this you will find my neglect repair'd. I have peculiar pleasure in sending you a Copy while I am this very day answering the letters of half a dozen noble personages, & three times as many other people who fancy it is in my power to furnish them with books because I reservd abt 40 Copies — for 58 Gentlemen who had consulted me & omitted to become subscribers — the Caution you gave me has been verified, as my publisher has desired a remittance of £200 balance — thus I am dunn'd by the bookseller & damnd by the reviewer — without the hope of reaping fame or profit — this however is not quite the Case. my fame is not to be hurt by the jealous nibbling of a rival Critic — who is puffing himself into notice under the title of Rural Artist — Marshall I suppose has reviewd my work, as he did Knights & Prices — & this will account for all the malice & pecking of this Critique.

The Compliments I daily receive from literary Correspondents & the more solid proof of its merit by the increase of my professional engagements — leaves me no reason to shrink from the detection of grammatical errors — in a work that teaches to improve Scenery & not language — & I will fairly own that I never saw more than 3 sheets of the work while it was printing — Excuse me my dear Sir for the apparent neglect which a constant moving from place to place has occasiond & believe me very sincerely & faithfully Yours

H Repton

at Corsham I confirm your opinion that the Stables should not be removed.

Appendix II

Extract from a draft agreement between
Mssrs. Jenkins & Lovell and John Scandrett Harford,
dated 1796

Gloucestershire Record Office, Gloucester,
Harford Papers D2957 160 (25)

Articles of agreement indented made and entered into this [*space*] day of [*space*] in the Year of our Lord 1796 Between Richard Jenkins & Joseph Lovell both of the City of Bristol House Carpenters and Joiners of the one part and John Scandrett Harford of the said City of Bristol Esqr. of the other part

Whereas the said John Scandrett Harford being about to erect a new House and Offices upon his estate at Henbury in the County of Gloucester called Blaze Castle Estate according to a Plan elevation & sections drawn by William Paty of the sd City of Bristol Architect the said Plan Elevation and Sections with the particulars for the Carpenters and Joiners work of the said intended new House and Offices have been delivered to the said Rd. . Jenkins & Joseph Lovell for their consideration in order to their delivering to the said John Scandrett Harford an Estimate for doing the said Carptenters & Joiners work for him, and after duly considering & perfectly understanding the said Plan Elevation and Sections and all the particulars of the said Carpenters and Joiners work which they do hereby admit. They having delivered their estimate to the said John S. Harford to do and perform all the Carpenters & Joiners work of and for the said new House and Offices [. . .]

Appendix III

Notes accompanying G.S. Repton's drawings for Rose Cottage, Blaise Hamlet

Art Gallery and Museums and the Royal Pavilion, Brighton: Notebook by G.S. Repton

The drawings for Rose Cottage appear on four pages. Three of these pages include notes. Those on the second page of drawings read:

Scantings of Timbers. Joists of Chamber floor 10 by 2½ — plates under Do. 5 by 4 — quarter partitions 4 by ½ — plates under roof 5 by 4 —

purlins 6 by 6 & to project out 9 in beyond the walls & the tiling 3″ farther —

principals 7 by 3 at top 9 by 3 at bottom —

Jack rafter under foot of principal 5 by 3. tie beams 9 by 3 common rafters 5 by 2½ —

the middle wall to be carried up in lieu of a principal rafter close up to the tiles but only 12 inches thick —

The flues to be 12 by 12 & turned angular ways in the shaft & these to be 10½ by 10½ with 4½ brick work round them — each flue in the shaft part to be 3 inches as under & the brick cornice over them to unite the Chimney Shafts to be set in Parker's cement — chimney pots on each shaft.

Notes on the third page of drawings read:

The walls built of rough Stone — the quoins to be toold true & good joints but to be rough on the face & to be irregular in length and courses — the whole of the bow window & dormers to be of toold stone in the like manner — the roof to be tiled with stone — the eaves of the house to project 12 inches and of the leantoo & dormers 9 inches — the rafter feet to be seen & to come within 3 inches of the eaves of the tiles & to be regularly spaced and to be cut off like an OG — the purlins of the dormers are to be 4 by 4 and to project within 3 inches of the face of the tiling — the purlins of the gable end to be 6 × 6 & to project within 3 inches of the Tiling — the rafters under the purlins to advance within 3 inches of the face of the walls and to be seen — the Chimney shafts to be of brick & the flues well pargetted — the shafts above the roof to be formed of brick & set with Parkers Cement. the shafts to be colord like the stone of the House — stone steps to the doorways — the Kitchen & Scullery & pantry to be paved with 10 inch brick tiles & the Cellar & Shed paved with Stock bricks — a stone Mantle Jambs & shelf to the kitchen chimney & the like & a stone slab to the Chamber — the Chambers to be floord with inch white deal folding — deal linings to the dormers & other windows — deal skirting to the rooms — deal steps risers & bearers to the Staircase — deal linings rounded edges to the inner doorways — the walls & partitions plaisterd & whited — shelves put up in the Pantry — all the wood work to be painted 3 times in oil & the outside wood work painted twice with stone color anti [corosian?] — and every thing done in the several trades of Digger Mason Bricklayer Carpenter Plaisterer Plumber Glazier & Painter requisite to make the Cottage in all respects compleat for Habitation — the hips ridges & Valleys coverd with Milld lead 5lbs to the footSup — Door frames 4 by 4 wrought ribd and [beaded?] to all the doorways — outside doors 2 inches 4 pand [bead?] butt & square an 8 inch draw back spring lock 3″ butt hinges & an inside bolt — inner doors 1½ 4 pand. square 2½ butts & a thumb latch to each —

Notes on the fourth page of drawings continue:
window frames 4½ by 3 rebated & to have 2″ deal casement sashes glazed in lead & hung with 2 inch butts — iron turnbuckles to fasten them within & iron spring stays to keep them open — stone step and paving to Seat —

Repton noted on one of his drawings for Double Cottage that these particulars applied to it also.

Appendix IV

Correspondence between G.S. Repton and J.S. Harford, with an inventory of defects

Bristol Record Office.
28048, Harford Papers P52/1-6, 8-10

P52/1: Addressed to J.S. Harford Esqre. Blaize Castle Bristol

Sir,

I expect to receive the designs for one or two of your Cottages from Mr Nash by tomorrow or Saturdays post, when I will lose no time in drawing them out, and forwarding them to you. I shall be obliged to you to inform me if you wish to have shaded drawings of all the Cottages like those you have already received.

Mr. Nash has desired me to say, that as he considers the chimneys to be a great feature in the Cottages, he recommends you to have Moulded bricks Made for them, which will very much increase their effect — should you wish it I will send you 2 or 3 different designs for them, which may be executed without much additional trouble.

I have the honor to be
Sir
Your obedient humble Servant
G S Repton

29 Dover Street
Aug. 9th. 1810

P52/2: Addressed to J.S. Harford Esqre Blaize Castle near Bristol

Sir,

Enclosed I have the honor of sending you a drawing [*] for a Cottage which I have received from Mr. Nash. he has promised to send me the sketches for another in a post or two, when I will lose no time in forwarding them to you. I have thought it better to draw them upon writing paper for the greater convenience of conveying them to you by the post. I will in a day or two send you the sketches for the chimney stacks — in the mean time I will again repeat to Mr Nash, your wish to have the drawings for all the Cottages — and I hope you will attribute my not sending them sooner to you to the great distance Mr Nash is at present from home, and the length of time necessarily taken up in conveying letters to him, and receiving his answers.

I have the honor to be
Sir
Your most obedient humble Servant
G S Repton

29 Dover Street
Aug. 15th 1810.

[* *The drawing is not with the Harford Papers.*]

P52/3: Draft letter from J.S. Harford to G.S. Repton

Blaise Castle 18 Aug 1810

Mr George Repton

Sir

I received your letter of the 15th. inclosing the Working Drawings for another of the Cottages but we shall not be able to proceed in it till we have the number as marked in Mr Nash's general Sketch of the Village not knowing to a certainty which he means or where to place it and wch. way lies our proposal in order that there might be no mistake that I would wish you to write him as soon as possible that it may be ascertained and at the same time shall be obliged to you mention that in the plan you have sent me I observe there is a room appropriated for a Cellar and Pantry which is [an unnecessary?] one and not wanted as in the other plans the Pantry is taken out of the Scullery and if this mode is adopted it will very much lengthen out the Building and enhance the expence, perhaps Mr Nash may be able fully to explain it to you but that about the number for each Cottage must be strictly adhered to or we shall always be at a loss

P52/4: Addressed to J.S. Harford Esqre. Blaize Castle near Bristol

Sir,

By the Plan of the enclosed Drawing for the Chimneys you will perceive the form in which the Bricks should be moulded. on the two plans [*] of the shaft I have drawn the different courses of the bricks to form the bond — those in the middle of the enclosed paper will require 3 different formd Bricks — but the other two stacks would require but one brick placed differently on each course as shewn upon the enclosed Plans — I am rather inclined to prefer the middle design of the enclosed three — though as you have so many opportunities of using them you will perhaps think it better to adopt them all in different parts of the Village rather than adopt the same for all the Cottages — these kind of Chimney stacks are frequently seen in old Cottages — and generally in old Manor Houses and buildings of the reign of Queen Elizabeth and invariably produce a picturesque effect — their character requires they should be very high — even more so than I have described upon the enclosed drawing — should you desire me to send you further instructions for carrying them into execution I shall be happy to do so, and will send you other designs for them should you wish to have every Cottage of a different design for the chimney stacks

I have the honor to be
Sir
Your most obedt. humble Servant
Geo Stanley Repton

29 Dover Street
Aug. 18. 1810

[* *The drawings are not with the Harford Papers.*]

P52/5: Addressed to J.S. Harford Esqre. Blaise Castle Bristol

Sir,

Your letter which arrived yesterday I immediately forwarded to Mr Nash in Ireland — who has sent me the sketches for another Cottage the working Drawing for which I have now the honor of enclosing to you [*] — in answer to what you mention in your letter that the Pantry and Cellar in the first designs you received were placed in the Cottage itself — if we make them all so it will very much injure (if not entirely destroy) the picturesque effect of the different Cottages where so much depends upon the leantoo's and Sheds etc to make a variety in their form — more particularly where the number and scale of the rooms are so similar and the pantry and Cellar projecting from the Cottage is not more expensive than if it were in the body of the building where you must still occupy [*word missing*] space, and must increase the Upper Rooms — which is not necessary where the Cellar and Pantry are formed by a leantoo shed without any building over it.

Mr. Nash in his letter says he has written to you for a figured Plan of the Field, with the pegs laid down as he put them into the Ground — which it is necessary to have before he can put in all the Houses.

I hope you will not let them carry the Chimneys above the roof untill you have decided if you will have the ornamented Chimney Stacks which will certainly very much improve the external effect of the Cottages.

I have the honor to be
Sir
Your most obedient humble Servant
G S Repton

29 Dover Street
Aug. 23. 1810

[* *The drawing is not with the Harford Papers.*]

P52/6: Draft letter from J.S. Harford to G.S. Repton

Blaise Castle Sept 1. 1810

Mr George Repton

Sir

I received your Letter of the 23rd Ult. inclosing another Sketch of a Cottage and though it is designated under the term "Second Cottage from the top North side looking South East" we are not quite sure where to place it for want of the number being specified but that will be obviated now by inclosing a Figured Plan of the Field with the Pegs laid down as Mr Nash put them into the Ground as requested by him I have also sent a facsimile of the general Plan of the Village as numbered by him and which Foster brought from London so that I think there cannot now be any mistake in designing the remainder of the Cottages but I am still anxious to have the Numbers forwarded to me as early as you can of the first and second Sketches which you sent me that there may be no blunder and I shall very soon be obliged to stand still with the Mason if I do not receive them I have not received any letter from Mr Nash from Ireland so I suppose it has miscarried I have fixed for the chimnies of the double and Single Cottages now nearly ready for tiling so that any conclusion about those that are not already begun may be left for a time

P52/8: Unsigned notes headed 'Directions about Coppers & Ovens & Privys'

Each paragraph has been identified in this Appendix for convenience of reference and is shown in the text (e.g.) — [14]

October 1811

Directions about Coppers & Ovens & Privys

[1] The Coppers and Ovens can have but little spaces allowed for them. the gardner must therefore enquire and find out the smallest sized coppers and ovens that will be sufficient for the sort of people who are to live in the Cottages and let them be built accordingly —

[2] In the Cottage No. 2 next to the double cottage the South leantoo is to be carried to the back front of the building — but the middle part must break forward a foot farther than the present leantoo in order to give width for Oven & Copper the eaves therefore of such projecting part will come a foot lower as the surface of the tyling is to be continued all along the same as the present leantoo — the privy is to have the well dug so as to admit the shoot of the privy in the angle to enter the bog — and the rest of the bog is to stand farther out in order not to come too near to the angle of the building —

[3] NB all the Bogs to be 4 feet diameter & 6 or 7 feet deep & to be [stoned?] & domed over except where the shoots from the privys enter them and to be kept as far from the body of the building —

[4] The angular Cottage No. 8 on the South east side to have the boiler and Copper in the open shed behind — and a flue carried up — the shaft of the flue to be angular & to stand in the most convenient place for the oven & copper

[5] NB a steam hole may be made in any of the external walls most convenient to carry off the steam of the copper — and one flue will do for copper and boiler having a proper damper in it

[6] The Copper and oven of No 9 to be built in the Scullery by the side of the stairs making use of the present flue intended for them —

[7] The privys of No 8 & No. 9 to be back to back and the seats in the angle & the Bog so made that the shoots of the privys in the angles may enter them — the walls are 9 inch brickwork — & the scullery roof continued round the privys and hipped all round

[8] The oven & Copper in No. 7 to be built in the open shed behind the Kitchen Chimney making use of the flue intended for them and behind the Copper and oven in the remaining part of the shed the privy is to be the seat on the angle and the bog so placed that the shoot may go into it

[9] The Crosses in the 2 Door entrances to be altogether omitted —

[10] The oven and Copper in the round cottage No. 4 — to be by the side of the stairs in the Shed originally intended for them kept clear of the stairs —

[11] The privys of the Cottage No 4 & No 5 to be back to back close in the hedge as sketchd on the colourd plan & the bog made so as to take the shoots of both privys to be 6:3 high to the eaves & hipped all round the walls of 9inch Brickwork

[12] The Chimney of Copper and oven in No. 5 to go up in the middle of the [*word illegible*] end of that building & to be built in the same manner and to the same heigth as the other Chimney shafts of that Cottage — the Copper and oven of course to be also in the middle of that [*word illegible*] end and the space beyond of the leantoo to be left open as a shed —

[13] The Copper and Oven for No. 3 to be built in a shed to be made for them behind the stairs the Walls to be 9 inch Brick and 6:3 to eaves and the roof hipped all round — the privy to be under the same roof the seat of it in the angle and the Bog made so that the shoot may go into it

[14] The privy of No. 6 to be built at the N W corner of the scullery building by the extension of the N W wall and the continuation of the roof so far that the Eaves may be 6:3 high over the privy — and the seat placed in the angle and the bog so formed that the shoot of the privy may go into it

[15] the Copper and oven to be in the scullery behind the stairs & a Chimney stack made for it unless the old flue can be made use of with safety to the stairs —

[16] The Copper and oven in the double Cottage to be built back to back in the sheds behind them — and the flue made use of as originally intended — and the 2 middle openings of the shed to be brought forward to form 2 privys back to back and one bog made to take both privys 5 feet diameter & 6 or 7 feet deep the seats to be in the angles & the bog so placed that the shoots of each privy may go into it

[17] NB. the plans cannot be found but on the back of the Colourd plan the intention is sketched though not to a scale — the 2 middle openings give the length of the 2 privy and the privys are to be 3 feet wide [in the clear?] and the Eaves to correspond with the present eaves with a pediment or gable [end in the front?]

[18] The Coping of the 2 porches made thicker by the addition of an ovolo under the projection —

[19] The bathstone pediments to the Chimney shafts to be cut away — and the Stone colourd like the building stone

[20] the Bathstone round the arrowslits in No 7 may remain but must be colourd like the stone walls

[21] the pidgeon houses to be made in point of number like the plans — the perching boards to project 4 Inches & to Slope ¾ of an Inch — & to have no uprights to support them —

[22] a penthouse to be put over the South West window of No 6 composed of the continuation of the lower course of Eaves tiles of the penthouse over the seat and the addition of another (lower) course of Tiles underneath supported by 4 brackets as shewn by the Sketch on the plan — the window in the pediment over it to be heighthend to the dimensions on the plan —

[23] The window in the Cottage No 3 to be alterd to conform to the plan it being now too low — the margin of the 6 inches round the frame to be the same all round —

[24] The dormer window in the circular cottage to have the stone work above the lintel taken away and the Eaves brought down to the top of the lintel — and the thatch over the circular penthouse to have the Eaves cut horizontal and level with the top of the lintel

[25] the Eaves of all the thatch to be cut level or nearly so in the under side —

[26] The dormer window in the front of the double cottage to be made higher to correspond with the plan

[27] the glazing is very badly done and the panes of the diamond glazing are too large they should have one more in number in width of each casement

[28] Bird [pottles?] to be put in the edges of the gables where shewn in the plans

[29] small blockings to be put under the circular brackets & at the heads of

them thus
[*A simple curved wooden bracket is shown in side elevation.*]

[30] The entrance porch of the northermost double cottage is not according to the design — the plan must be found and the porch made conformable to it

[31] If gutters must be made I recommend them to be made according to the drawing and placed as marked on the several plans.

[32] Query is the Penthouse at No. 5 fixed — the gate [was hence?] set out wrong — vide the plan No 5. but the gardner will alter it

P52/9:Addressed to J.S. Harford Esqre. Blaise Castle Bristol

Dear Sir

I have taken the liberty to enclose you our account for the professional assistance we have had the honor to afford you — not knowing the exact amount of the expenditure upon which the perCentage is charged you will perhaps have the goodness to fill up that Sum.

I have the honor to be, Sir
(for Mr Nash and myself.)
Your obliged and faithful humble Servant
G S Repton

Dover Street
Nov. 22. 1812

J.S. Harford Esqre.

To Messrs. John Nash & George S Repton Architects.

working Drawings and instructions for a Village containing 1 double Cottage and 8 single Cottages & a Sundial, with a Design for the general disposition of the same at 5 per Cent.

Two fair Drawings for the Cottages No. 1 and 2		5. 5. 0
Mens time and Materials making Moulds for the ornamental Chimney Stacks, and packing case for the Same		3.14.10
Estimate of double Cottage amounting to 407.7.0 at 1½ per Cent		6. 0. 0
Two Journeys Mr Nash —	£. s. d.	
124 Miles posting	12. 8. 0	
same Back	12. 8. 0	
3 days travelling and 1 day there	8. 8. 0	66. 8. 0
each Journey	33. 4. 0	
		£81. 7.10

P52/10: Draft letter from J.S. Harford to Messrs. Nash & Repton

Blaise Castle Dec. 2 1812

Messrs Nash & Repton

Gentm.

In consequence of the Reciept of your Letter of the 22nd Ult° I have been looking into the Account of the Expenditure of the Cottages etc done for me and find that though the original Estimates did not amount to £2000 that I have already expended upwards of £3000 but part of that Amount had nothing to do with the Building, that if it is agreeable to you to settle it at that Amount say 5 pc on £3000 amt to £150 I will immediately Remit you wch added to £81.7.10 which your account amounts to will make £231.7.10 the balance due from me

Appendix V

The Red Book for High Legh,
prepared by Humphry Repton for George John Legh
Dated 10 October 1791: Extract

With acknowledgements to Mr. Charles Cornwall-Legh

N.B.: earlier in the 'Red Book' Repton recommends developing an approach from the South

Approach from the North

I think in this case it is not advisable to make one approach answer every purpose, because if we break from the road where the house is nearest to it we show at once the defect of the place, yet it is not allowable to make those who come from the North go some hundred yards out of their way to enter the south gate, besides a back way to the offices &c, is absolutely necessary. I therefore propose to enter in the hollow as I have shewn in the map, and this approach may be made an object of great beauty. The whole village may be so picturesquely ornamented as to mark that it belongs to the person whose name it bears, at this gate a porters lodge may be hereafter placed with great propriety, and utility [. . .]

Appendix VI

Letters, Draft Letter and a Copy Letter:
Correspondence between G.J. Legh, H. Repton and J. Nash

John Rylands University Library of Manchester
Cornwall-Legh Papers (uncatalogued)

Letter [1]: Addressed to: Captain George John Legh of the Chesire Regt., at or near Newcastle upon Tyne, from H. Repton, dated 4 May 1797 & posted at St. Albans, 5 May 1797: Extracts

May 4th. in my Chaise.
betwixt High Legh & the post Town
from whence this letter will be sent

Sir,

The letter you were so good to direct to me at Harestreet demands my very sincere thanks & as you desire that subject may be drop't, I will only make this acknowledgement of my gratitude & pass on to the letter I found at High Legh — where I did not arrive so soon by many days as I expected because Lord Berwick could not keep his appointment with me in Shropshire but Mr. Nash & I have spent two days on the Spot & I shall give you the result of our operations under the seperate heads which you have mark'd.

1st The Village — I believe I have already hinted my wish that you would consent to remove the Inn entirely — but under the idea of saving expence by preserving the great room etc — I have acquiesced in your determination to add to it — Mr. Nash on inspecting the dampness of the walls — is of opinion that the present materials may be moved to another Site without any great difference in the expence — & I believe generally speaking it is always more safe — more satisfactory & more economical to build a new thing than to alter or add to an old one & on considering the effect of removing the opposite cottages to enlarge the Area of High Legh Green — we observe that the Inn would stand so high above the Lodge — & be evidently so near the mansion that its back yard would appear to extend into the pleasure ground & if any building must be there at all — an Inn of all others would be the least proper —

we therefore beg you will seriously weigh the trifling saving of one damp room against the advantage to be expected from continuing the wall or fence of the plantation from the Lodge quite round to the Corner of the Chappel — leaving only the way to it for Mr E. Legh, & the Villagers — then the whole of that side of the area would be appropriated to the mansion & the Inn might have the advantage of standing at the Lower Corner by the roadside — diagonally oposite the Entrance — but I will explain by a sketch (if the Jolting of the Chaise will permit me).

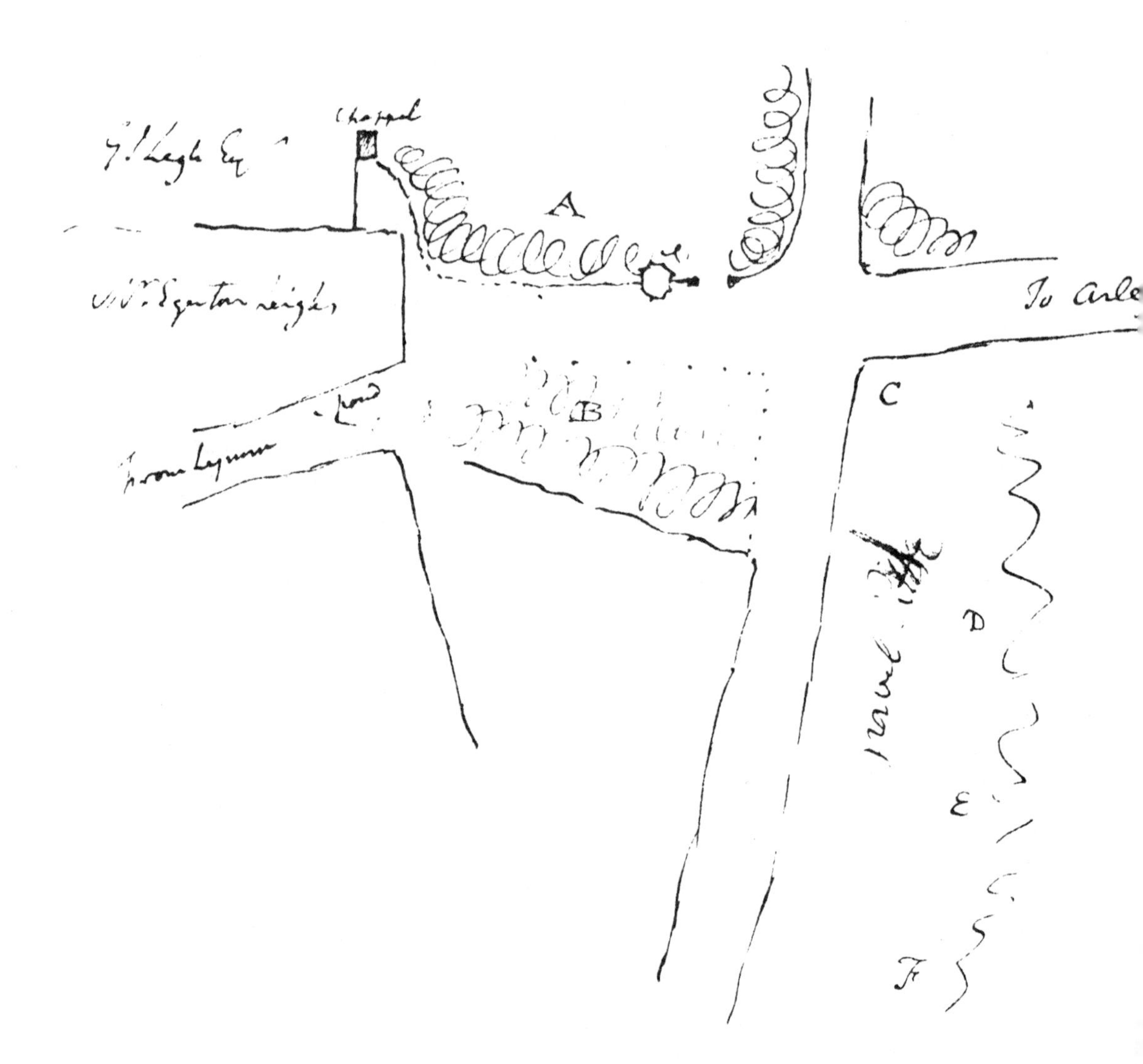

If you should consent to plant all the quarter A & have no building but the Lodge on your side the Cross road — we then shall further suggest that it would be still better to have no other building on that side the turnpike at B — but plant the rough ground where the Smith's shops now stand & in this case you want nothing from Mr Egerton Leigh, but you leave the area as broad or as narrow as you please

Then The Inn would be most commodiously situated for the publick & least in your way at the Corner C. — & the rest of the space — D.E.F. [etc?] might be occupied with houses — & gardens in front — but both Mr. Nash & I shrink from the idea of a row like almshouses — or the appendages of a manufactory & therefore we fear this space would not contain all you want — especially as we should like to make the doors open on the sides or back of the houses that the fronts to the gardens & Turnpike might be kept Neat but as the whole of this arrangement can now be made on paper as well as on the spot — having both made ourselves thoroughly acquainted with it — the further consideration, will wait your determination whether the Inn may be removed or not, as upon that will depend the whole disposition of the ground — [. . .]

I come now to the building which I agree with Nash — wants not only effect, but it wants Character — if it is not a temple what ought it to look like ? — for a keepers house it is too near — & a Labourers Cottage is less in Character — it should be a shed — or hovel — or deer Court to fodder the Cattle of the park, & this I think it may be made with little alteration — as Mr. Nash will have the honor of shewing you — & I am more than ever convinced that something ought to be in this place to give breadth to the Lawn which is already in some degree done by this building even in its present motly garb of red & thatch —— but such is the effect of Colour that both Mr. Nash & I are most fully convinced — little else is wanting to the house to make it one of the best houses in Cheshire — since its Architecture is far better than any of Sam Wyatts in that County — [. . .] [*]

Having now finishd my observations on the place permit me Sir to thank you for the Reception we experienced & the Cordial manner in which you desired us to take the Command of your house & all the good things it containd — a permission of which I availd myself in two instances — the first in desiring a bottle of Claret to celebrate the 2nd of May 1797 when I enterd my 45th year & secondly by begging Mr Newton to lend me money enough to carry me home — as by the failure of seeing Lord Berwick or his agent & being out a week later than I expected I had exhausted my Note case & could not have paid my way home

This Letter which has been written by piece meal on the road — is at length brought to a Conclusion near Daventry — but as I wish Nash to see it

Letter [2]: Copy of a letter from J. Nash, 'Sent 24th June 1797', with note stating 'Rcd. August 5th': Extracts

[. . .] Mr. Repton & myself considerd in every point of view the subject of the Cottages or rather Village. He wishes to remove everything on that side of the road & to place them on the other. My department is only to consider expence. The effect he means to produce in lieu of the Rugged Cottages & broken ground he will no doubt explain to you. The Part of the Inn which would remain is the new building & to take that down & rebuild it in another situation without altering the dimensions and form cd. not be more than £100 my only fears (not doubting Mr Repton can appropriate the scite of the present Village to a good effect) is that there will not be sufficient space for all the Cottages you want on the opposite side. Mr Repton suggested the putting them in a Row but I must step out of the slippers and inveigh against so alms house an idea. The Inn and Two Cottages are all that can be placed on the low ground on the left of the road and I presume to place Cottages in the field behind would be placing them too conspicuously & subject them to be seen from the ground of the House. if you think otherwise a Village may certainly be formd on the higher grd: with assistance of plantatn. be made picturesque tho' situated so high it can never have the snugness of one —

In case you should not approve of removing the Inn, Mr. Repton's objection to Cottages on left side of the road will be done away in that case four cottages (with the blacksmith's shop) may be placed without having any thing to do with your name sake in the way of exchange & Mr Repton & myself in case of such a determination on your part [what ?] the Inn shd be & where the cottages shd. be placed. — I am sorry to say I do not like the lodge but it may be helped by the form of the Piers and a little change in the outer form to give it less the appearance of the small octagon tea Caddies. If you would wish me to consider how that shd be done it will be necessary to send me the working drawings, It may be done now at a little expence as the building is but just coverd in and no Stucco done [. . .] The Hurdles on each side of the [Great?] road are the ugliest grotesque things I ever saw. they shd. be Park Hurdles strong enough as a fence agst animals of every kind. They may be fixed yet have the appearance of temporary separation, be as light as Park Hurdles are ever made yet as strong as any other fence [. . .]

Letter [3?]: Draft Letter from G.J. Legh [to Humphry Repton]: Undated [14 Aug. 1797?]. (The original MS is heavily altered and scored, leaving ambiguities. Some deleted words are illegible. Some others, if they aid continuity or add interest, have been included below, as indicated): Extracts

Dear Sir

Having now receivd Mr Nash's letter & sent my answer to it I shall beg to take up a little of yr time in answering yr letter of [*word illegible*] written in yr Post Chaise — relative to the Village & one or two other points not considerd in my former letter —

The Village I am sorry to say I do not entirely agree with you in the propriety of the removal of all the Cottages or placing plantation in their stead on the east side of the High Road. The Genl. Principle I wish to be acted on is to make the [*deleted:* whole of] the Green of High Legh a Village & surely this was the idea that first struck you as mentiond in yr Book — As far as Mr Leigh's House is to be considerd. It is a [fresh ?] reason for acting on this idea. Without much vanity I think it is not advisable to give the property of others close to you more consequence than it has. Surely the taking away the Cottages would be giving his house additional consequence as the [resouring? — restoring?] of them would be [drowning?] it. The original object was to have this entrance go out into the Village — But exclusive of other reasons convenience requires more Cottages than can be placd on the ground you have allotted for them — . I will therefore tho' paying the highest deference to all yr opinions lay it down as data to go on that there should be Cottages on each side of the road — The Question then therefore to be considerd is realy where the different buildings should be placd & what those buildings shd be. In determining on which The first thing I wish you to settle is this — Whether the Look & beauty of the Village would be diminishd or increasd by enlarging the area of the Green & throwing back the Cottages to L. You have misunderstood the business between Mr Legh & myself He has made a request to me to have the area enlarged & laid open as far as L. where he is to give me land enough of L. backwards, for Cottages & Gardens that the area may be bounded by my property as it is now, which request I should wish to come into if it can be done without materially [hurting?] the look of the Place —— I must own myself that as far as I can judge the enlarging the area will be of no [diservice?] but the contrary & will certainly add a little to the convenience as it will afford a larger space before the Entrance

The next thing to be determind is. Whether in case of enlarging the [area?] It will be then advisable to take down the Inn. I do not object to taking it down in case you think it material. If the expence In this case will be more than £100 I am inclin'd to think it will be better on every account to rebuild it

[*deleted*: I think it will be better to have a Cottage in the] place of it or at [*deleted*: least some building such as] a small stable to the Inn I beg to suggest too the idea of a kind of Gate or Porch on this side of the Green that would be an entrance to the path leading to the Chapel — To mark it as private Property which it is & wd be only opend when [wanted?] for divine Service

The Question then to be considerd & for you to determine on May the Cottages A B be thrown back to L—? & thus the area be enlarg'd Is the Inn to come down. How many Cottages shd be placed at L. L. L., D E F — & where Blacksmith Shop — ?

Mr Nash observes that 4 Cottages may be fixed without interfering with Mr Leigh — But you now understand me that I rather want to accomodate Mr L. in this wish of laying more Green open in case you approve of the appearance of it — [*deleted*: I have desird Nash to send me a rough sketch of what he means to do with the Inn] [. . .]

Fence

I did not admire those small upright poles in the Hurdle and to me — They are if you & Nash will not be offended very like the fence of Mr. — who was a [grocer?] & is now retird from business to [Turnham?] Green [. . .]

The building. I have desird Mr Nash to send me a rough sketch of what he intends to do with it. — & quite agree with you and him that it ought to be a shed, Hovel or to feed Cattel in — [. . .]

Letter [4]: Addressed to: George John Legh Esq. Blythe Bay Camp Near [*deleted* Newcastle], Glasgow [*added*], from H. Repton, Aylsham, dated 26 September 1797: Extract

Sir,

The honor of your letter dated 14 August should have been sooner noticed — but that I have not been two days at home since I received it — & there were some points on which I wish'd to consult with Mr Nash —

1st. — The Village —

There can be no objection to the idea you propose of putting houses opposite to your Entrance Lodge — & the larger the area of the Village Green — the more airy & cheerful it will make it — but I think in your wall there should be no other building than your Lodge — except indeed — as you very judiciously suggest — a gothic porch to the Chapel — of course the inn is out of the question — for I still continue to think that of all the buildings that can be placed in your park — an Inn — would be the most objectionable — But Mr Nash desired me to explain what he meant by £100 — lest you should conceive that he said the removal of the Inn would only cost £100 — — He means that if the whole present Inn & Stables are to be pull'd down except the two rooms in front — he thinks the removal of those same rooms to another Site would not cost more than £100 — —

Mr. Nash having the exact measure of the Space — will best answer your queries respecting the number — situation — & disposition of the several Cottages — — The Corner of the Cross road will be the best place for the Inn — & the Corner of the area or green — next the High road would be the place for the BlackSmith's Shop — but I could never have settled with Nash what would be the effect of altering the Inn — as I always hoped you would give it up [. . .] . . .

Letter [5?]: From J. Na[sh] to G.J. Legh. Undated (possibly 17 January, 1798)

Dear Sir

Agreeable to my promise I have sent the plan [*missing*] of the intended village, every part of which as well as the particular form of each cottage has been studied for effects, but in the compass of a letter or by any written description it will be almost impossible to set forth all the circumstances which occured and gave rise to those different shapes you will perceive in the plans — but the principal objects we had in view I will endeavour to describe and refer the rest to some opportunity of talking over the design with the plan before us.

in the first place Mr Repton will not hear of a cottage on the lodge side of Mr Egertons vista — he wishes to mark a distinct [*deleted*: broadness] and the appearance of an extensive boundary to the property of high Legh both of which a cottage on that side would certainly interupt besides the unpleasant intrusion of a cottager under your pales — to this reasoning good in itself we had only to oppose the want of Cottages — of course being convinced I gave way —

in the disposition of the village after much debate we settled that the Cottages should be scattered and intercepted by plantations and that they should be set back as far as possible in order that a considerable Area or space might be between them in the manner of a green or portion of common surrounded by Cottages

the first difficulty which occurd was how to secure the plantations from depredation and as the clumps of plantation would be disjunct to avoid so great a quantity of paling as there would be was each clump to be enclosed — we therefore agreed upon one open pale boundary to enclose the green from the road which by precluding Cattle and every thing that annoys trees & shrubs — would make it unnecessary to fence round each clump — this pale you will find distinguished in the plan & you will perceive that it occupies the least possible space — the next object was to prevent the nuisances of cottagers entering into the view of the Village this consideration occasiond the particular forms you will see of the Clumps which are so managed as to screen the gardens and yards of all the Cottages — at the same time that the view of the Cottages themselves are not intercepted but are seen through the glades formed by the clumps the yards and gardens of each Cottage must necessarily be paled or enclosed — and the space between those pales and the paling of the roads should not be left to the mercy of the cottagers but kept clear or at all events no cattle should be allowed to come into that spot — in the disposition of these plantations you will perceive a studied intention to shew the Cottages in the most favourable points of view and as the traveller passes along as he loses one Cottage others will unfold themselves — — the next object was to give a background to the whole scenery which is proposed to be done by sloping the gravel under the hedge about 10 or 12 feet and plant it as thick as possible with trees on the flat or field above the gravel pit — — the next object was to make the lodge of high legh the termination of the picture when you enter the village which you will perceive the plantations admit whilst the blacksmiths shop on the right and Cottage on the left will be the foreground of the picture — — another object was Mr Egerton Leighs house in front of which an ample avenue is formed and from which the new plantation on the right and your plantation on the left will lead the sight to a perspective view of the Inn as a termination with the cross and upper cottage as the foreground — the next object was going from high legh & in coming out of the lodge it was intended the Inn the single Cottage, the double cottages & blacksmiths shop with the background plantation of the village should burst together on the sight — — the next object was where to place the buildings — the Inn we placed at the corner that it might take the advantage of all the roads — the blacksmiths shop as the next most picturesque object and requiring to be near the road we placed at the other corner & we turned the smiths shop to look up the road so that the fire may illuminate the whole length of road and give a chearfulness at night to the whole village the upper cottage next the Cross is so placed as to allow the Cross to be seen in the group of the village from the road & form part of the picture and if a cupola was on the chapel that would be seen among the trees also — the entrances to the Cottages No. 5, 6, 7, & 8 on the upper side of the road are made from the road in order that the green might not be cut up by footpaths — the cottages on the righthand side of the road are one single Cottage & 1 double Cottage placed so as to divide the ground pretty equally among them — in the detail of the Inn many picturesque circumstances and conveniences have been attended to — in Scattering Cottages without any principle to go by — confusion instead of picturesque intricacy is often produced — for the mind though fond of variety and to be kept in suspence with always something to expect loves nevertheless to comprehend what it does see — and when it is not the result there is what is termed confusion — to avoid this though the Cottages vary in form and position. the traveller will easily see why each Cottage is so placed — the Inn conforms itself to the road — the Cottage No. 1 stands square with the road it looks on — the blacksmiths shop and cottage takes its direction by its boundary behind and the double cottages No. 2 & 3 being placed in an angle between the two last mentiond looks straight between them to the road — the Cottages No. 5, 6 & 7 — square themselves with the road on which they front and the Cottage next the Cross conforms itself to the angle in which it stands.

You must excuse my not correcting and writing fair this description of our Labours — but if I had done so I must have broke my word as to sending the plan this evening which I hope you will receive as an apology —— much of the effect of this village will depend on the detaild form of the cottages — if you wish me to make them out, it will be necessary for you to inform me — not being willing to put you to any unnecessary expence — the expence of working drawings compleat will be 3 Gns. each Cottage. if a painting of each Cottage such as you have seen 3 Gns. each but if painting and working drawgs. of each Cottage the whole will be 5 Guineas each — I am sure you will conceive my reason for apprizing you of the expence to be such as it is namely — the anxiety to preserve your friendship and esteem — I am trying to lick into shape that [monster?] in the field — in which I am sorry to say I shall not have Reptons concurrence for he is determined it should be a Temple — but I think with you it should be an hovel which I am making it & I think I shall succeed — I wish I could say as much for the lodge — but it is incorrigible — and so like the small oblong octagon tea cadies that I wonder you can bear it

the ground work of the house is advancing fast [*word missing*] completion

I shall be happy if our village proves to be what you expectd it to be & that it will meet with the approbation of your friend also

I have the honor to be
Dear Sir
Your most obliged [*word missing*]
obedient hum[ble]
J Na[sh]

Letter [6]: Addressed to George Legh, from John Nash 28 Dover Street, dated 2[1?] January 1798

Dear Sir

Mr Pit did me the honour of calling yesterday and we spent several hours on the subject of your Village —

Certainly if gardens can be provided in the field behind the quarry the cottages may be placed farther back with advantage to the general Area — I also understood that the old road on the other side was to be preserved otherwise I should undoubtedly have placed the cottages on that road — it will elevate them and contribute very much to the effect of the village. but I think some little plantation at the back of them or at least at the back of some of them will be necessary — and this removal of those cottages farther back will enable you to shift the Cottage by the Cross in the way you want it may be moved 20 or 30 feet — the Inn I have supposed to consist of a tap room about 18 feet square a parlor of 18 by 14 a passage and stairs a Bar a kitchen washouse & brewhouse Cellars Stabling for about 12 horses and some open sheds to put Coaches or Carts under — the taproom & parlor are the only parts which go up & have rooms over the other buildings are merely sheds — the Cottages consist of a single room below divided into two above a small pantry a backshed by way of washouse & a place for their coals and wood — — some of the Cottages I made double that is to say joind two cottages together to vary the size of the buildings as well as their forms — — Mr Pit seemed to think the clumps in the middle of the Area very small. they are only intended for [present as?] it was meant that when the standards planted among them should have attaind a certain height the fences should be removed the underwood cleard away and the trees stand unprotected on the green between the stems of which the village should be seen — those parts of the plantations only which screen the yards from the road & those which form the back ground of the buildings should be permanent — Mr Pit seems to think we need not continue your boundary wall home to the chapel but stop it at the division between Mr. Egerton Leighs ground & yours from whence through a gate and between 2 paled fences the public might go to the chapel — this is a circumstance so immaterial to the general effect & which you are yourself the most competent to decide on that my opinion can be of no consequence — I find by the same gentleman that you are determined to remove the Tea Caddy lodge I congratulate you on that determination and I should recommend that in future no lodge be seen but only a handsome Archway and the lodge a mere leantoo building against the wall withinside which will in a great measure bring back the expence you have incurrd in so much of the lodge as is done by adopting a cheaper kind of building

Mr Repton did not insist on the open hurdles extending farther than where the view on each side of the road was open as soon as it comes where there is any plantation on either side he recommends a close fence so that at the end where the hurdles join the plantation he would begin the close fence and carry it to the gate, & from the gate again at the back of the plantation adjoining the road till it joins the wall that goes on to the lodge and [on?] the other side of that road when [*one or two words obliterated*] is plantation behind it he recommen[ds a?] close fence

I have the honour to be Dear Sir

Your most obedient
humble Servant

Jno Nash

2[1?] Jany 1798

No 28 Dover St

Appendix VII

Manuscript material referred to: some major sources

The Harford Papers. Two Collections have been consulted.
One is at Bristol Record Office, Bristol. Items are listed in the 122pp. *Report on the Papers of the Harford Family, Baronets of Falcondale, Cardigan (q.v.)* under the accession number 28048.

The other Collection is at Gloucestershire Record Office, Gloucester. This includes, among other documents, many deeds relating to Henbury and Westbury-on-Trym.

The Cornwall-Legh Muniments. These are at The John Rylands University Library of Manchester, Manchester. The Collection includes a number of letters and copy letters that passed between H. Repton, G.S. Repton, J. Nash and G.J. Legh, of High Legh, Cheshire.

G.S. Repton's Notebooks. Two have been referred to in this book. One — the earlier — is in the Drawings Collection of the Royal Institute of British Architects, London. It is referred to in this book as the *RIBA Notebook*, to distinguish it from another in the keeping of Art Gallery and Museums and Royal Pavilion, Brighton. This is referred to in this book as the *Pavilion Notebook*.

The RIBA Notebook is signed 'G.S. Repton' and is undated except by the paper watermark — 1798. It was in use from shortly after that date until about 1805 and measures 100mm x 160mm. It contains ninety-four leaves. An annotated list of the drawings will be found in John Summerson, *John Nash — Architect to King George IV (q.v.)*, and in the *Catalogue of the Drawings Collection of the RIBA* (O—R), *(q.v.)*, edited by Jill Lever.

The *Pavilion Notebook* is similar. It is signed 'George.Stanley. Repton.' and dated 'January.1805'. Fragmented watermarks appear to make up 1799 : the last figure is least clear. The pages have not all been used. One drawing is dated October 1818. Between them, the two Notebooks appear to span, more or less, the years spent by Repton in Nash's office.

Bibliography

Printed works referred to in the text or in the Notes are listed below in two sections. First are items published contemporaneously with or at about the time of events discussed. Second are works published from about 1860 to date.
Manuscript material referred to is identified in the text or in the Notes.

1 Printed Works published before *c.* 1860

Committee — Report from the Select Committee on Crown Leases (London, Reports & Committees, 1829).
Matthews's New Bristol Directory, for the Year, 1793-4 (Bristol, Matthews, n.d.).
Miscellany of Valuables, the Property of the Late Mrs. Beaumont, at Bretton Hall . . . ((London, Robins), 1832).
New Annual Register, or General Repository of History, Politics, and Literature For the Year 1789 (London, Robinson, 1790).
The New History, Survey and Description of the City and Suburbs of Bristol (Bristol, Matthews, 1794).
Nine Lithographic Views of the Cottages, composing Blaise Hamlet, with a Ground Plan of each, and a general Ground Plan of the Whole, situated in the grounds of Blaise Castle, Near Bristol, etc. (Bristol, Bedford, n.d.).
Sketchley's Bristol Directory (Bristol, n.p., 1775).

ANTROBUS, J., *Clifton; or Thoughts and Scenes in two Cantos* (London, Longman, Rees, 1834).
ATKYNS, R., *The Ancient and Present State of Glocestershire,* second edition (London, Herbert etc., 1768).
AUSTEN, J., *Mansfield Park* (London, Egerton, 1814).
BURKE, E., *A Philosophical Enquiry into the Origin of our Ideas of the Sublime and Beautiful* (London, 1756).
BUSBY, C.A., *A Series of Designs for Villas and Country Houses* (London, Taylor, 1808).
CHALMERS, A., *The Works of the English Poets, from Chaucer to Cowper* (London, Johnson, etc., 1810).
[COMBE, W.], *The Tour of Doctor Syntax, In Search of the Picturesque,* fifth edition (London, Ackermann, 1815).
COOKE, W., *A New Picture of the Isle of Wight,* second edition (Southampton, Baker, etc., 1813).
(CRABBE), (editor), *The Life and Poetical Works of the Rev. George Crabbe* (London, Murray, 1847).
CUMBERLAND, G., *An Attempt to Describe Hafod, and the Neighbouring Scenes about the bridge over the Funack, commonly called the Devil's Bridge, in the County of Cardigan* (London, Egerton, 1796).
CUMBERLAND, G., *A Poem on the Landscapes of Great Britain* (London, for the Author, 1793).

DYER, J., *Poems,* collected edition (London, Dodsley, 1761).
EVANS, J., *A Chronological Outline of the History of Bristol, and the Stranger's Guide through its Streets and Neighbourhood* (London & Bristol, Evans, 1824).
EVANS, J. (the Revd.), *The Picture of Bristol,* second edition (Bristol, for W. Sheppard, 1818).
GILPIN, W., *Observations on the River Wye, and Several Parts of South Wales, & c. relative chiefly to Picturesque Beauty; made in the Summer of the Year 1770* (London, Blamire, 1782).
GILPIN, W., *Observations, Relative Chiefly to Picturesque Beauty, made in the year 1772, on several parts of England; particularly the Mountains, and Lakes of Cumberland, and Westmoreland* (London, Blamire, 1786).
GOLDSMITH, O., *The Deserted Village* (London, Griffin, 1770).
HARFORD, J., *Address Delivered in The Assembly Room of Aberystwith on October 18 1849, by John S. Harford, Esq., on presentation of Testimonials from the Conservative Electors of the borough of Aberystwith, and of Cardigan, Adpar and Lampeter* (1849).
HARFORD, J., *Illustrations, Architectural and Pictorial, of the Genius of Michael Angelo Buonarroti* (London, Colnahgi, Longman, 1857).
HASSELL, J., *Tour of the Isle of Wight* (London, Hookham, 1790).
HEATH, C., *Descriptive Accounts of Persfield and Chepstow* (Monmouth, 1793).
JOHNSON, G., *A History of English Gardening* (London, Baldwin & Craddock and Longman, 1829).
JONES, H., *Clifton* (1766).
KENT, N., *Hints to Gentlemen of Landed Property* (London, 1775).
KNIGHT, R., *An Analytical Inquiry into the Principles of Taste,* fourth edition (London, Payne and White, 1808).
KNIGHT, R., *The Landscape, a Didactic Poem. In Three Books,* second edition (London, n.p. 1795).
Le ROUGE [G.], *Détail des Nouveaux Jardins à la Mode* (Paris, le Rouge, 1776-87).
LESLIE, C., *Memoirs of the Life of John Constable, Esq., R.A. Composed Chiefly of His Letters* (London, 1843).
LOUDON, J., *An Encyclopaedia of Cottage, Farm, and Villa Architecture and Furniture* (London, Longman, etc., 1833: second edition, 1835 and 1842 Supplement).
LOUDON, J., *An Encyclopaedia of Gardening,* new edition (London, Longman, etc., 1835).
LOUDON, J., *The Landscape Gardening and Landscape Architecture of the late Humphry Repton, Esq.* (London, Loudon, 1840).
LOUDON, J., *The Suburban Gardener, and Villa Companion* (London, Loudon, 1838).
LOUDON, J., *A Treatise on Forming, Improving, and Managing Country Residences* (London, Longman, Hurst, Rees and Orme, 1806).
LOUDON, J. (edited by LOUDON, Mrs.), *The Villa Gardener,* second edition (London, Orr, 1850).

MALTON, J., *An Essay on British Cottage Architecture* (London, for Hookham & Carpenter, 1798).
[MARSHALL, W.], *Planting and Rural Ornament*, second edition (London, Nicol, 1796).
MASON, G., *An Essay on Design in Gardening*, new edition (London, White, 1795).
MASON, W., *The English Garden*, books 1-4 (London, Dodsley, Cadell, 1777 - 81 editions referred to).
[MATTHEWS, J. (attr.)], *A Sketch, from the Landscape, a Didactic Poem* (London, Faulder, 1794).
NASH, J., *A Statement* (privately printed, 1829).
PAPWORTH, J., *Rural Residences, consisting of a series of Designs for Cottages, Decorated Cottages, Small Villas, and other Onamental Buildings* (London, for Ackermann, 1818).
PLAW, J., *Ferme Ornée; or Rural Improvements* (London, Taylor, 1795).
POCOCK, W., *Architectural Designs for Rustic Cottages* (London, Bensley for Taylor, 1807).
POPE, A., 'Moral Essays: Epistle IV — Of the Use of Riches', *The Works of Alexander Pope, Esq.* (Edinburgh, Donaldson, 1767).
PRICE, U., *An Essay on the Picturesque* (London, Robson, 1794).
PRICE, U., *Essays on the Picturesque* (London, Mawman, 1810).
[PÜCKLER-MUSKAU, H.], *Tour in England, Ireland, and France, in the years 1828 & 1829* (London, Effingham Wilson, i, ii, 1832) : (iii, iv, published as *Tour in Germany, Holland and England in the Years 1826, 1827, & 1828).*
PUGIN, A.C., *Specimens of Gothic Architecture* (London, Taylor, 1821-23).
PUGIN, A.W., *Contrasts; or, a Parallel between the Noble Edifices of the Fourteenth and Fifteenth Centuries, and Similar Buildings of the Present Day* (Salisbury, Pugin, 1836).
PUGIN, A.W., *The True Principles of Pointed or Christian Architecture* (London, Weale, 1841).
REPTON, H., *An Inquiry into the Changes of Taste in Landscape Gardening* (London, 1806): incorporating an edited version of *Sketches and Hints.*
REPTON H., *Designs for the Pavilion at Brighton* (London, Stadler, 1808).
REPTON, H., *Observations on the Theory and Practice of Landscape Gardening* (London, Taylor, 1803).
REPTON, H., *Sketches and Hints on Landscape Gardening* (London, Boydell, [1794/5]).
REPTON, H. and J., *Fragments on the Theory and Practice of Landscape Gardening* (London, Taylor, 1816).
ROBINSON, P., *Designs for Village Architecture* (London, Carpenter, 1830).
ROBINSON, P., *Rural Architecture; or, a series of Designs for Rural Cottages,* second edition (1826), fourth edition (London, Bohn, 1836).
SMITH, J., *Remarks on Rural Scenery* (London, Smith, 1797).
SOANE, J., *Sketches in Architecture; containing Plans and Elevations of Cottages, Villas, and Other Useful Buildings, with Characteristic Scenery* (London, Taylor, 1793).

STORER, J. & H. & BREWER, J., *Delineations of Gloucestershire* (London, Sherwood, Gilbert & Piper, 1824).
WALPOLE, H., *Anecdotes of Painting in England* (Strawberry Hill, 1762-71).
WALPOLE, H., *Essay on Modern Gardening* (Strawberry Hill, 1785).
WEALE, J. (editor), *Designs and Examples of Cottages, Villas, and Country Houses, being the studies of several eminent Architects and Builders* (London, Weale, 1857).
[WHATELY, T.], *Observations on Modern Gardening* (London, Payne, 1770).
WHITEHEAD, W., *The Removal of the Village at Nuneham* (1771).
WOOD, J., *A Series of Plans, for Cottages or Habitations of the Labourer, either in Husbandry, or the Mechanical Arts* (London, Taylor, 1781).
WRIGHT, T., *Six Original Designs of Arbours* (1755).
WRIGHT, T., *Six Original Designs of Grottos* (1758).
WRIGHTE, W., *Grotesque Architecture, or, Rural Amusement* (London, Webley, 1767).
YOUNG, W., *Guide to the Beauties of Glyn Neath* (London, Longman, etc., 1835).

Periodicals, Journals, etc., published before *c.* 1860

Felix Farley's Bristol Journal, 9 May, 16 May, 20 June 1789; 13 December, 27 December, 1800; 28 February, 1801.
The Gentleman's Magazine, 1835.
Hereford Journal, 18 January, 1826.
Morning Post, 6 September, 1799.
The World (No. 15), 12 April 1753; (No. 76), 13 June 1754: quoted from the edition of Adam FITZ-ADAM (London, Dodsley, 1789).

2 Printed Works published from *c.* 1860

A Guide to Henbury, second edition (n.p., Hallen & Henbury W.I., 1970).
Report on the Papers of the Harford Family, Baronets of Falcondale, Cardigan (London, R.C.H.M., 1976).

BARRETT, C. (editor), *Diary and Letters of Madame D'Arblay* (London, Macmillan, 1904-1905).
BATEY, M., *Nuneham Courtenay: an Oxfordshire 18th-Century Deserted Village,* reprinted from *Oxoniensia,* xxxiii (1968).
(BATEY, M.), *Nuneham Courtenay Oxfordshire* (n.p., Oxford University Chest Estates Committee, 1970).
BECKETT, R. (editor), *John Constable's Correspondence* (London & Ipswich, Suffolk Record Society, 1962-68).
BROWNELL, M., *Alexander Pope and the Arts of Georgian England* (Oxford, Clarendon Press, 1978).
BUTLER, E. (editor), *A Regency Visitor* (London, Collins, 1957).
CAVE, C., *A History of Banking in Bristol* (Bristol, Privately Printed, 1899).

CLARK, K., *The Gothic Revival*, new edition (Harmondsworth, Penguin, 1964).
COLVIN, H., *A Biographical Dictionary of British Architects, 1600-1840* (London, Murray, 1978).
COLVIN, H. & HARRIS, J., *The Country Seat* (London, Allen Lane, Penguin Press, 1970).
COPELAND, T. (general editor), *The Correspondence of Edmund Burke*, volume iii, GUTTRIDGE, G. (editor), (London, Cambridge University Press, 1961).
CORNFORTH, J. & GORE, St. J., *Attingham Park Shropshire* (n.p., National Trust, n.d.).
CRICK, C., *Victorian Buildings in Bristol* (Bristol, Bristol & West Building Society and City Art Gallery, 1975).
CRONIN, V., *Louis & Antoinette* (London, Collins, 1974).
DARLEY, G., *Villages of Vision* (London, Architectural Press, 1975).
DAVIS, T., *The Architecture of John Nash* (London, Studio, 1960).
DAVIS, T., *John Nash — The Prince Regent's Architect*, second edition (Newton Abbot, David & Charles, 1973).
FENDALL, C., & CRUTCHLEY, E. (editors), *The Diary of Benjamin Newton* (Cambridge, University Press, 1933).
FERRY, B. (introduced by WAINWRIGHT, C.), *Recollections of A.W.N. Pugin and his father Augustus Pugin* (London, Scolar Press, 1978).
FOX, C., *Ancient Monuments . . . South Wales and Monmouthshire*, third edition (London, H.M.S.O., 1955).
GERMANN, G. (translated by Gerald ONN), *Gothic Revival in Europe and Britain: Sources, Influences and Ideas* (London, Lund Humphries — Architectural Association, 1972).
GLOAG, J., *Mr. Loudon's England* (Newcastle upon Tyne, Oriel Press, 1970).
GOMME, A., JENNER, M., LITTLE, B., *Bristol: an Architectural History* (London, Lund Humphries — Bristol & West Building Society, 1979).
GREIG, J. (editor), *The Farington Diary* (London, Hutchinson, 1922-1928).
GUNNIS, R., *Dictionary of British Sculptors 1660-1851* (London, Odhams, n.d.).
GUTTRIDGE, G. (editor), *The Correspondence of Edmund Burke* (1961): (see COPELAND).
HARFORD, A. (editor), *Annals of the Harford Family* (London, Westminster Press, 1909).
HEBDITCH, M., *Blaise Castle House Museum: The House and its Collections* (Bristol, City Museum, 1971).
HIPPLE, W., *The Beautiful, The Sublime, and the Picturesque in Eighteenth Century British Aesthetic Theory* (Southern Illinois University Press, 1957).
HITCHCOCK, H.-R., *Architecture: Nineteenth and Twentieth Centuries*, third edition (Baltimore, Penguin, 1968).
HOWITT, W. & M., *Ruined Abbeys and Castles of Great Britain* (London, Bennett, 1862: second series, including Ireland, 1864).
HUSSEY, C., *English Gardens and Landscapes 1700-1750* (London, Country Life, 1967).

HUSSEY, C., *The Picturesque: Studies in a Point of View* (London, Putnam, 1927).
HYAMS, E., *Capability Brown and Humphry Repton* (London, Dent, 1971).
INGLIS-JONES, E., *Peacocks in Paradise* (Shoreham-by-Sea, Service, 1971).
ISON, W., *The Georgian Buildings of Bristol* (London, Faber and Faber, 1952).
JONES, B., *Follies and Grottoes,* second edition (London, Constable, 1974).
KALNEIN, W. & LEVEY, M., *Art and Architecture of the Eighteenth Century in France* (Harmondsworth, Penguin, 1972).
LEMMON, K., *The Covered Garden* (London, Museum Press, 1962).
LEVER, J. (editor), *Catalogue of the Drawings Collection of the RIBA* (O - R), (Farnborough, Gregg, 1976).
LITTLE, B., *The City and County of Bristol* (London, Laurie, 1954).
LODWICK, J. & V., *The Story of Carmarthen,* second edition (Carmarthen, Lodwick, 1972).
MALDEN, E. (editor), *Victoria History of the County of Surrey* (London, Constable, 1902-12).
MALINS, E., *English Landscaping and Literature 1660-1840* (London, Oxford University Press, 1966).
MALINS, E., *The Red Books of Humphry Repton* (London, Basilisk Press, 1976).
MANWARING, E., *Italian Landscape in Eighteenth Century England* (London, Cass, 1965).
MARSHALL, P., *Bristol and the American War of Independence* (Bristol, Historical Association, 1977).
PAGE, W. (editor), *Victoria History of Hampshire and the Isle of Wight* (London, Constable, 1900-12).
PEVSNER, N., *Buildings of England: North Somerset and Bristol* (London, Penguin, 1958).
PEVSNER, N., *Studies in Art, Architecture and Design,* volume i (London, Thames & Hudson, 1968).
PHILLIPS, D. RHYS, *History of the Vale of Neath* (Swansea, 1925).
PLOMER, W. (editor), *Kilvert's Diary* (London, Cape, 1938).
POUNTNEY, W., *Old Bristol Potteries* (Bristol, Arrowsmith, 1920).
PRITCHARD, E., *Penoyre* (Brecon, n.p., 1969).
RICHARDS, R., *The Chapels of the Blessed Virgin Mary and St. John at High Legh, Cheshire,* reprinted from the *Transactions of the Historic Society of Lancashire and Cheshire* (1949).
RICHARDSON, C., *The Englishman's House,* new edition (London, Chatto & Windus, 1898).
RUSKIN, J., *The Seven Lamps of Architecture*, seventh edition (London & Orpington, Allen, 1897).
(SANDERSON, J.), MORGAN, G. (editor), *Rural Architecture; being a Series of Designs for Rural and Other Dwellings*, second edition (London, Rogerson and Tuxford/Houlston and Wright, 1860).
SANECKI, K., *Humphry Repton* (Aylesbury, Shire, 1974).
SAUNDERS, A., *Regent's Park: a Study of the Development from 1086 to the Present Day* (Newton Abbot, David and Charles, 1969).

SHERWOOD, J. & PEVSNER, N., *The Buildings of England: Oxfordshire* (London, Penguin, 1974).
STEVENS, F., *Normandy, its Gothic Architecture and History* (London, Bennett, 1865).
STROUD, D., *Capability Brown*, new edition (London, Faber and Faber, 1975).
STROUD, D., *Humphry Repton* (London, Country Life, 1962).
SUMMERSON, J., *Architecture in Britain 1530-1830* (London, Penguin, 1953).
SUMMERSON, J., *John Nash — Architect to King George IV*, second edition, (London, Allen & Unwin, 1949).
WATERS, I., *Piercefield on the Banks of the Wye* (Chepstow, Comber, 1975).
WATERS, I., *The Unfortunate Valentine Morris* (Chepstow, The Chepstow Society, 1964).
WATKIN, D., *The Life and Work of C.R. Cockerell* (London, Zwemmer, 1974).
WATKIN, D., *Thomas Hope 1769-1831 and the Neo-Classical Idea* (London, Murray, 1968).
WIEBENSON, D., *The Picturesque Garden in France* (Princeton, Princeton University Press, 1978).
WILENSKI, R., *English Painting* (London, Faber & Faber, 1933).
WILLIS, P. (editor), *Furor Hortensis* (Edinburgh, Elysium Press, 1974).
WINSTONE, R., *Bristol as it was, 1866-60* (Bristol, Winstone, 1967).
WOODFORDE, J., *The Truth about Cottages* (London, Routledge & Kegan Paul, 1969).

Periodicals, Journals, etc., published from *c.* 1860

Architect and Building News, 17 September, 1943.
Architectural History, xi, 1968; xviii, 1975; xix, 1976; xx, 1977.
Architectural Review, May, 1938; August, 1976; September, 1977.
Art Bulletin, xxxi, 1949.
Connoisseur, December, 1956.
Country Life, 3 September, 1943; 4 July, 1952; 9 September, 1971.
Field, 9 October, 1943.
Garden History, ii, no. 3, Summer 1974.
Illustrated London News, 11 September, 1943.
South Wales Daily News, 25 March, 1911.
Sphere, 14 August, 1943.
Transactions of the Cambrian Antiquarian and Field Society, 1939.
Transactions of the Honourable Society of Cymmrodorion, 1977.
Y Cymmrodor, xxxv, 1925.

Index

The Index includes those book titles (under authors when applicable) that appear in the text or Notes and also in Section 1 of the Bibliography: that is, those books published before *c.* 1860. The source of a reference not stating the book title, and books listed in Section 2 of the Bibliography, may normally be traced via the Notes. Some titles appearing in the Index are in shortened form.

Plates

Plate 1. Blaise Hamlet, Bristol: the cottages, drawn on stone by J. Horner and dedicated by the Bristol publisher George Davey to John Harford. Several variations on nine such miniature views appeared between *c.* 1825 and *c.* 1835, one set published in Bristol by T. Bedford being dedicated to Mrs. Harford.

Plate 2. Blaise Hamlet, Bristol: a drawing of Jasmine Cottage, from an album of about 1820. It appears to have been copied in pencil from a miniature lithograph by J.B. West Junior, of Bath.

Plate 3. Milton Abbas, Dorset: looking up the gently winding village street.

Plate 4. Nicolas Poussin. *Gathering of the Ashes of Phocion.*

Plate 5. Downton Castle, on the Herefordshire-Salop border. The valley across which it looks is to the right.

Plate 6. Vignette from the title page of *A Sketch from the Landscape*, 1794: Lancelot Brown's memorial besmirched.

Plate 7. 'Dr. Syntax Drawing after Nature', by Thomas Rowlandson, from *The Tour of Doctor Syntax, in Search of the Picturesque.* Here he studies animals — picturesque and beautiful — as Gilpin might have suggested he should.

Plate 8. 'Aberystwith Castle and Church'. To the left is Castle House, designed by Nash for Uvedale Price. Picturesque ruins were conveniently nearby.

Plate 9. Hafod — Thomas Johnes' mansion in Wales — as rebuilt after the fire of 1807 and enlarged to the design of Anthony Salvin.

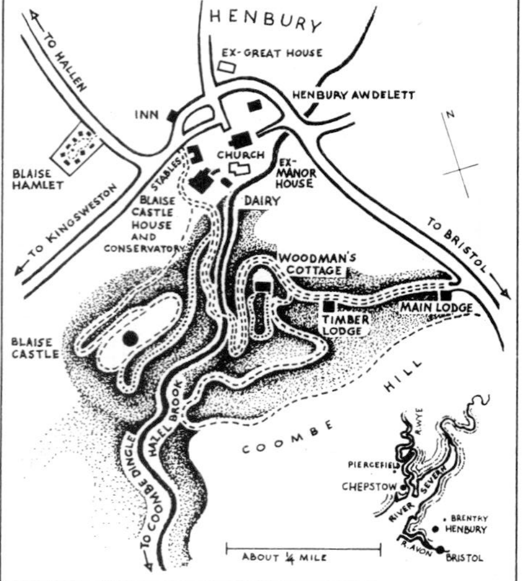

Plate 11. Blaise Castle Estate: a plan showing the drive (as suggested by Repton), major buildings and Blaise Hamlet. The Severn estuary is about three miles to the west.

Henbury The Seat of Mr John Sampson

Plate 10. Henbury, Bristol: Kip's view of about 1710, showing the avenue, the hill on which Farr later built his tower, and (left) the ravine: also the Vicarage, Church, Henbury Awdelett (foreground) and the Great House. The Severn estuary and Wales lie beyond. Harford built his mansion between the churchyard and the avenue.

Plate 12. Blaise: the Main Lodge, with Anne Lodge and her descendants posing.

Plate 13. 'Blaze Castle': detail of an aquatint dated 1786, by F. Jukes. 'Picturesque' cows ruminate: one notices a 'beautiful' horse passing from the view: there is a promise that 'terrifying' landscape features are there to be explored.

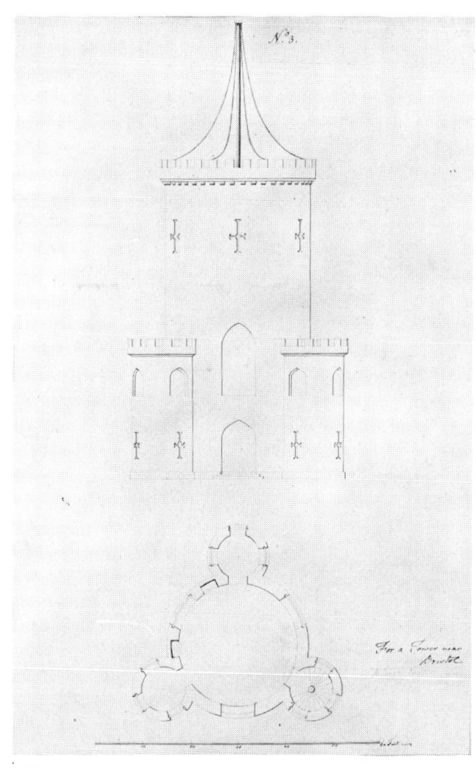

Plate 14. A drawing by Robert Mylne 'For a Tower near Bristol'. The flagstaff, with slack ropes (?), gives the appearance here of a turret-like roof line.

Plate 15. Blaise Castle: Farr's tower, now in a more ruined state.

Plate 16. Blaise Castle: the Circular Centre Room in 1919.

Plate 17. Blaise: the Main Lodge as envisaged by Humphry Repton in the *Red Book for Blaise*. The dwelling and tower had their positions reversed when built and the tower was heightened.

Plate 18. Blaise, the Main Lodge: an undated drawing attributed to John Repton. The paper is watermarked 1830. There are minor differences between the building depicted in this drawing and the Main Lodge as shown in Plates 12 and 19.

Specimen, with the Engravings plain.

202 REPTON'S LANDSCAPE GARDENING, &c.

In determining the sort of entrance proper for BLAIZE CASTLE, the name of the place caused some difficulty; the

[Fig. 87. View of the entrance to Blaize Castle before the lodge was built.]

house to which the castle belongs, neither does nor ought to partake of any Gothic character, yet there appeared some incongruity in making the entrance in the Grecian style of architecture to accord with the house, which is nowhere seen from the road [see fig. 87], while the castle is a conspicuous feature, and gives a name to the place; I, therefore, recommended the design [fig. 88], as a proper object to attract

[Fig. 88. Entrance lodge to Blaize Castle.]

notice in the approach, which is one of the most interesting and romantic.

Plate 19. Blaise, the Main Lodge: the reverse of an undated prospectus for J.C. Loudon's '*Repton's Landscape Gardening, and Landscape Architecture*': 'To be completed in Twelve Numbers'. In Loudon's book two wood-engravings were needed (as here) to achieve what Repton had done by using one 'slide'.

Plate 20. Blaise Woods, Timber Lodge: a delicacy of knots and rods standing alongside Harford's drive, probably dating from the earlier half of the nineteenth century.

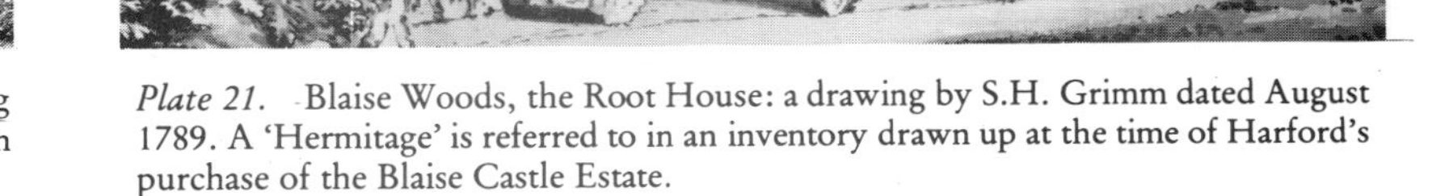

Plate 21. Blaise Woods, the Root House: a drawing by S.H. Grimm dated August 1789. A 'Hermitage' is referred to in an inventory drawn up at the time of Harford's purchase of the Blaise Castle Estate.

Plate 22. Blaise Woods, Woodman's Cottage: Repton's visualisation in the *Red Book for Blaise* is very much like the building depicted in this anonymous aquatint.

Plate 23. Blaise Woods, Woodman's Cottage.

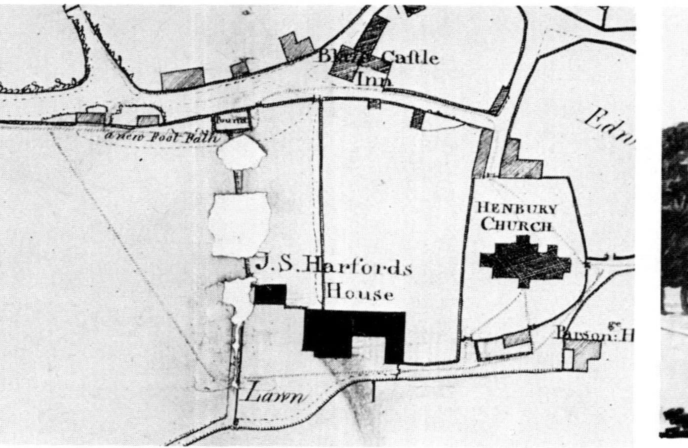

Plate 24. Blaise: detail from a plan dated 1790, locating the house Harford bought and later demolished. The footpath cutting across his park to the church is indicated, as is the proposed replacement for it, alongside the highway (top). The new mansion was to be built a little to the north of this house, roughly where the large tear appears on the plan; Blaise Hamlet by the road forking top left.

Plate 25. Blaise: the house Harford bought, as seen from the woods and recorded by Repton in the *Red Book*. A slide, hinged to the right, can be seen overlaying the water-colour painting.

Plate 27. Blaise Castle House: a view from the south showing the Gallery added by John Harford junior, to Charles Cockerell's design.

Plate 26. Blaise: the slide lifted to reveal the scene as it would be on completion of Blaise Castle House. A conservatory is shown where Nash was later to provide one.

Plate 28. Blaise Castle House, the Conservatory.

Plate 29. Blaise Castle House, the Dairy: a drawing attributed to John Repton.

Plate 30. Blaise Castle House, the Dairy: drawings from George Repton's *RIBA Notebook*.

Plate 31. Blaise Castle House, the Dairy.

Plate 32. Study for a Druid Temple, for 'Mr Harford'. On the verso of this leaf from the *RIBA Notebook* are drawings for Blaise Dairy.

Plate 33. Henbury, Blaise Hamlet: an early photograph taken from inside the entrance, with Oak Cottage (left), and Dial Cottage (right). The Pump, topped by a weather vane, can be seen. It existed in this form by 1826. Harford, the father, marked the spring with an 'obelisk'. His son had a memorial tablet inscribed. This names Nash as designer of the cottages as well as John Harford senior, the benevolent parent. The inscription is dated August 1859. The earlier wooded setting can be appreciated. It has been replaced largely by neighbouring rooftops and a field, which jointly contribute to the loss of essential intimacy and the exposure of several cottage backs.

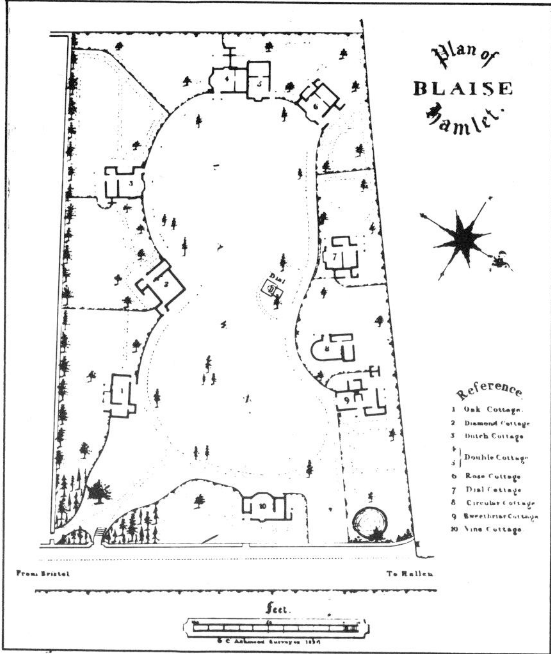

Plate 34. Blaise Hamlet: a plan by G. Ashmead, dated 1826, which shows garden boundaries, planting and the Pump, or 'Dial'. There is a pond in the north-east corner and two small entrances are indicated in the east angle.

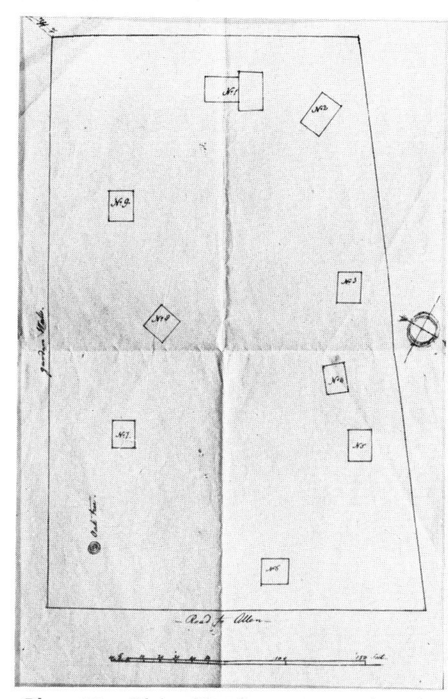

Plate 35. Blaise Hamlet: a manuscript plan with the John Harford — George Repton correspondence. The numbering of cottages is as followed in this account. They are set out as built. While the oak tree is shown, there is no sign of the sundial charged for in Nash's account of 1812.

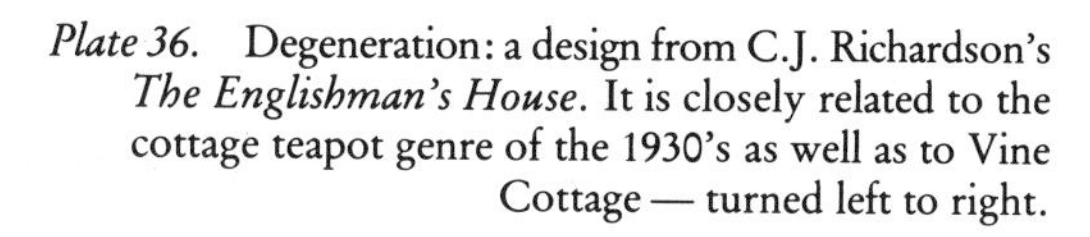

Plate 36. Degeneration: a design from C.J. Richardson's *The Englishman's House*. It is closely related to the cottage teapot genre of the 1930's as well as to Vine Cottage — turned left to right.

Design No. 3.

A PICTURESQUE COTTAGE.

Perspective view.

Ground-floor plan

Upper floor

A PICTURESQUE COTTAGE. 63

This design for a peasant's cottage possesses no architectural feature beyond what could be given

Elevation of front.

to it by any common country village carpenter. It was made from the recollection of one at Blaise Hamlet,

Side front.

near Blaise Castle, in Gloucestershire, the seat of John I. Harford, Esq., to whom the hamlet belonged. This

Plate 37. Blaise Hamlet: one of a set of undated lithographs by James West. Looking towards Double and Rose cottages on having passed through the entrance gate.

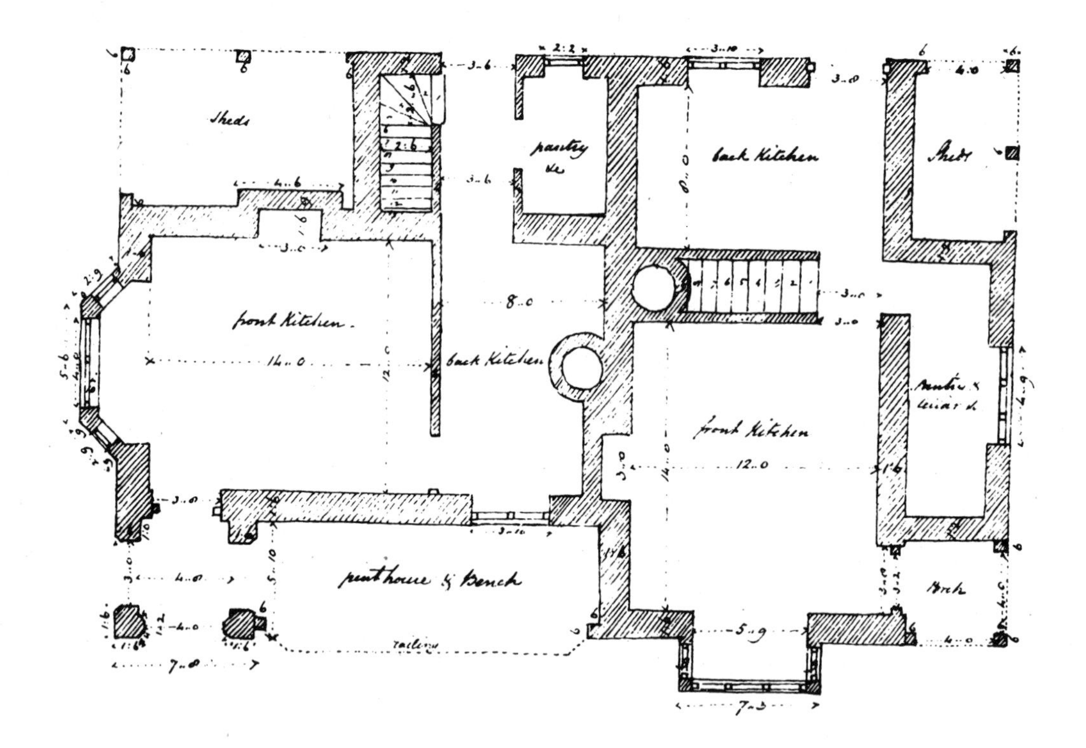

Plate 38. Blaise Hamlet, Double Cottage: a plan from the *Pavilion Notebook*. It differs from the dwellings as built in the placing of stairs, the arrangement of offices and by the presence of a pantry behind the north porch.

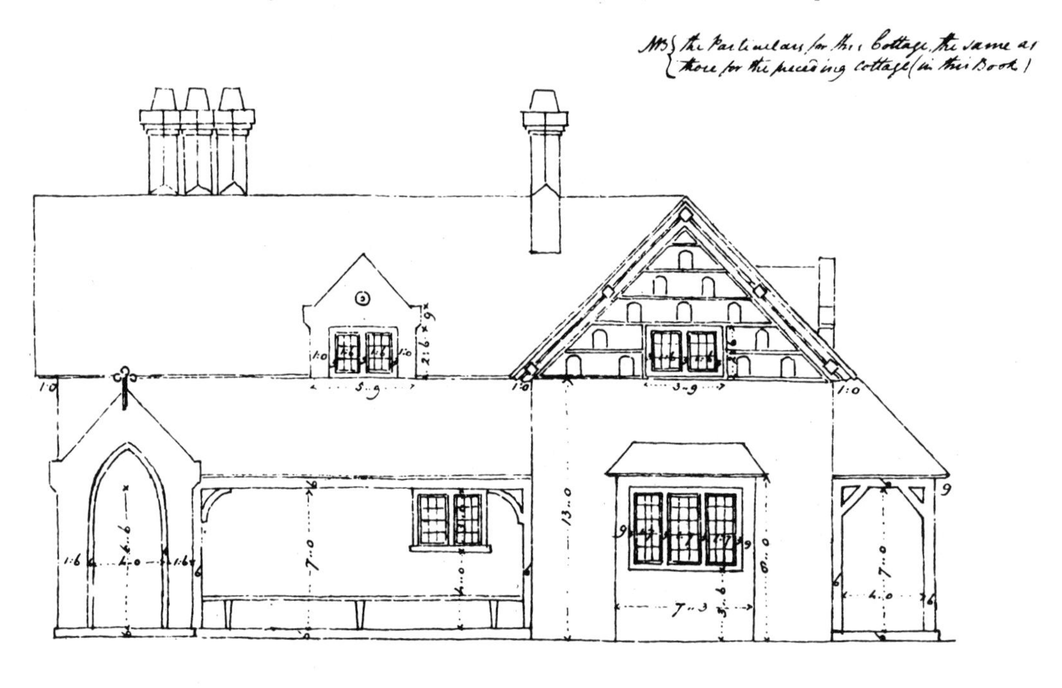

Plate 39. Blaise Hamlet, Double Cottage: an elevation from the *Pavilion Notebook*. Apart from lacking its decorative chimneys, the drawing is very close to the cottage as built. The south porch has a finial. A bay window has been omitted.

Plate 40. Blaise Hamlet, Double Cottage: an undated drawing attributed to John Repton. The window placed centrally over the seat does not comply with the accompanying plan — watermarked 1830 — which places the window as built, to the right. The north porch is open, exposing the pantry wall to view. Yet this was not built. The chimneys are as in Repton's drawing, but the upper casements are of different depth.

Plate 41. Blaise Hamlet, Double Cottage: an undated and anonymous watercolour not agreeing fully with Repton's working drawings, or with the completed building. The north porch is open and the south one sports a finial like the one in Repton's elevational drawing. The chimneys are plain and of modest height. While the front bay window has only two casements looking on to the green, the south porch entrance is like that built at Rose Cottage next door — Tudor rather than Gothic in form. Perhaps this is an early visualisation, with ashlar in mind.

Plate 42. Blaise Hamlet, Double Cottage. The two now form a single dwelling. The repetitive shapes of six tall slim shafts add a commanding quality not apparent in Plates 39, 40 and 41.

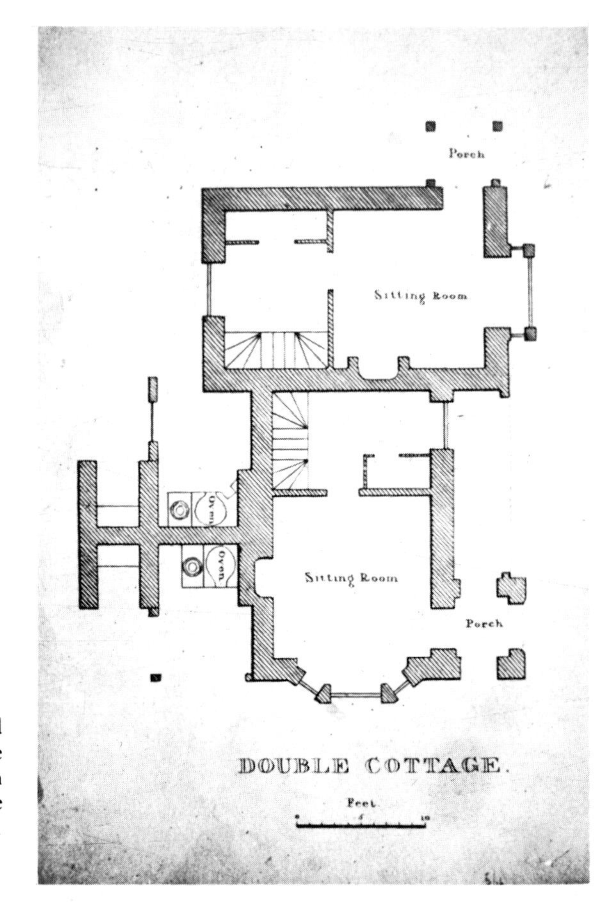

Plate 43. Blaise Hamlet, Double Cottage: ground plan, from *Nine Lithographic Views* of *c.* 1826. The rearranged stairs, ovens and out houses are shown and the north porch, no longer backed by the pantry, can be seen standing proud.

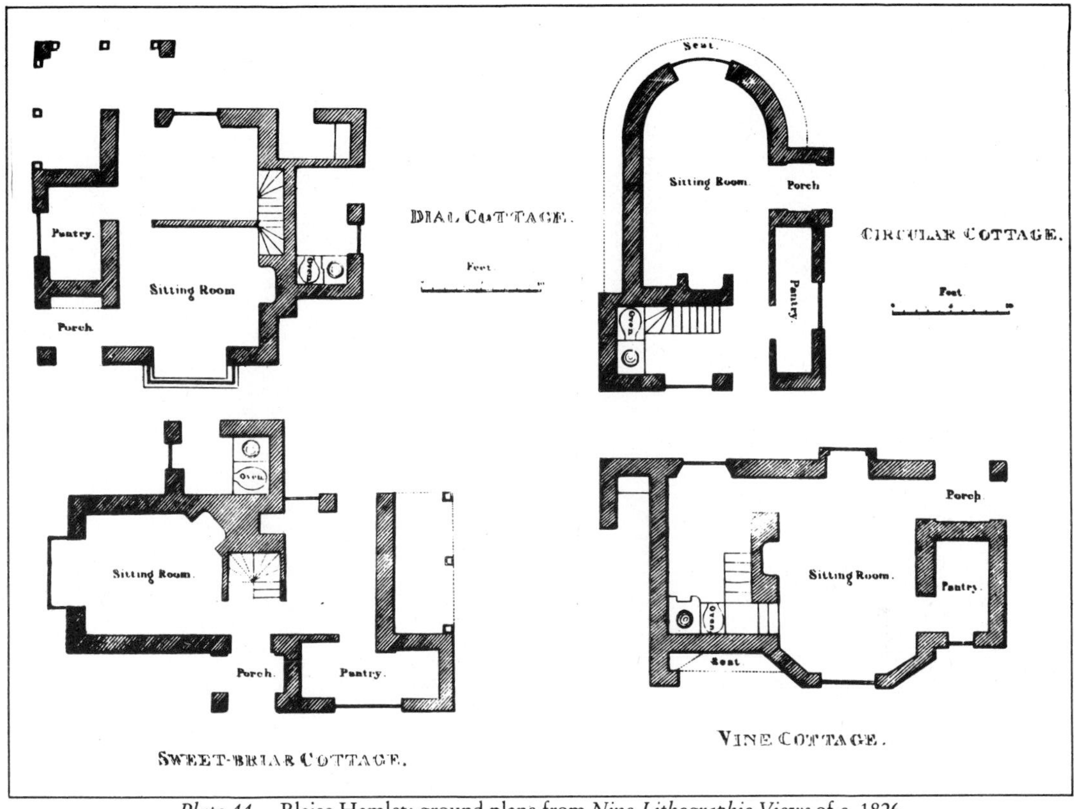

Plate 44. Blaise Hamlet: ground plans from *Nine Lithographic Views* of *c.* 1826.

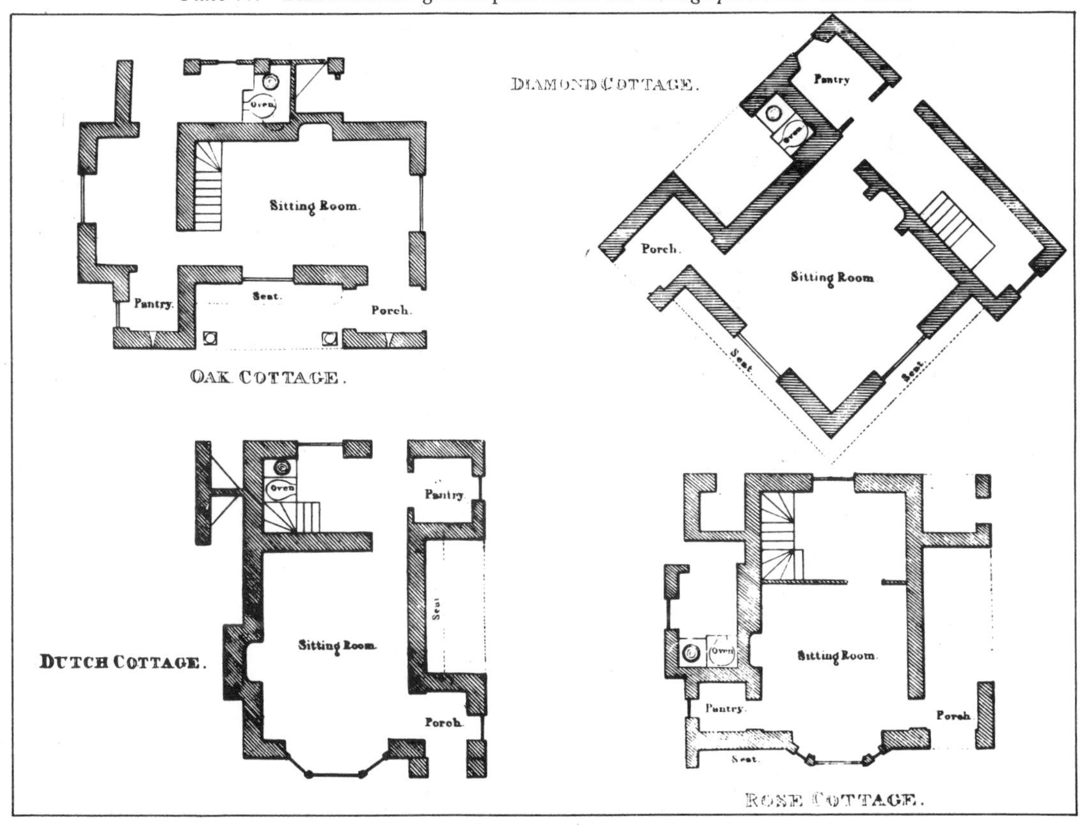

Plate 45. Blaise Hamlet: ground plans from *Nine Lithographic Views* of *c.* 1826.

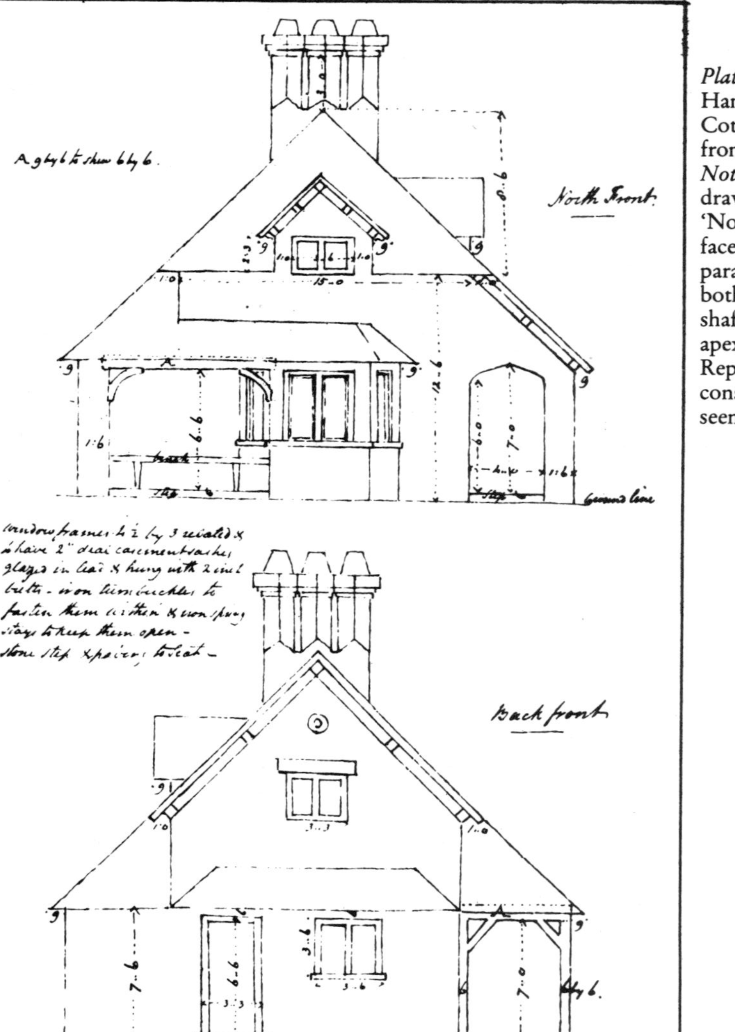

Plate 46. Blaise Hamlet, Rose Cottage: elevations from the *Pavilion Notebook*. The top drawing is captioned 'North Front'. It faces east. The parallel elevations both show three shafts above the apex. Some of Repton's notes on construction can be seen on this page.

Plate 47. Blaise Hamlet, Rose Cottage: an undated drawing attributed to John Repton. It shows chimneys astride the main roof. They were built to the left, as can be seen in Plates 48 and 50. Only two shafts are shown here.

Plate 48. Blaise Hamlet, Rose Cottage: one of O'Neill and Harding's *Nine Lithographic Views*. The 'dormer' then contained a pigeon loft not shown in Repton's elevation or Plate 47. As there was no other window the bedroom was presumably given over to the pigeons.

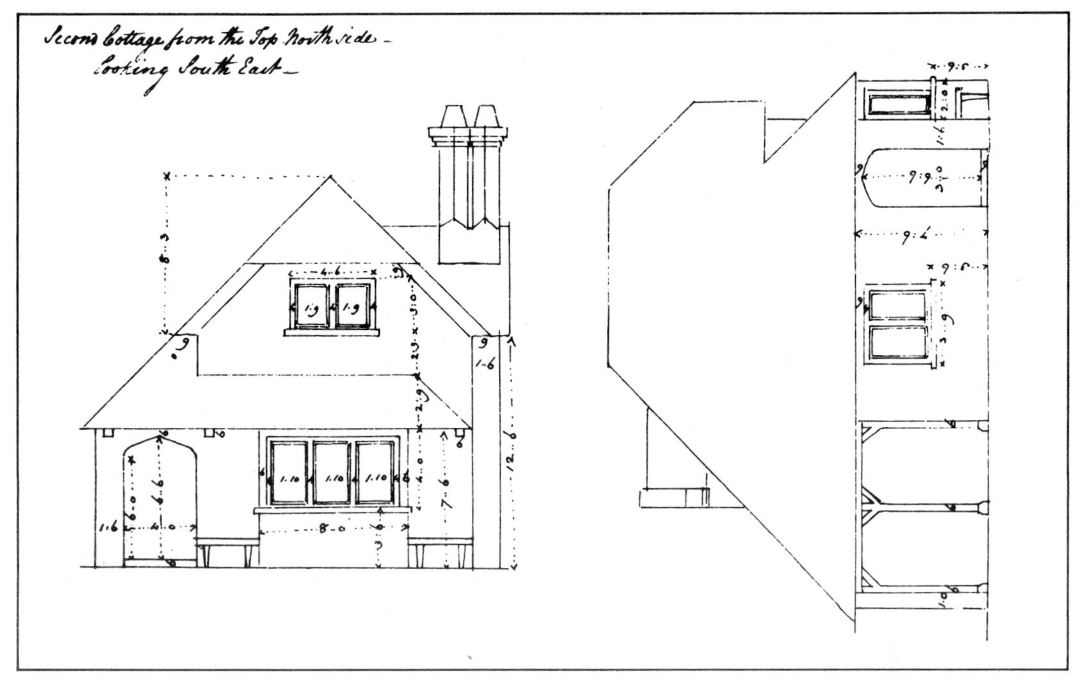

Plate 49. Blaise Hamlet, Dial Cottage: the south-east elevation (left) and south-west elevation, from the *Pavilion Notebook*.

Plate 50. Blaise Hamlet: Rose Cottage, Dial Cottage, and the Village Pump. The extension housing the oven, copper and privy required by the inventory of defects can be seen. The main wall and stack against which it is built is the only instance of brick being used conspicuously in a main wall, the remainder being of local pennant.

Plate 51. Blaise Hamlet, Dial Cottage: the triple shafts not indicated on Repton's drawings, which required only two, of standard form — as at Rose Cottage. Their height, mass and grandeur add great distinction to the cottage and endorse the narrow axis of the green with authority.

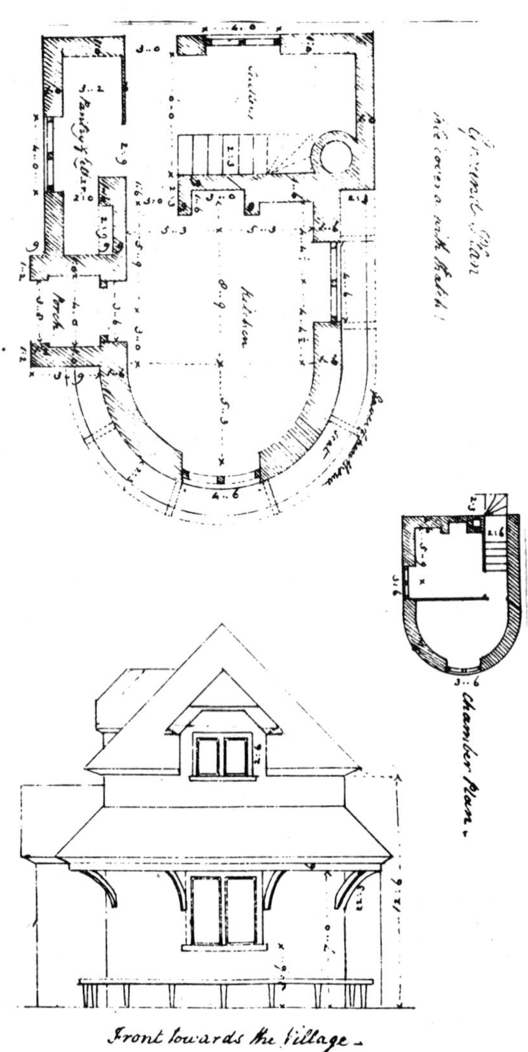

Plate 53. Blaise Hamlet, Circular Cottage, showing a dormer window complying with Repton's amended drawing and the inventory requirements. See also page 97 (south-west dormer).

Plate 52. Blaise Hamlet, Circular Cottage: ground and chamber plans, with south-east elevation. Thatch is specified and indicated. Pencilled amendments to the dormers can be seen and they were finished accordingly.

Plate 54. Sarsden, Oxfordshire; the Keeper's House: an undated drawing attributed to George Repton. Compare with Plates 53 and 88.

Plate 55. Blaise Hamlet, Sweet Briar Cottage: south-east and north-east elevations, showing the projecting window long since removed. Both drawings are identified as being for the 'Front towards the South'. From the *Pavilion Notebook*.

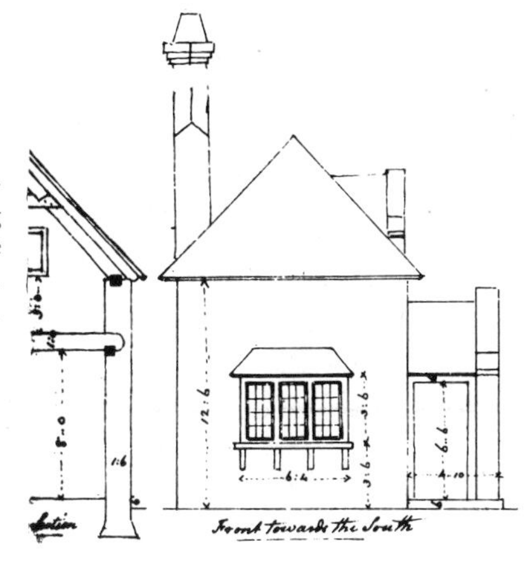

Plate 56. Blaise Hamlet, Sweet Briar Cottage, showing the bracketed window once looking out on the Green. Compare the porch, seat and pent with those shown in Plate 79 and the building in Plate 80.

Presented in folio printed boards, *Nine Lithographic Views of the Cottages, Composing Blaise Hamlet* appeared in at least two editions (with plates according to a range of choices). While the main title (above) was the same, there were variations in secondary titling, one (later?) version implying that Ashmead, of Bristol, drew the cottage plans, although they remained undated and unsigned in the stone.

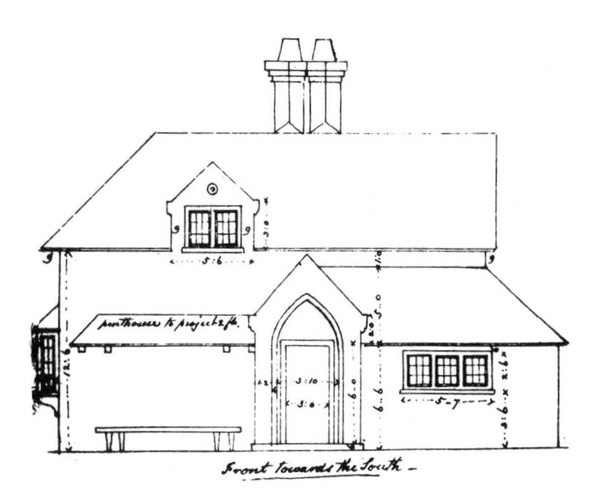

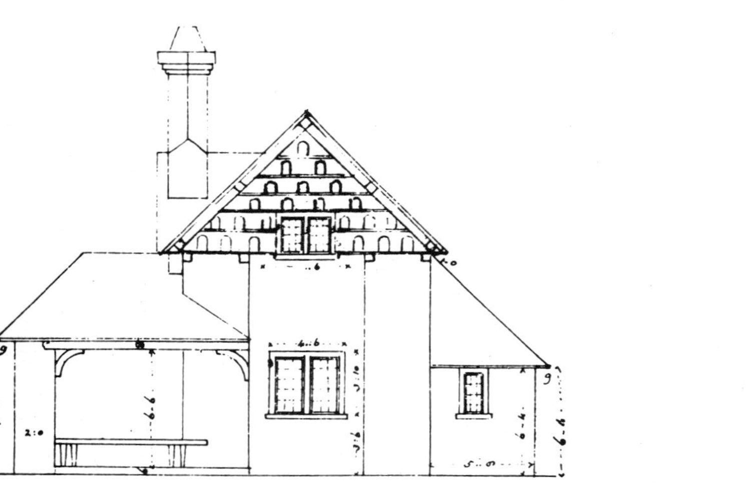

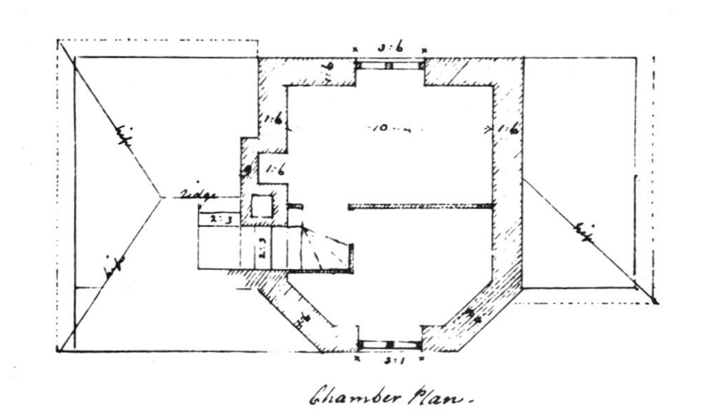

Plate 57. Blaise Hamlet, Vine Cottage: south-west elevation and chamber plan, from the *Pavilion Notebook*. The gable end with pigeon holes is responded to by the same device at Double Cottage. The two serve to emphasise the major axis of Nash's plan. One welcomes: one bids *adieu*.

Plate 58. Blaise Hamlet, Vine Cottage: south-west elevation, showing an additional chimney and extended canopy to the right of the seat. There is an extra row of pigeon holes that influence qualities of pattern and scale.

Plate 59. Blaise Hamlet, Vine Cottage: north-east elevation — facing the road — suggesting that it might have doubled as a lodge.

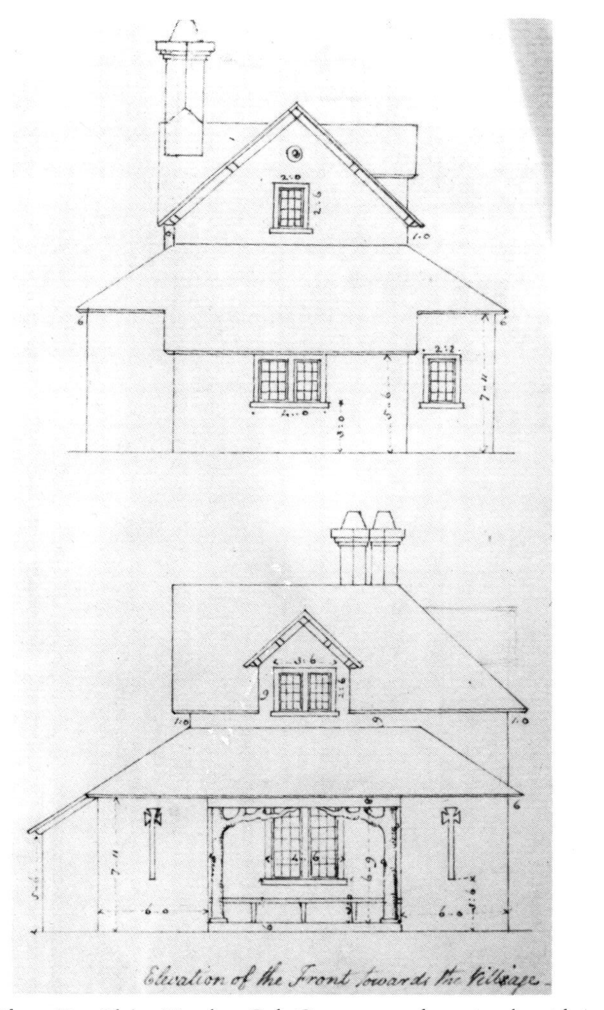

Plate 60. Blaise Hamlet, Oak Cottage: north-east and north-west elevations, from the *Pavilion Notebook*. There was no door leading from the right of the seated porch in Repton's drawings.

Plate 61. Blaise Hamlet, Oak Cottage, photographed in 1972, before restoration by the National Trust. Such tiles, popular in the Bristol area, had an extremely dulling effect on the appearance of this cottage.

Plate 62. Blaise Hamlet, Oak Cottage, photographed in 1974, after restoration by the National Trust. Its visual vitality has been recaptured. All the cottages have been restored by the National Trust and now appear very much as they did when newly built.

Plate 63. A pencil drawing, perhaps of Oak Cottage, or of a similar one built elsewhere. There is no suggestion that the original was in a village setting. Windows are out of scale. See Plate 60 and front end paper.

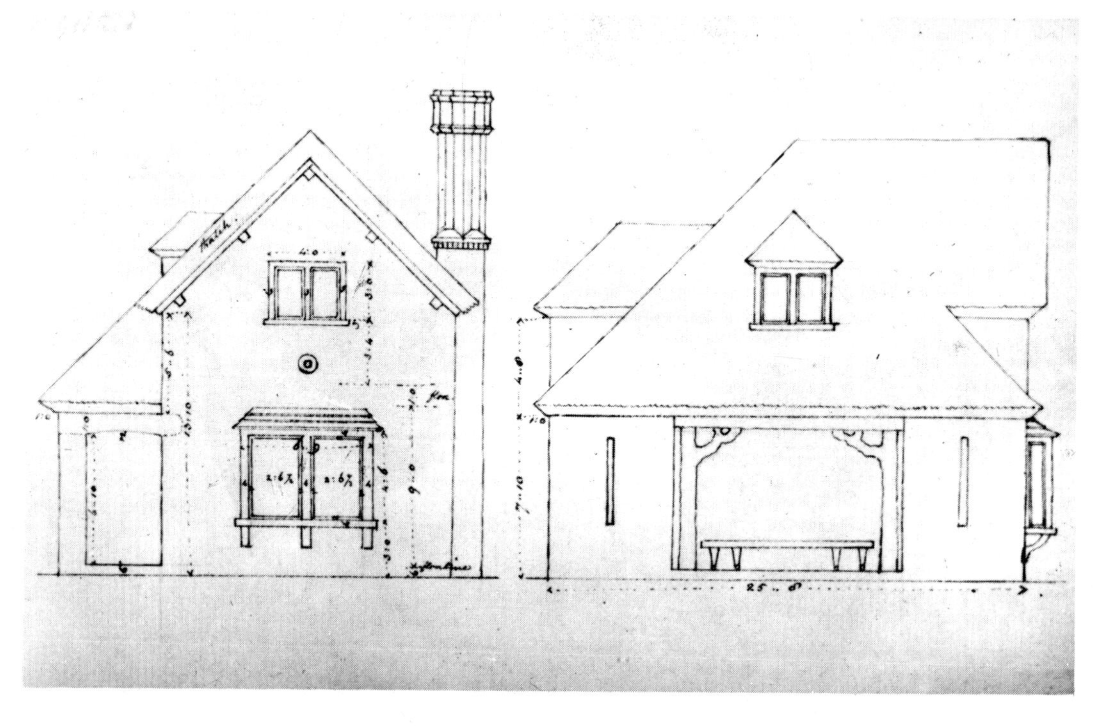

Plate 64. Elevations for a thatched cottage for Mr G. Ward, from the *Pavilion Notebook*. George Ward was one of Nash's wealthy neighbours on the Isle of Wight. George Repton also produced for him drawings for a thatched building with a first-floor balcony supported by branching tree trunks.

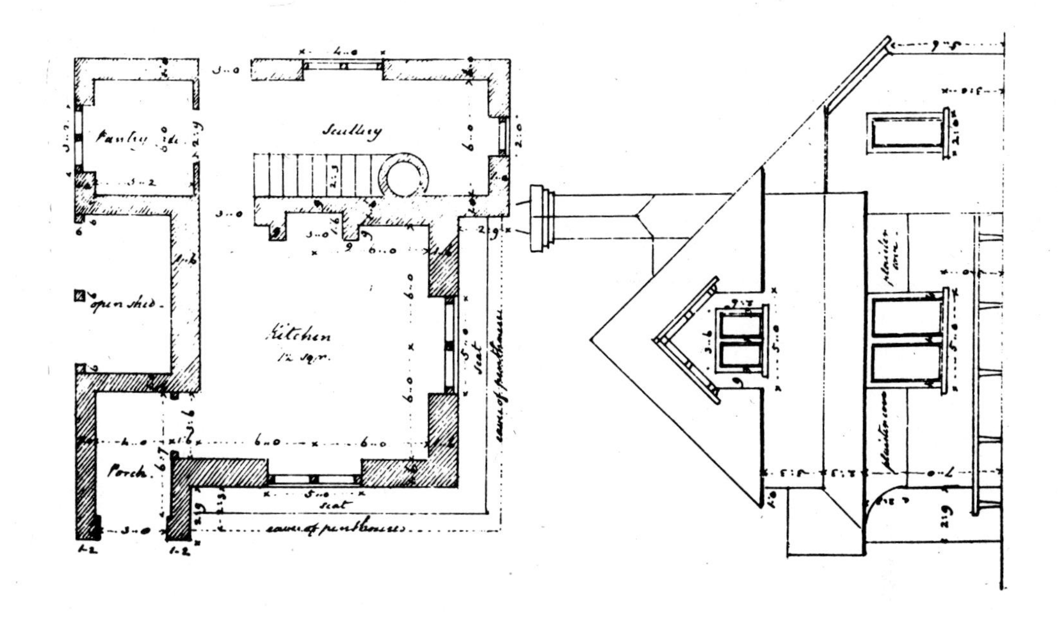

Plate 65. Blaise Hamlet, Diamond Cottage: ground plan and west elevation, from the *Pavilion Notebook*. A dormer has been omitted. See also the inside back wrapper of this book. Diamond Cottage, by means of its assertive placing, simple geometry and apparent near symmetry, contributes a stabilizing influence on the group. With the Pump and Dial Cottage it marks the minor axis of the village plan.

Plate 66. Blaise Hamlet, Diamond Cottage: a view from the north, with the chimneys of Jasmine Cottage to the left.

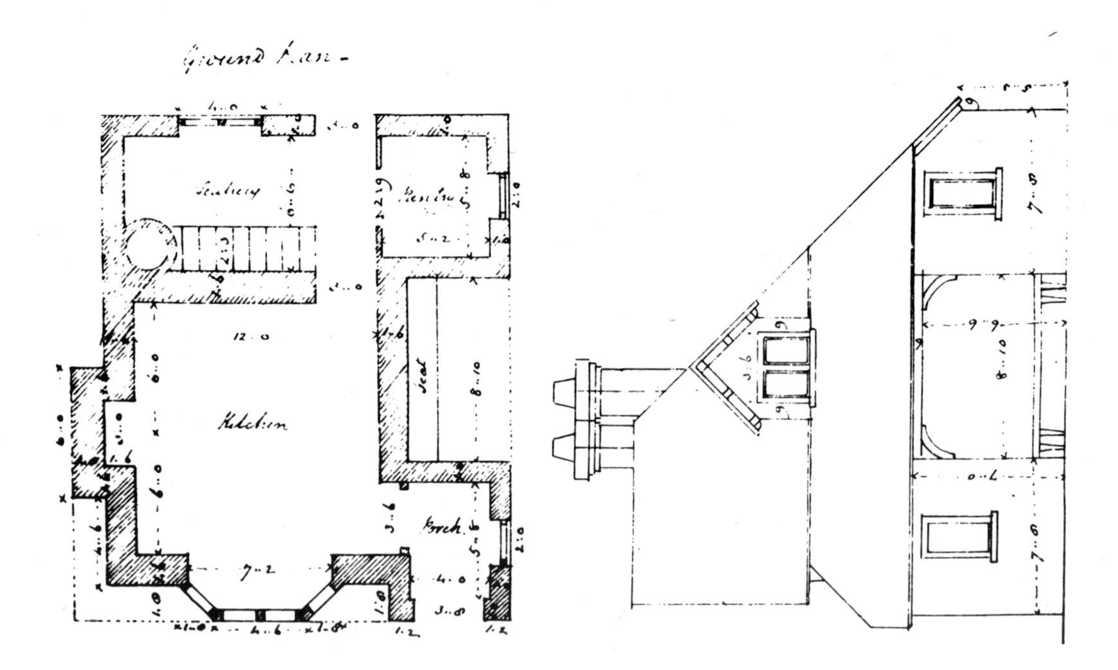

Plate 67. Blaise Hamlet, Jasmine Cottage: ground plan and south-west elevation, from the *Pavilion Notebook*. See also Plate 2. Here, as at Rose, Circular and Oak cottages, simple, diagonally-set chimney shafts, as in Repton's drawings, were actually built and survive.

Plate 68. Blaise Hamlet, Jasmine Cottage: new thatch in 1973, and the south-west dormer window. Treatment of the roofing, as at Oak Cottage, is of vital importance to both the cottage and its neighbours.

Plate 69. Isle of Wight, East Cowes Castle: the seat of John Nash.

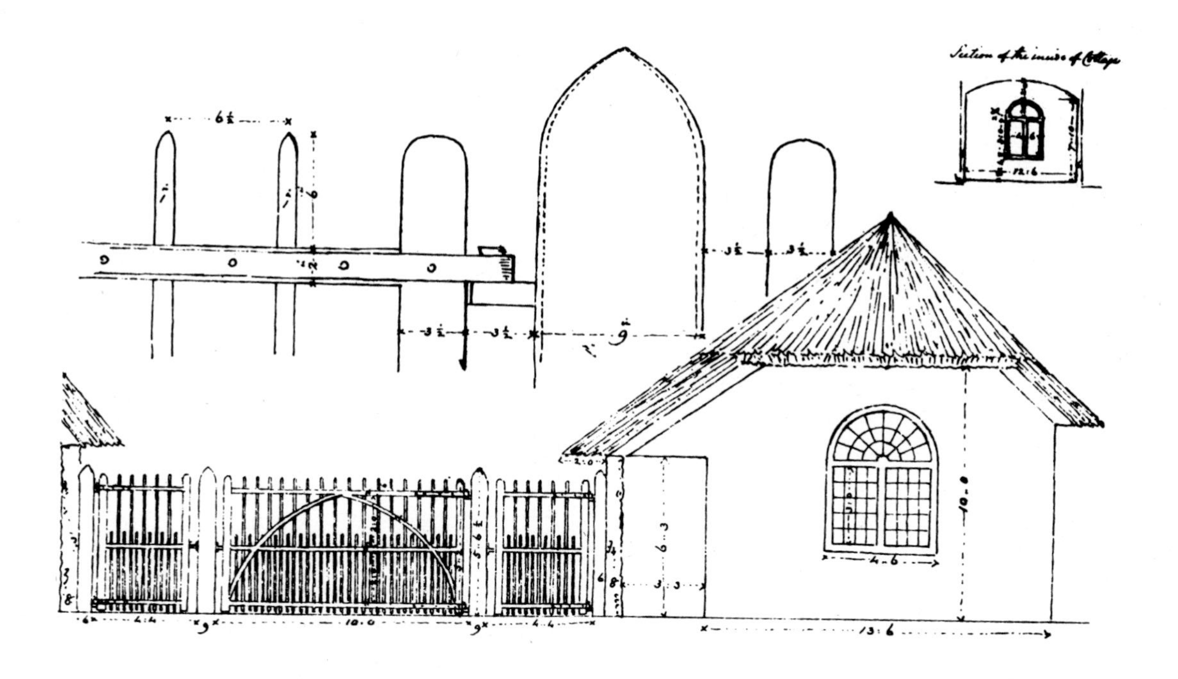

Plate 70. One of a pair of thatched lodges from the *Pavilion Notebook* for an un-named client. The second (facing) lodge is indicated to the left. Another drawing shows the porch roof rising under thatch on the return (inward) elevation and a chimney set on the ridge, to its rear.

Plate 71. Isle of Wight, St. John's: 'Lodge or Cottage Entrance' to the estate of George Simeon, from *A New Picture of the Isle of Wight* (1813).

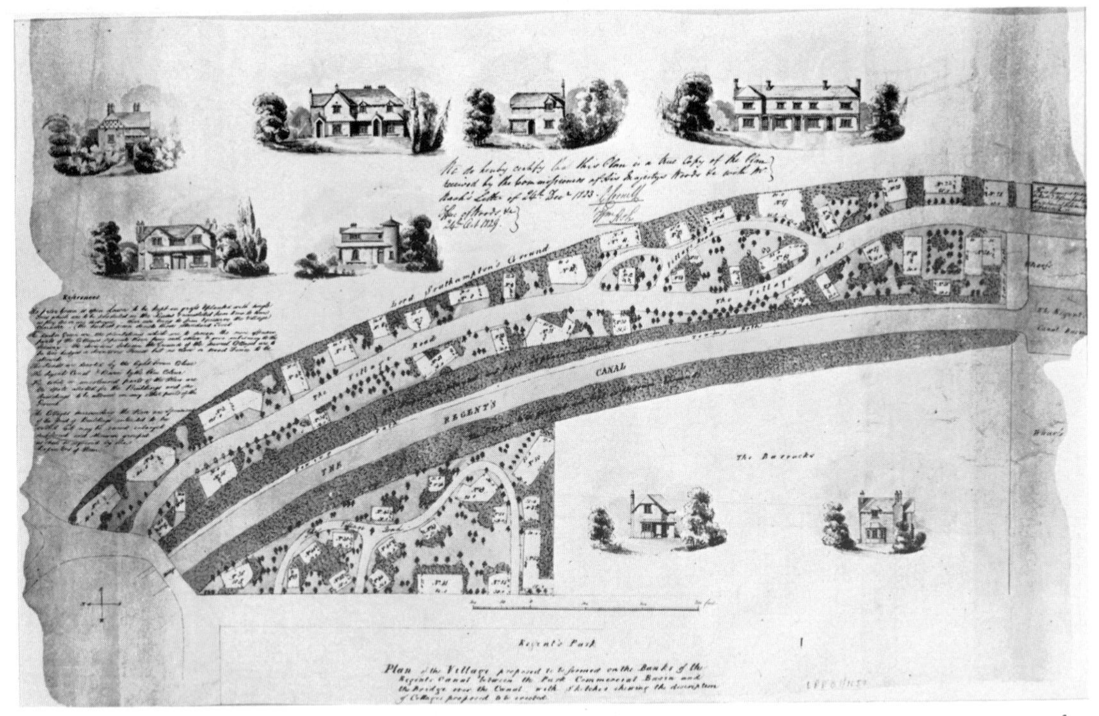

Plate 72. The original from which this copy plan of the Park Villages area was made was received by the Commissioners of Woods, Forests and Land Revenues with a letter from Mr Nash of 1823. It shows meandering village roads, irregular plots. Specimen designs include features found at Blaise, although none has conspicuous chimneys. Planting would screen offensive details, enrich pleasure grounds, form and preserve the village character of this post-Blaise Hamlet suburban proposal. *Public Record Office. Crown Copyright.*

Plate 73. Elevation of a dwelling complying with a plan inscribed as being for Mr. Edwards, from the *Pavilion Notebook.*

Plate 74. Resolven, Rheola House: the west front. The house, as later enlarged by Nash, was very much like a design for Burgh Hall, Aylsham.

Plate 75. An undated drawing attributed to George Repton of a house with a rustic-columned loggia and a bay window. See Plates 76, 77 and 78.

Plate 76. Rheola, 'Brynawel': a house complying with the design in Plate 75 and with working drawings in the *Pavilion Notebook*. The loggia was enclosed long ago and the bay window was removed more recently.

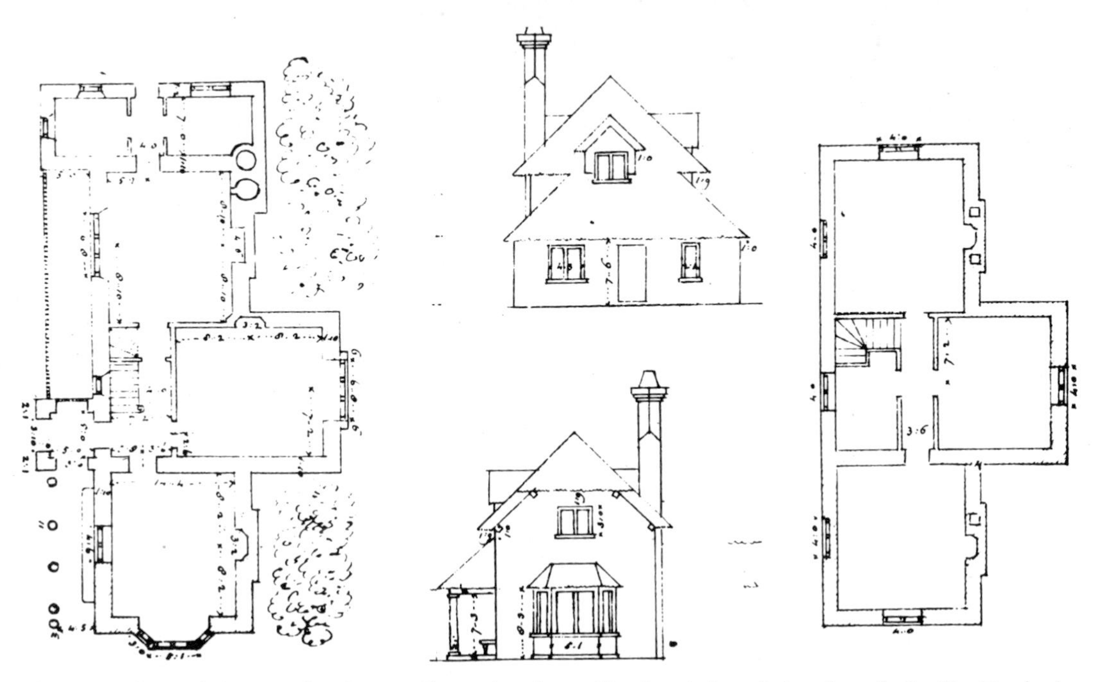

Plate 77. Plans and elevations for a house with a rustic-columned loggia and a bay window, from the *Pavilion Notebook*.

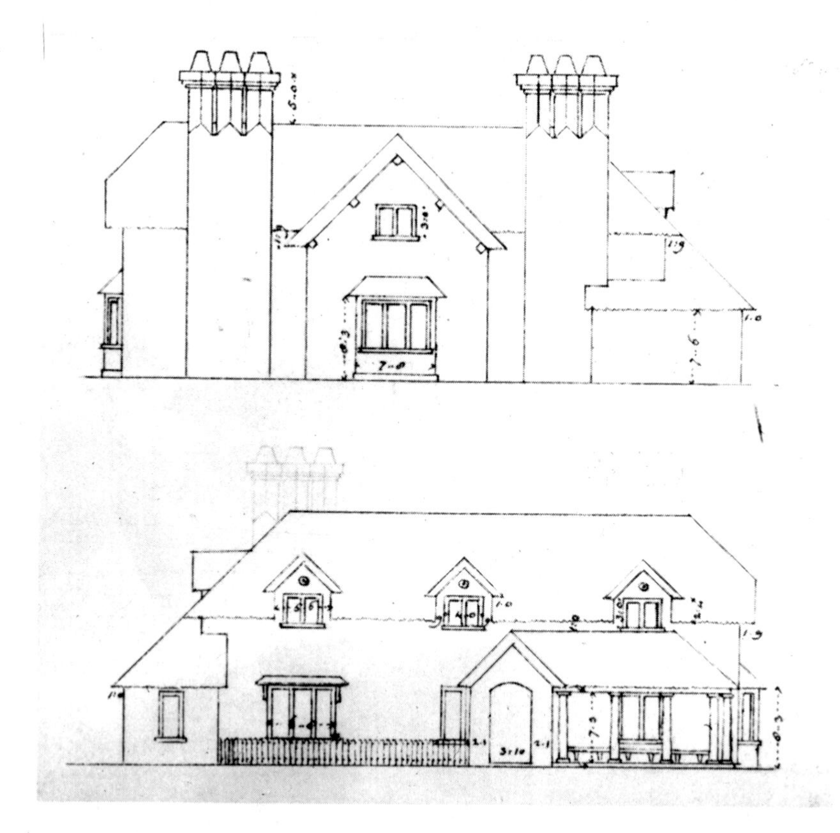

Plate 78. Elevations, dated 1818, for a thatched Steward's House at Rheola, from the *Pavilion Notebook*.

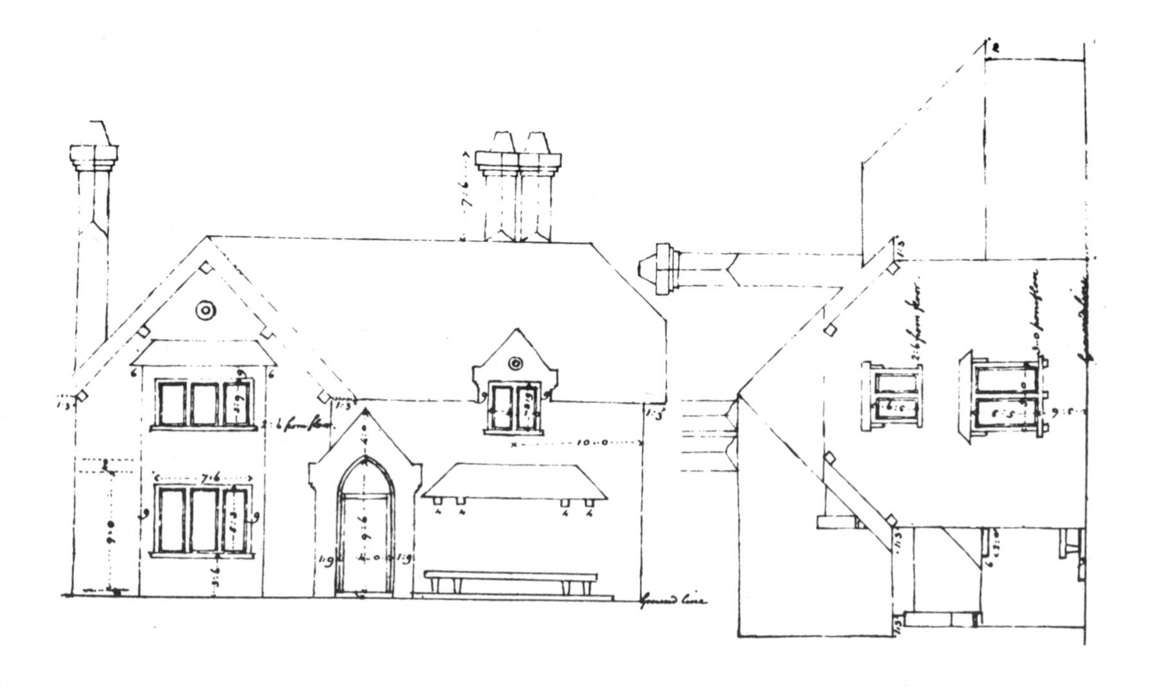

Plate 79. Elevations for a 'Farm House for John Edwards Esq', from the *Pavilion Notebook*. By the porch is a canopied seat.

Plate 80. Rheola, the Lodge: this seat canopy, supported by paired brackets, appears to have survived from the farmhouse shown in Plate 79. See also Plate 55.

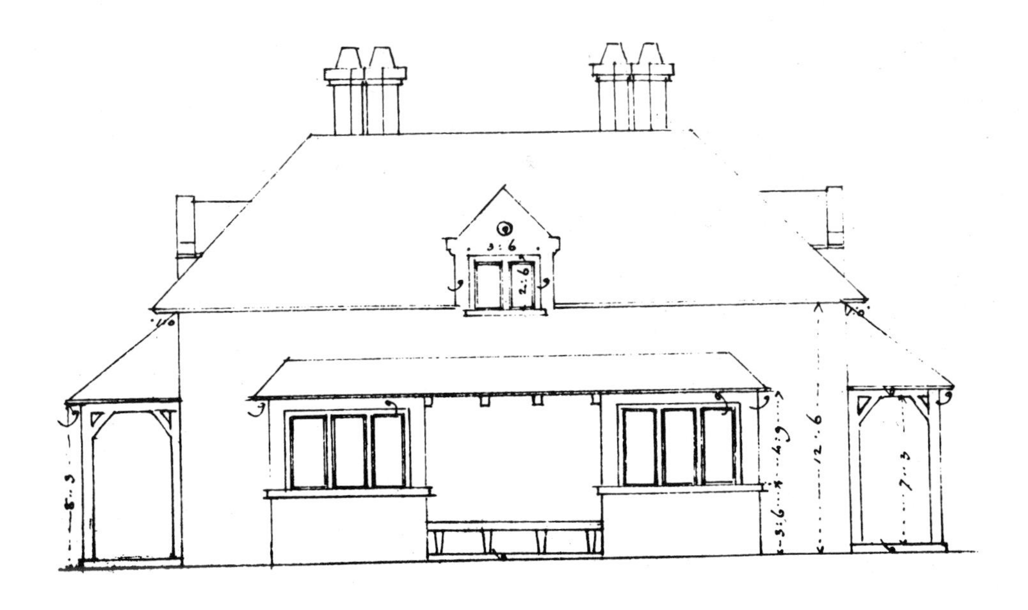

Plate 81. Elevation of a double cottage, inscribed 'Col Matthews', from the *Pavilion Notebook*.

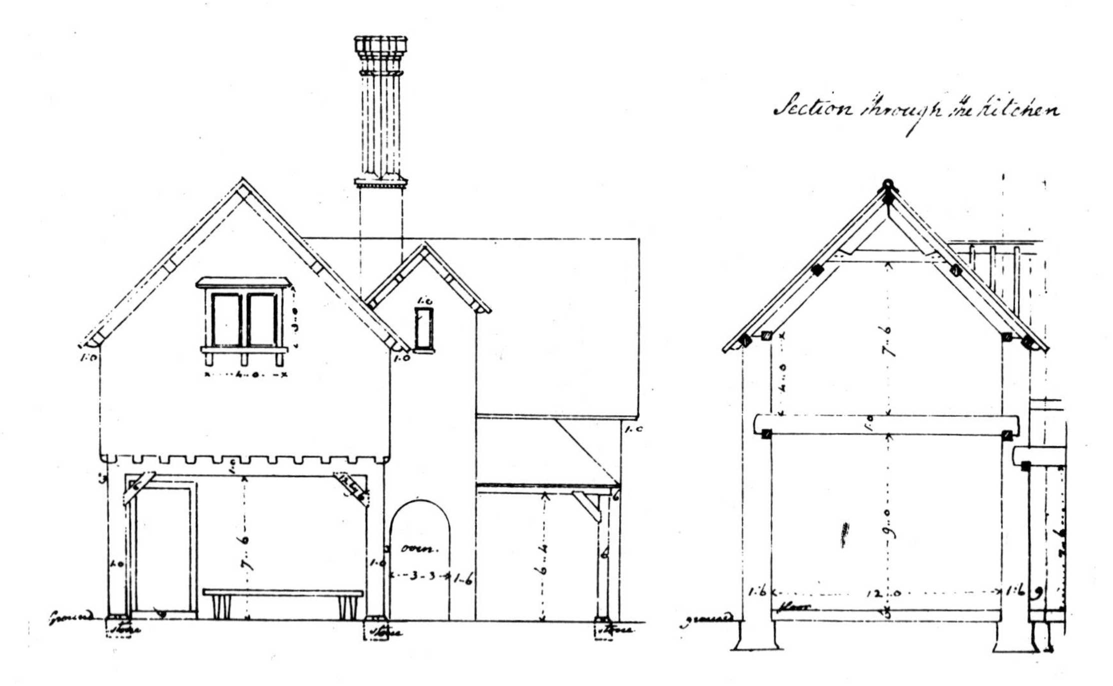

Plate 82. Elevation and section of a cottage, inscribed 'Mr. Matthews. No. 2 Spring Grove', from the *Pavilion Notebook*. The door is set back under a deep open porch. See figures on pages 105 and 125.

Plate 83. Belmont, Herefordshire: a photograph taken in 1964 of a derelict cottage which complies with the design in Plate 82. The large porch had been enclosed (extreme left) and a new front doorway added. This view shows the back.

Plate 84. Belmont, Post Office, Herefordshire: a photograph taken in 1964 of cottages sharing features with the design shown in Plate 81.

Plate 85. Belmont, Lake Cottage (once Woodman's Cottage): a view from the south-east. Thatch and decorative chimneys have been removed, the columned loggia enclosed and a porch bricked in.

Plate 86. Belmont, Woodman's Cottage (now Lake Cottage): enlarged detail from a lithograph dated 1821.

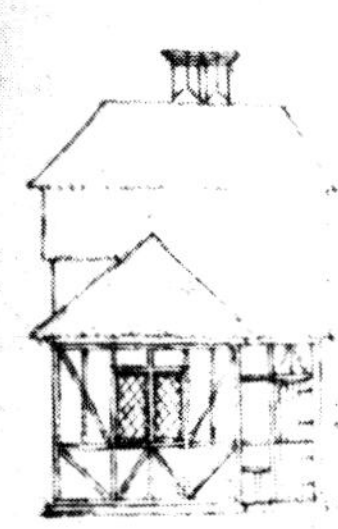

Plate 87. A cottage for U. Price featuring a five columned loggia (seen in end elevation, right of centre drawing) like that shown in Plate 86, once at Lake Cottage, Belmont. From the *RIBA Notebook*.

Plate 88. Callow, Herefordshire: Dewsall Lodge, which earlier photographs show to have been thatched, topped with decorative brick chimneys and to have had a complete thatched semi-circular pent roof. At the rear is a recent extension. See Plates 52, 53, 54. Unlike Circular Cottage at Blaise Hamlet, it has a second (once blind) dormer window, facing to the right.

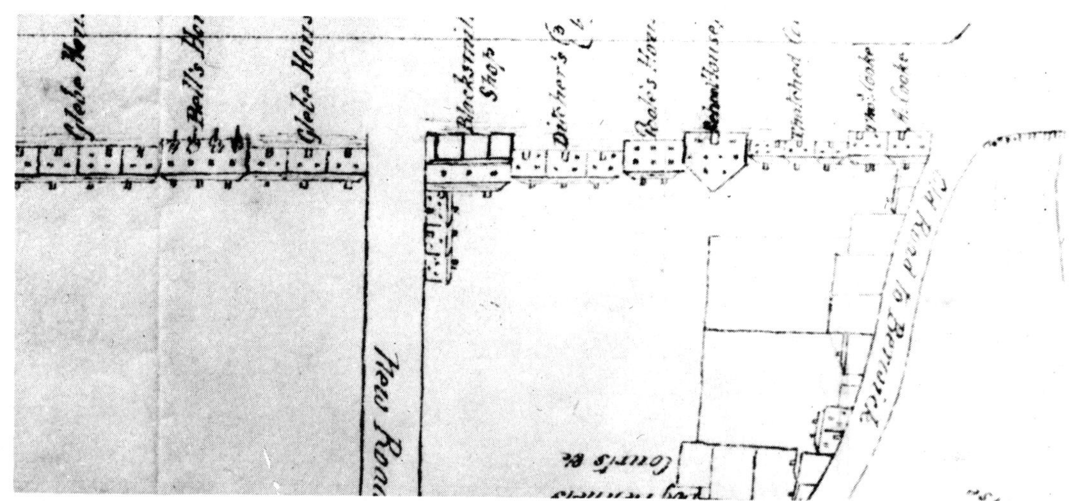

Plate 89. Atcham, Salop: an undated plan (detail, inverted to comply with Plates 90, 92-95), evidently of post-1789 origin. Information recorded on it suggests that the plan was prepared in connection with the development of this approach to Attingham Park.

Plate 90. Atcham, Salop: a plan dated 1793 (detail). Many buildings shown in Plate 89 have gone. Some remain (bottom left). The terrace is immediately above 'Atcham': the *Mytton and Mermaid* (once *Talbot*), above 'AGE' of 'Village'.

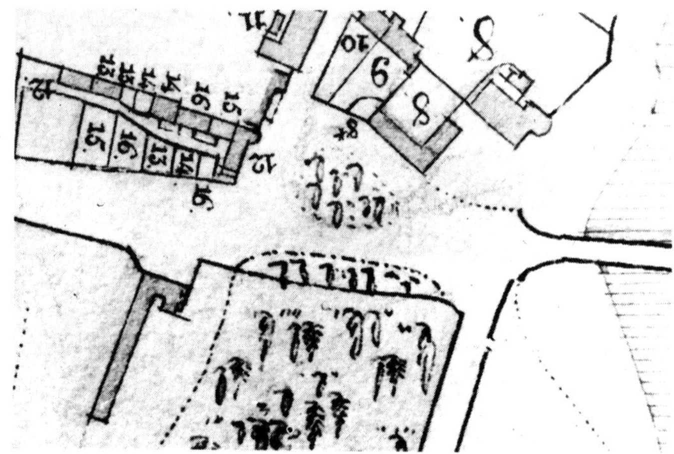

Plate 91. Atcham, Salop: a plan dated 1807 (detail, inverted). Bottom, right of centre, the new road. Plots 12-16 include a terrace. Where buildings had been removed there has been roadside realignment and planting. All but one of the other park side buildings have gone.

Plate 92. Painted panel showing a picturesque-village scene. It includes a terrace with porches and a gothick bay window, a plantation encircled by road, and an heraldic sign.

Plate 93. Detail of a painted panel showing a terrace generally like that in Plate 92. It is also similar to the building photographed in Plates 94 and 95. Compare proportions, chimneys, dormers, fenestration and bay window.

Plate 94. Atcham, Salop: a terrace opposite the entrance to Attingham Hall, photographed in 1972. There is a simple brick dentil course behind the gutter. Wide transoms and mullions of the paired windows suggest that one might have been a door.

Plate 95. Atcham, Salop: the same terrace, photographed from outside the *Mytton and Mermaid* in 1975.

Plate 96. Painted panel: detail of a shop included in the village group (Plate 92), and reminiscent of Blaise Hamlet cottages.

Plate 97. Painted panel: view of a riverside cottage not shown in Plate 92. On the back is a label bearing Nash's name and London address.

Plate 99. 'Elevation of the Inn to be built in Cheshire', showing a grand display of picturesque devices, from the *RIBA Notebook*.

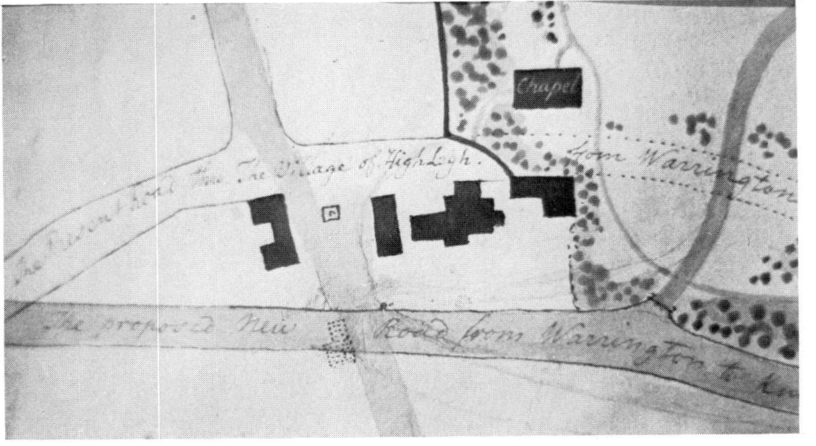

Plate 98. High Legh, Cheshire: detail of a plan in the *Red Book for High Legh* (1791). Repton's proposed diversion of the Knutsford-Warrington road is shown below the cottages, Village Cross, *Red Lion* and Chapel (top). The upper road was to be closed. West Hall lies off this detail (top), and High Legh Hall similarly (upper right).

Plate 100. High Legh, Cheshire: a plan, *c.* 1886, of the Village Green area. The Cross is marked (below 'No 11.'), but the *Red Lion* and stables have gone. The road has been re-routed and a smithy is shown to the left, but there is no evidence to suggest that the Repton-Nash plan was realised.

Plate 101. Painted panel, anonymous and undated, depicting a gated arch and towered lodge (detail).

Plate 102. High Legh: the Village Cross, around which Legh, Nash and Repton planned their village. The photograph was probably taken in the mid-1880s. The Cross was removed in recent years.

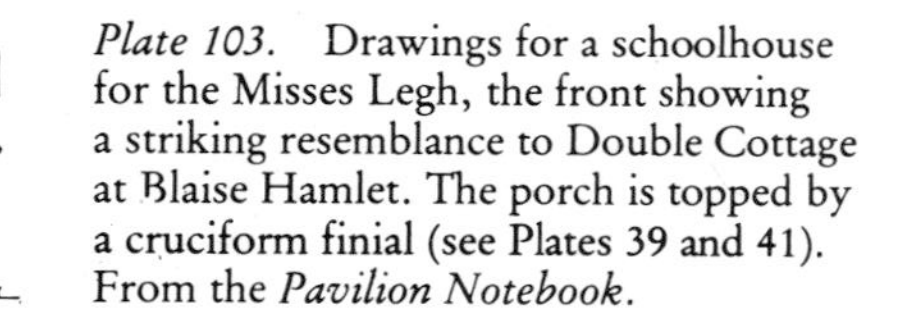

Plate 103. Drawings for a schoolhouse for the Misses Legh, the front showing a striking resemblance to Double Cottage at Blaise Hamlet. The porch is topped by a cruciform finial (see Plates 39 and 41). From the *Pavilion Notebook*.

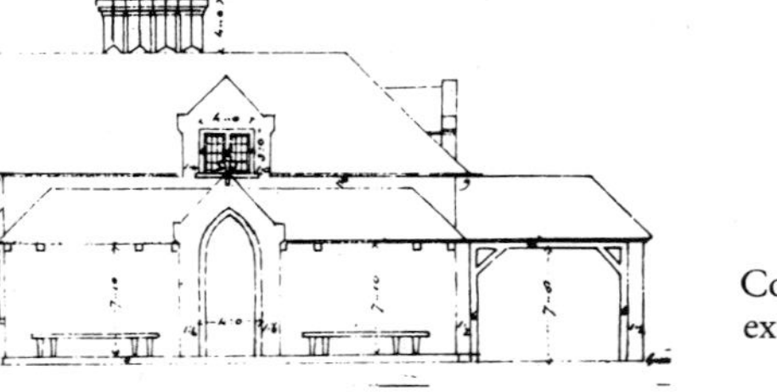

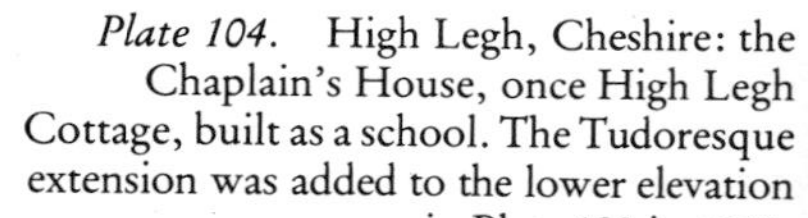

Plate 104. High Legh, Cheshire: the Chaplain's House, once High Legh Cottage, built as a school. The Tudoresque extension was added to the lower elevation in Plate 103 in 1862.